Ruth

TRAPPED

Essays on the History of the Czech Jews, 1939–1943

This publication was supported by a grant
from the following organizations:

The Conference on Jewish Material Claims Against Germany

The Memorial Foundation for Jewish Culture
The Adelson Family Charitable Foundation

Ruth Bondy

TRAPPED

Essays on the History of Czech Jews, 1939–1943

Yad Vashem ⋆ Jerusalem ⋆ 2008

Ruth Bondy

Trapped

Essays on the History of the Czech Jews, 1939–1943

Translated from the Hebrew by Chaya Naor

Language Editors: Heather Rockman and Leah Goldstein
Managing Editor: Daniella Zaidman-Mauer

P.O.B. 3477, Jerusalem 91034, Israel
publications.marketing@yadvashem.org.il

ISBN 978-965-308-322-6

Typesetting: Judith Sternberg
Produced by: Offset Shlomo Nathan Press

Printed in Israel

Table of Contents

❖ ❖ ❖

Preface

The chapters of this book cast light on certain events in the history of Czech Jews, in particular from 1939 to 1945, and reflect their situation, mood and actions until they were annihilated. It is not, however, an inclusive historical study of the history of the Jews in the crown lands of Bohemia and Moravia, which later became the western part of Czechoslovakian Republic, and finally, during the Holocaust, a protectorate of the Reich. Such a book, amazingly enough, does not yet exist, neither in Hebrew nor in any other language, except for H.G. Adler's book, *Theresienstadt 1941–1945*, published in German in 1955, which contains a great deal of information. Obviously, however, in the more than fifty years since that book appeared, much documentary material has been published and documents have been discovered that were not available then, and from the perspective of time passed, things look different today than they appeared to the emotionally involved Adler.

Many books have been written on the Terezin ghetto, in different languages, and from different vantage points: on the children's education, on the children's drawings and newspapers, on the artists, the music, and the cabarets. Memoirs, diaries and biographies have been published; collections of poetry written in the ghetto have been printed. However, a concise one-volume book, containing not only the history of the Jews of Bohemia and Moravia in the Terezin ghetto, but also what preceded it during the occupation and what followed it in all the extermination and labor camps, is still lacking. For this reason I saw fit to at least attach a brief calendar of the events of those fateful years.

Most of the studies included in this book appeared between

1994 and 2001 in the annual, *Studies and Documents of Theresienstadt,* published in Prague, in German and Czech, by the Terezinská Iniciative Foundation and edited by Dr. Jaroslava Milotová and others. One chapter, on the women of the Terezin ghetto in the family camp in Birkenau, is based on my lecture at a conference on women in the Holocaust, held in 1993 at the Hebrew University of Jerusalem and included in the anthology, *Women in the Holocaust.* The chapter on the children's section of the family camp at Birkenau is based on my lecture at an international conference on the family camp held in Prague in March 1994, and published that same year in a collection edited by Toman Brod, Miroslav Kárný and Margita Karná. I am grateful to the editors of the collections for agreeing to include the studies published at their initiative in my Hebrew book and later in its English version.

I am thankful to Anita Tarsi, the director of Beit Terezin at Kibbutz Givat Haim-Ichud, and its entire staff for their help in collecting the required material. I remain indebted to the late Professor Leni Yahil for reading the Hebrew manuscript and her comments on it. My thanks also to the members of the board of the Theresienstadt Martyrs Remembrance Association for their willingness to help finance the publication of this book in its original Hebrew version.

I also wish to thank the members of the publications committee of Yad Vashem who approved the manuscript for publication, in particular the past director and editor in chief, Dr. Bella Gutterman, as well as Avital Saf, for the extremely professional work they invested in the original Hebrew publication, and Daniella Zaidman-Mauer for preparing the English edition of *Trapped.*

The Changing Image of the Terezin Ghetto

In the fifty-five years since the end of World War II, the image of the Holocaust survivor in the eyes of Israelis has undergone many changes, and that is also true of the image of the Terezin ghetto. Despite all the solemn declarations regarding the homeland awaiting the "embers snatched from the fire," a sentiment commonly voiced at the time, the *Yishuv* in Eretz Israel was apprehensive about the arrival of the survivors of the Holocaust. In internal discussions, the leaders of the *Yishuv* spoke about "human dust," and regarded their survival as the result of primeval natural selection: apparently the only ones to survive were those who were cruel, selfish, and prepared to step on corpses. And the accusation hung over all of them, the living and the dead: why didn't they fight? Why did they go like sheep to the slaughter? Only the rebels in the ghettos and the partisans could stand tall; they fought heroically. Hence a day of commemoration was devoted not only to the Holocaust, but also to heroism, the Holocaust belonging only to the submissive, and the heroism to those who fought with weapons.

The Terezin ghetto, or Theresienstadt in German, did not become a part of the broad Israeli public consciousness. It remained a negligible footnote, devoid of any rebellion, the sole ghetto in Central Europe, not comparable to the ghettos in Poland, a ghetto for the privileged, as the Nazis presented it and as the representative of the International Red Cross defined it after he visited there in June 1944, not wanting to see the reality behind the show prepared for him and the members of his delegation.

The former inmates of the Terezin ghetto, most of them young, who immigrated to Israel after the State was established, wished most of all to be integrated into Israeli society, to acquire a profession, to find housing and a source of livelihood, to establish families. They were preoccupied with their day-to-day existence, and among themselves or with their spouses who had not experienced the Holocaust, they spoke very little about what they had undergone during the German occupation, in the Terezin ghetto and, especially, after it. Of the 150,000 prisoners from Bohemia and Moravia, Germany, Austria, Holland, Denmark and other countries who passed through Terezin, more than 33,000 died in the ghetto itself, 88,000 were sent to extermination camps, and only 3,500 of those survived.

To some extent, the inmates of Terezin were the ones who created the image of the Terezin ghetto as a place to look back at with longing. There they were still near their parents, siblings and friends; many of them experienced their first love there, lived with peers of their own age, studied, believed it was possible to overcome the tribulations, and knew nothing about the existence of a mechanized extermination in gas chambers.

Only years later, a decade after their liberation, was the first national conference of former Terezin ghetto inmates held. The conference took place in Israel in May 1955 at Kibbutz Givat Haim-Ichud, where one group of survivors had gone to live. There too there was a sing-along around a campfire, as in the days of the Zionist youth movement, a soccer game in memory of the games in the ghetto, and the joy of the reunion. However, alongside these activities, the first buds emerged of a feeling that they ought to organize to memorialize those who perished in the ghetto, in particular their comrades from the Zionist youth movements and *Hechalutz*, most of whom did not survive; that they ought to commemorate another aspect of the Holocaust – the attempt to preserve human dignity, the concern about educating the children and the youth as the seed for the future growth of the Jewish people, and the force of creativity under conditions of hunger, friendship and responsibility for one another.

This aspect of the ghetto first came to the knowledge of the broad Israeli public in the first half of the 1960s, with the publication by Sifriat HaPoalim of the Hebrew editions of *There Are No*

Butterflies Here, a collection of drawings and poems by children of the Terezin ghetto translated by Leah Goldberg and Tuvia Ruebner, and *A Requiem to Terezin*, by Josef Bor, that tells about the performance of Verdi's *Requiem* in the ghetto. Under the influence of the Eichmann trial, personal memoirs and biographies brought the individual forth from the haze of the terrifying, incomprehensible number of six million, and Israelis slowly began to see the Holocaust, the survivors – as well as the heroism – through different eyes.

The Terezin ghetto was not destroyed and continued to exist until the end of World War II, although most of its inmates were annihilated. Therefore, more material was preserved there than in the ghettos of Poland that were set on fire or razed to the ground. Exhibitions of paintings by artists of the ghetto and drawings by the children of Terezin, a performance of music composed in the ghetto, the mounting of the children's opera *Brundibár* in several Hebrew versions, the dramatization of the story of Verdi's *Requiem* in the ghetto performed by Naava Shan, the publication of the diary of Egon (Gonda) Redlich, head of the department for youth in the ghetto, a Hebrew edition of the children's newspaper *Kamarád,* and cabarets based on texts from Terezin – all these created a new image of the Terezin ghetto.

However, this image, too, is distorted to some extent. The Terezin ghetto is often described in the Israeli media as a place "in which the Germans concentrated the finest artists of Central Europe," but that was not the case. In the Terezin ghetto, the Germans concentrated, at least for a period of transition, all of the Jews of Bohemia and Moravia and most of the elderly Jews from Germany and Austria – and because of the character and composition of Central European Jewry prior to Nazi rule, they included many members of the learned professions, scientists, intellectuals and artists. The impression may be that the inmates of the ghetto went from theater play to opera performance, from lecture to lecture, from one concert to another, or from cabaret to cabaret. But the reality was different. In the eighteen months I spent in the ghetto, I saw one opera performance and one play, and many prisoners were not fortunate enough to see any, and not because they took no interest in culture. The hard labor, the hours standing in line for food, at a water faucet, for a toilet; the efforts undertaken to see parents or one's husband, wife, children, or a friend before the curfew, which usually began at 8 p.m.; the widespread illness; the dread of the transports; mourning for a father or a mother who died in the ghetto – in short, the strength needed, first and foremost, for day-to-day existence prevented much cultural activity. Added to this was the technical difficulty of obtaining a ticket to a performance in the small improvised halls, and the prohibition against being in the street after dark. All of these reduced the audiences to a few inhabitants of one barracks or another, to those who had connections with the *Freizeitgestaltung* (the Administration of Free Time Activities).

It seemed as if everyone had forgotten the thousands of elderly Jews dying from malnutrition and disease, the lack of will to go on living, the eternal dread of separation from loved ones looming over the ghetto like a cloud and the transports leaving for an unknown destination or one known only by a disguised name – the Birkenau bei Neu-Berun labor camp which was none other than Auschwitz. The frayed nerves from standing endlessly in lines; the feeling of constant hunger, not hunger that drives one mad as it did in other places, but hunger that gnaws like a small mouse; the series of incessant diseases among children and young people – impetigo, encephalitis, typhus, scarlet fever, infectious jaundice, diarrhea; the fleas and bedbugs that were irritating especially at night – all of these supposedly never existed.

Perhaps if one wishes to preserve the memory of the Terezin ghetto's uniqueness, that's the only way. Suffering, distress, diseases and hunger existed wherever Jews were concentrated throughout Eastern Europe during the German occupation, but such a large number of artistic treasures, poems, musical works, children's drawings and newspapers of the children's homes, diaries and notes were preserved only there.

Another aspect of the Terezin ghetto also seems to have been forgotten: the attitude towards work. Most of the ghetto's inmates worked for the general good, without supervisors, without a whip over them, and without the presence of an SS man or a Czech gendarme (there were no kapos there at all). They worked faithfully (inmates aged sixty and over worked voluntarily), according to their ability, in workshops, in the children's homes, in hospitals, in agriculture, in transport, in offices, in cleaning, in sewing shops, and in scores of other jobs, because in their previous lives they had been educated to regard work as a value and a privilege. Their work was important in their own eyes, not only because of the small food supplement given to workers, but because it gave them the sense that they were benefiting others; it was a support, it created a way of life and strengthened relationships, it filled the day.

I would like the Terezin ghetto to be remembered the way it was: a place of uplifted spirit as well as toughness, of pettiness and of generosity, of mutual help and of ignoring the suffering of others – a kaleidoscope of human beings trapped in a distressful situation, most of whom knew how to preserve human dignity, who were not cruel to one another, who hoped to hang on until the yearned-for end of the war, which for the majority came too late.

And that is also why I think it is so important to pass down the material about the Terezin ghetto to the coming generations: not only as a testimony to the period, but as testimony of the readiness of individuals to accept responsibility for the lives of all, and not to give up; a testimony of people's ability to learn, to create, to laugh and to love life, even in the most difficult conditions.

The History of the Closing Gates
Jüdisches Nachrichtenblatt – Židovské Listy
The Jewish Newspaper in Prague during the Occupation Years, 1939–1945

It's almost incredible: throughout all the years of the war, under the Nazi regime, even after nearly all the Jews in the Protectorate of Bohemia and Moravia had been sent to the Terezin ghetto and extermination camps, a Jewish newspaper came out in Prague. Even after only a handful of Jews who were married to non-Jews remained in the Protectorate and the paper had shrunk to one page, the weekly *Jüdisches Nachrichtenblatt – Židovské Listy* continued to exist.[1]

The newspaper was a logical and natural continuation of the past. From 1907, two Jewish weeklies, *Selbstwehr*, the German newspaper of the Zionist movement, and *Rozvoj*, the paper of the Jews who regarded themselves as Czechs of the Mosaic religion,

1 A complete collection of all the issues of the weekly *Jüdisches Nachrichtenblatt – Židovské Listy* year by year does not exist in Israel. The volumes in the Zionist Archives and in the National Library in Jerusalem supplement one another until 1943. A collection of its issues from 1943 to 1945 is not complete (the issues found in Yad Vashem are not accessible to readers for technical reasons). But since hardly any Jews were left in the Protectorate of Bohemia and Moravia from 1944, and in those years the newspaper consisted of only one information sheet, I saw no need to follow up its publication until the end. According to official figures, from 25 March 1945, two months before the end of the war, 3,030 Jews, 2.5 percent of their number at the beginning of the occupation, remained in the area of the Protectorate (with the exception of the Terezin ghetto and prisons) (*Terezinská Pamětní kniha*, Prague: Melantrich, 1995), p. 54.

were published in Bohemia and Moravia, then crown countries of the Austro-Hungarian monarchy. In 1918, when the Czechslovakian Republic was founded, a third newspaper was added: *Židovské Zprávy*, a Czech Zionist weekly. *Selbstwehr* stopped printing in the fall of 1938, the time of the Munich crisis and the Czechs' hatred of the Germans, when it seemed impossible to carry on publishing a Jewish newspaper in German. The other two newspapers continued until March 1939, when the German occupation began and the Protectorate was established in Bohemia and Moravia.[2] The new situation called for a temporary halt in publication.

On Friday, 24 November 1939, the first issue of the new German-Czech weekly appeared: *Jüdisches Nachrichtenblatt – Židovské Listy*, a joint organ of the Jewish community and the Zionist movement in Prague. The third partner, secret but influential and not mentioned on the paper's masthead, was the Center for Jewish Emigration, the kingdom of Adolf Eichmann. Not only was he the one who chose the name of the newspaper, but the weekly *Jüdisches Nachrichtenblatt* also came out under his direction in Berlin and Vienna. German was also the preferred language of *Jüdisches Nachrichtenblatt – Židovské Listy*; its regulations, laws, instructions and important articles also appeared in Czech translation, but there were items, readers' letters and advertisements that were printed only in one language – Czech or German.

Common interests intersected: in those difficult early days of Nazi rule the Jews needed something to rely on that would reinforce their sense of belonging. The Zionists wanted to encourage immigration to Palestine, and the occupation authorities were anxious to hasten the departure of Jews from their territory, in the framework of the "solution of the Jewish problem." Judging from the appeal to all the Jews of the Protectorate featured on the first page, the date of the new weekly's appearance was not accidental: "Every Jew must be aware of his responsibility for Jewry as a whole. In certain circumstances, the actions of every Jew are apt to be catastrophic for all the Jews. Hence we must avoid any act that

2 Avigdor Dagan, *The Jews of Bohemia and Moravia*, vol. 1 (Philadelphia: The Jewish Publication Society of America, 1968), pp. 524–525.

might endanger the Jews. This is particularly relevant in relation to any political or pseudo-political activity." This was a clear allusion to the anti-German demonstrations held a month earlier, on 28 October, the national holiday of the former Czechoslovakian Republic, and to the mass arrests that came in its wake, when some politically active Jews were also arrested.

Just a short time earlier, it had seemed unthinkable, in fact impossible, that two such different institutions as the Jewish community and the Zionist Federation could publish a joint newspaper. In the new situation, however, the old antipathies between the Zionists and the non-Zionists became blurred. František Weidmann, secretary of the Jewish community in Prague, was a nationalist Czech Jew, who felt deeply rooted in the soil of Bohemia. Now, in the main editorial (in German, signed Franz Weidmann) in the first issue of *Jüdisches Nachrichtenblatt,* he stated that the major role of the Jewish community was to encourage emigration and deal with all the issues it involved.

Before the war, the office of the secretary of the Jewish community in Prague was not an especially lofty position. Now, in the absence of the elected head of the community, 27-year-old Weidmann, a plump man, honest but hesitant, suddenly bore the responsibility for all the Jews of Czechoslovakia. In September 1939, Dr. František Kafka, head of the Jewish community in Prague, was in Paris dealing with matters of emigration and preferred not to return. From now on, Dr. Franz Kahn, who for many years was the Secretary-General of the Zionist Federation in Bohemia and Moravia, would be Weidmann's mainstay.[3]

In March 1940, by order of the German authorities, Weidmann was appointed head of the Jewish community in Prague, and Jakob Edelstein, Director of the Palestine Office in Prague and now the chief Zionist personality, was appointed his deputy. *Jüdisches Nachrichtenblatt* informed its readers that the leadership was being reorganized; from now on all the Jewish communities and Jewish organizations in the Protectorate (namely all the Jews of the Pro-

3 Ruth Bondy, *Elder of the Jews: Jakob Edelstein of Theresienstadt* (New York: Grove Press, 1989).

tectorate), including all of the issues involved in emigration and the handling of all those regarded as Jews under the racist laws of Nuremberg even if they belonged to other religions, would be subject to the Jewish community in Prague. According to the *Jüdisches Nachrichtenblatt,* a five-member advisory committee would assist Weidmann and Edelstein, and no changes would take place in the departments of the Jewish community in Prague.[4] However, Dr. Oskar Singer, chief editor of *Jüdisches Nachrichtenblatt,* in an editorial entitled "Responsibility," reacted with surprising candor: "In 1939, the elected representatives of the Jewry of Bohemia and Moravia did not foresee the events to come: a totalitarian reversal in the framework of a totalitarian state. The Jewish side cannot insist on a democratic leadership. The sole possibility is this: we will place our trust in them, we will help them."[5]

In July 1940, in his summary, "One year of the New Arrangement and the Wandering," Singer wrote with no less frankness:

> Only one office exists that has authority in all Jewish affairs: the Center for the Emigration of the Jews. The authority that passed from it to the Jewish community in Prague, as well as to all the communities in the provinces, is an innovation in the history of Diaspora Jewry. The great wish and the firm hope of the leadership is that this innovation will act solely for the good of all.[6]

In an interview, Weidmann also confirmed the lines of action of the new set-up: "The organization of the community is also based on the principle of personal responsibility. Every section director reports to the general secretariat on the achievements and actions of his department…it turns out that the great tasks cannot be carried out by honorary officers, but almost only by professional officials." According to Weidmann, the area of the Jewish community's activity had expanded in the past year twenty to twenty-five fold, but

4 *Jüdisches Nachrichtenblatt,* 15–22.3.1940.

5 *Jüdisches Nachrichtenblatt,* 12.4.1940.

6 *Jüdisches Nachrichtenblatt,* 26.7.1940.

the number of officials had increased only twelve-fold, and "thanks [to them] enormous achievements were attained."[7] The impression almost created that there was some cause for joy: "The surroundings of the Jewish municipality have awakened to new life," an editorial stated on 3 July 1940. "The Jewish community is no longer a mechanism devoid of content. It is our community, an iron ring of a shared fate that encircles us all."

♦

When reading the *Jüdisches Nachrichtenblatt* or writing about it, it is very difficult – almost impossible – to wrest oneself free of the knowledge of what happened two or three years later. The newspaper's naiveté is often scathingly painful in the shadow of the mechanized extermination of the Jews. One needs to keep reminding oneself that then it was still something indescribable; even in Nazi ideology it had not yet been fully developed. There was still hope of emigration and career retraining.

The optimism reflected on the pages of the newspaper in the first and second years of its existence, which now seems so totally groundless, was then entirely fitting for the difficult times. Publication of the story of two flies that fell into a full cup of milk is a telling example:

> One sank and drowned, because it told itself there was no way it could escape its fate. But the other fly moved its legs incessantly, although it too knew that would not do it much good. It fought hour after hour, and the following morning it was sitting on an island of butter. Everyone must become an optimist. The harder we take life, the harder it becomes. We have to find a new homeland somewhere in the world. Optimism fuels hope as oil fuels the wick.[8]

The important thing was to imbue the Jews with psychological

7 *Jüdisches Nachrichtenblatt*, 15.3.1940.
8 *Jüdisches Nachrichtenblatt*, 9.2.1940.

strength. Moreover, anyone who viewed the future as bleak did not write articles to raise morale. There was no lack of Jewish writers and editors in search of employment, since in 1939 they were all fired from the general press, both the German and the Czech. The first chief editor of *Jüdisches Nachrichtenblatt*, whose name appeared on the bottom of the last page, was Dr. Oskar Singer, former editor of *Prager Tagblatt,* who from time to time wrote the editorial column of *Jüdisches Nachrichtenblatt* and signed it with the initials O.S. He remained in this position until the fall of 1941 and then his name vanished without any explanation from the margins of the last page. Dr. Karl Fleischmann, until then the acting editor, was then given the title of Chief Editor.

In fact, it was impossible to write about any of the truly fateful matters in a newspaper that was completely censored. Nothing was written about the first five transports that left between 15 October and 3 November 1941 from Prague to the Łódź ghetto (or Litzmannstadt, as the Germans called it), or about the reason why Dr. Singer, whose position ought to have protected him from deportation at least for a time, was among the deportees. It turned out that one of the newspaper's employees, Heinz Schnabel, who was in the second transport, sent Singer a gloomy letter from the area of the commercial fair that was the assembly point of the outgoing transports, in which he described the harsh conditions there and the way the SS man Fidler abused the deportees. The letter came into Fidler's hands, and Dr. Singer was forced to choose: to leave with his family on the next transport to the Łódź ghetto or to report to a field tribunal. He chose the former option.[9]

The only mention of the Łódź ghetto appeared a few months later in a notice in the margins of *Jüdisches Nachrichtenblatt* about letters, including postcards from Łódź,[10] kept in the Department of

9 A conversation with Leah Rachman, the daughter of Oskar Singer, held in 1999 at Kibbutz Naot Mordechai. Singer (1892–1944) also wrote a daily chronicle in the Łódź ghetto. He and his family were among the last to remain in the Łódź ghetto until the summer of 1944 when they were transferred to Auschwitz. There Oskar's traces disappeared.

10 *Jüdisches Nachrichtenblatt*, 23.1.1942.

Residents Registration of the Prague community because the addressee could not be found.

Nor is the establishment of the Theresienstadt ghetto in November 1941 or its existence mentioned in the weekly. Only a small, nearly concealed notice on 12 December 1941 stated: "Notice: we have been informed by an authorized source that it is forbidden to send parcels to the Jewish camp in Theresienstadt."

Since the newspaper was bilingual, Dr. Singer or his representative would submit it first to the German censor in the Center for Emigration of Jews in the Střešovice quarter, and then to the Czech censor. According to Dr. Fritz Tauber, formerly an attorney in Olomouc and now the editor of *Židovské Listy,* the Czech part of the newspaper, the Czech censor often expunged more than his German counterpart did. In an article written to mark the festival of Chanukah, Tauber mentioned the war of the Maccabees against the Greeks and the victory of the few over the powerful, and the German censor remarked that he understood the innuendo very well. After this incident, Franz Kahn suggested that Tauber be declared "unsuitable for his job." In December 1939 he succeeded in joining one of the five groups that had certificates enabling them to go to Palestine, although his name appeared on the black list of those officeholders who were forbidden to leave the area of the Protectorate.[11]

♦

For years, the occupational retraining of the Jews had been one of the main issues in the Zionist ideology. According to the doctrine of Ber Borochov, the Zionist socialist thinker, the Jewish people could only be saved if the professional pyramid that prevailed among them was overturned. The wide base should comprise not only commerce, the learned professions and *luftgescheften* (literally, "air business"), as it did now, but rather the workers and farmers in Palestine. Now was the time for a professional revolution.

11 Dr. Franz Tauber (1903–1978), Moshe Tavor in Israel, a member of the *Davar* editorial board, in a conversation with the author, 1977.

The non-Zionist, Franz Weidmann, wrote in the same vein in his article, "On the Way": "The endeavor to retrain the Jewish community means rectifying the wretched, unnatural stratification of Jewry. One of the main tasks is to prepare the Jew to return to the soil."[12]

From the first issue of *Jüdisches Nachrichtenblatt,* one of the key topics was the retraining courses. Alongside general information about courses held under the auspices of the community, from short-term courses lasting three weeks to six-month basic retraining, detailed articles were printed about the various branches of study: fine mechanics, ironworking, soldering, carpentry, cattle raising and chemical cleaning as well as courses training men to be electricians and opticians, and dozens of other occupations. The women were offered courses in the care of infants, dietetic cooking, and training as manicurists and pedicurists. To encourage retraining and emigration, the weekly printed a regular section called "They achieved their goal," which told about Jewish emigrants in the past who had been successful in their new country, such as Isaac Merritt Singer, inventor of the sewing machine, or Helena Rubinstein, the cosmetics queen. In the Letters section of the paper, featuring letters from different countries in the world, emigrants from Bohemia and Moravia described how they had succeeded in their new homeland thanks to their inventiveness and the occupations and trades they had recently learned. An emigrant to Brazil began baking yeast cookies and other goodies from Czech cuisine that her husband sold outside factories during the lunch break. Now the two had opened a small bakery.[13] A couple from Prague, based on their retraining, opened a beauty parlor in the Far East and were also producing a substitute for cologne as well as a deodorant that were very popular in the local hot climate.[14]

The Prague community opened an office for occupational counseling managed by the graphologist Willy Schönfeld (later in the Terezin ghetto he also administered graphological tests to can-

12 *Jüdisches Nachrichtenblatt*, 24.11.1939.

13 *Jüdisches Nachrichtenblatt*, 15.12.1939.

14 *Jüdisches Nachrichtenblatt*, 23.8.1940.

didates for responsible positions). A guide written by Schönfeld to help in the choice of a profession was available for eighty kronen. The newspaper also printed a column entitled "The Small Theory of Professions," which included, in alphabetical order, the requirements for and opportunities offered by each and every profession and occupation overseas: lawyers would have no possibility of earning a living in their profession abroad, while physicians were advised to learn another trade closely related to their specialization, such as massage, gymnastics, podiatry, photography and dog breeding.[15] For all of them, courses were given in English, French and Hebrew. "It is never too late to learn Hebrew," the column stated.

Beyond their practical value, the retraining courses offered by the Jewish community in Prague was an occupational therapy of sorts. They were like a life raft to cling to in a collapsing world; they filled the time of those Jews who had lost their jobs, and provided them with hope. The courses continued even after there was no longer any possibility of emigrating. On 27 June 1941, these retraining courses in Prague still included 50 occupations and trades, such as repairing fountain pens, bookbinding, sewing eiderdowns, photographing advertisements and playing jazz.

During the years 1939–1941, the community was not dealing with questions of life and death, but rather with solutions for financial problems, loss of property and enforced proletarization, which could also be interpreted as a move towards a better future. "As absurd and daring as this may sound – even in this economic crisis, in the thick smoke rising from the Jewish heap of debris – again a glimmer of opportunity is visible," O.S. wrote in an editorial in December 1939.[16] Even the official Czech spelling came to the aid of the Jewish national consciousness. Under the order of the Protectorate authorities, from now on, *Žid* and *Židovka*, namely Jew and Jewess, had to be written with a capital letter, the way it was spelled to denote nationality, instead of *žid* and *židovka*, the usual way of denoting religion.[17]

15 *Jüdisches Nachrichtenblatt*, 23.2.1940.

16 *Jüdisches Nachrichtenblatt*, 22.12.1939.

17 *Jüdisches Nachrichtenblatt*, 12.6.1942.

The cooperation between the Jewish community in Prague, the Zionist Federation and the Palestine Office, which Weidmann noted with satisfaction, was also expressed in many articles and items about life in the "land of the forefathers," in particular in the choice of photographs: pioneers engaged in clearing the land, in agricultural work, in construction. The occupational retraining seemed first and foremost to be preparation for life in Palestine.

Fredy Hirsch, head of the united sports department of the Zionist youth movements, preached discipline, self-control, responsibility for others, learning Hebrew, and the pioneering ideal: "Our worker is a pioneer, a man who is settling the wilderness and the desert to make the land bloom, the land that will be an old-new homeland for his people."[18] The young immigrants going to an unfamiliar life must change their entire way of thinking and all of their preparations: they must become tough, train their bodies to attain higher achievements and perform supreme deeds.[19] In an article, "Healthy Youth – a Healthy Homeland," illustrated by him, Fredy Hirsch wrote:

> When a young Jew arrives at the decision, I want to devote my life to my people, he must also come to the necessary conclusions; go to a training farm, become a worker in Eretz Israel, to conquer the land and, first of all, overcome all his fears and his laziness – to engage in sport, exercise, toughen his body and respond to the competitive urge.[20]

In short, he should, encouraged by the accompanying photographs of Jewish athletes, join the Maccabee sports association, spend time at the "Hagibor" sports ground (meaning "the hero" in Hebrew, and the only one to which Jews, and only Jews, were admitted), and become strong for the future. Many of Hirsch's accomplishments in Prague in 1939–1940 were carried over directly to the Terezin ghetto: when he served as deputy head of the Department for

18 *Jüdisches Nachrichtenblatt*, 15.12.1939.

19 *Jüdisches Nachrichtenblatt*, 8.12.1939.

20 *Jüdisches Nachrichtenblatt*, 22.3.1940.

Youth in the ghetto and also when he managed the children's home in the family camp at Birkenau, Fredy Hirsch remained faithful to this principle until the day of his death.[21]

The joint fundraising project of the Jewish community in Prague as well as *Keren Hayesod* and *Keren Kayemet*, "To Sacrifice – To Build – To Live" managed by engineer Otto Zucker, one of the leaders of the Zionist movement and from 1940 chairman of the Jewish community in Brno, the capital of Moravia, also attested to the atmosphere that prevailed at the time – as if emigration meant first and foremost immigration to Palestine. The donations, collected under the Nazis' supervision, were partly intended for Palestine. This is also confirmed by the warning to fraudulent donors: "'To Sacrifice – To Build – To Live" is the only fundraising campaign that has been approved by the authorities.'"[22] In May 1941, *Jüdisches Nachrichtenblatt* was still writing: "Contribute generously to the joint campaign of the Jewish community in Prague, the Keren Kayemet and the Keren Hayesod, 'To Sacrifice – To Build – To Live.'"

From 1939, the British mandate government in Palestine drastically reduced the number of immigration certificates: only 15,000 Jews were allowed to immigrate each year. It seemed as if salt was being poured on the wounds of those waiting their turn when those happy few who had certificates took leave of their friends and acquaintances in notices printed in the newspapers, sometimes also adding: "See you soon."

♦

21 See the Chapter, "Games in the Shadow of the Crematoria."

22 *Jüdisches Nachrichtenblatt*, 26.1.1940. Absurd situations were created. Moshe Tavor told the author that in 1939 he served as a fundraiser for Keren Hayesod, and according to the orders of the Gestapo headquarters, wherever he went he had to report to the local Gestapo office in every city and present the list of contributors. Jakob Edelstein, Director of the Palestine office at the time, feared that the Gestapo might regard those who failed to contribute as violators of the emigration order, and he advised Tavor to evade handing over the list of contributors, with various pretexts – to say he hadn't had time to prepare the lists, he had received only commitments but no cash, and the like – to avoid causing any harm to the local Jews.

JAHRGANG II. • Nr. 40
ROČNIK II. • Čís.

Erscheint jeden Freitag
Vychází každý pátek

PRAG, MITTWOCH, DEN 2. OKTOBER 1940.
PRAHA, STŘEDA DNE 2. ŘÍJNA 1940.

Jüdisches Nachrichtenblatt
Židovské listy

ORGAN DER JÜDISCHEN KULTUSGEMEINDE – PRAG – ORGÁN ŽIDOVSKÉ NÁBOŽENSKÉ OBCE – PRAHA

PREIS CENA K 2·-

REDAKTION · REDAKCE TELEFON 601-28, ADMINISTRATION · ADMINISTRACE TELEFON 602-49

Hygiene der Kleidung in Erez Israel

Kampf der Wintersnot

Auf jeden von uns kommt es an

Die Zeit der regnerischen, naßkalten Herbsttage hat begonnen. Da die rauhen Wintermonate vor der Türe stehen, empfinden die Armen und Bedürftigen doppelt ihre Not. Lassen wir den jüdischen Menschen nicht unnötig unter der Kälte leiden! Geben wir ihm, was er in diesem Augenblick am bittersten entbehrt!

Schenket Kleider, Wäsche und Schuhe!
Viele Menschen aus unseren Reihen bedürfen der Hilfe.
Die Kleidersammel-Aktion beginnt am 14. Oktober 1940

Verfolgen Sie alle weitere Ankündigungen in diesem Blatte und die Flugschriften, die Sie noch erhalten werden! Auf jeden von uns kommt es an.

Auf jedes einzelne Kleidungsstück kommt es an!

Wir wissen, daß Sie für jüdische Zwecke schon oft geopfert haben. Wir wissen: Auch diesmal werden Sie nicht abseits stehen!

Durchsuchen Sie sorgfältig Ihre Kleiderschränke! Sie werden dort sicherlich alte Anzüge, Wäsche und Schuhe finden, die Sie noch entbehren können. Ein Bedürftiger jedoch wird sie mit Tränen des Dankes entgegennehmen, denn Ihre Opfergabe ist ihm Schutz vor bitterster Kälte. Denken Sie an das ewig wahre Sprichwort: Doppelt gibt, wer schnell gibt.

Unsere Helfer werden Sie besuchen. Lassen Sie sie nicht mit leeren Händen aus Ihrer Wohnung gehen!

Schenket den Armen!

Jüdische Kultusgemeinde Prag

Rhythmus des Aufbaues

„Das Land gab seine Früchte" (Tehillim 67/7)

Archiv: Jüdisches Nachrichtenblatt

Da lacht allen unseren Chaluzim das Herz im Leibe: Kohlernte in Daganiah

Jüdische Siedler nach San Domingo

• Auch in Prag wurde vor einigen Monaten bekanntlich eine Gruppe von Personen zusammengestellt, um in die jüdische Domingo-Siedlung an der Sosua-Küste zu reisen. Dort werden sie am Aufbau der mit großen Mitteln errichteten Siedlung mitarbeiten.

Jetzt eingetroffenen Nachrichten zufolge wird an der Verwirklichung der Reisemöglichkeit unablässig gearbeitet. Wir erfahren, daß es möglich sein wird, die San Domingo Siedlungsgruppe bis Ende dieses Jahres zur Ausreise zu bringen.

Bei Anmeldung jüdischen Schmucks Angabe des Bruttowertes

• Prag. Die Prüfungsaktion des Finanzministeriums teilt mit, daß entsprechend den Bestimmungen der Kundmachung des Finanzministeriums …

Jewish News Leaves, the weekly published in German and Czech by the Jewish Community of Prague under SS censorship, was the only newspaper Jews were allowed to read under the Nazi occupation 1935–1945. Yad Vashem Archives (YVA), 0.7, October 2, 1940.

JAHRGANG II. • Nr. 42
ROČNIK II. • Čís. 42

Erscheint jeden Freitag
Vychází každý pátek

PRAG, FREITAG, DEN 18. OKTOBER 1940.
PRAHA, PÁTEK DNE 18. ŘÍJNA 1940.

Jüdisches Nachrichtenblatt
Židovské listy

ORGAN DER JÜDISCHEN KULTUSGEMEINDE – PRAG – ORGÁN ŽIDOVSKÉ NÁBOŽENSKÉ OBCE – PRAHA

PREIS CENA K 2·–

REDAKTION – REDAKCE TELEFON 601-28; ADMINISTRATION – ADMINISTRACE TELEFON 602-69

Die Armen rufen!

Weit wichtiger ist im gegenwärtigen Augenblick soziale Betätigung als theoretischer Redekampf. Eine solche praktische soziale Tat ist gerade die Sammlung von Wäsche, Kleidern und Schuhen, zu der die Jüdische Kultusgemeinde in Prag aufruft. Sprechen wir offen: Für Bitten ist keine geeignete Zeit, geht es doch um Beschaffung von ein bißchen Wärme in guter Kleidung und guten Schuhen, dringendst benötigt von Leuten unter uns. Auch die außerhalb der jüdischen Religionsgemeinschaft Stehenden sind dieser Sache bedürftig. Darum erscheint es uns nicht am Platze, solche Sachen nur zu erbitten von Leuten, die sie entbehren und denen schenken können, welche sie unbedingt benötigen. Wir leben einfach nicht mehr in den idyllischen Zeiten scheinheiliger Philantropie — in einer Welt harter Tatsachen leben wir, die durchdachte soziale Tat verlangt. Bedürftigen Leuten einige der Dinge zu geben, wie sie die Jüdische Kultusgemeinde sammelt, dünkt uns der Maßstab für die soziale Reife der jüdischen Gesellschaft, der jetzt auch die konfessionslosen und die getauften Juden angehören. Der an die philantropischen Sammlungen der Vergangenheit Gewohnte muß sich in der heutigen Zeit von solcher Einstellung befreien. Einstmals fanden zugunsten der Armen pompöse gesellschaftliche Veranstaltungen statt, bei denen die Reichen Geld ausgaben, um die Armen wenn schon nicht leben, so zumindest vegetieren zu lassen. Mit dieser Form und Vorstellung von Wohltätigkeit ist jetzt endgültig Schluß, nicht würden wir damit erreichen. Es gilt, das Gefühl in praktische wirksame Tat umzusetzen. Diese Sammlung ist eine solche Gelegenheit. Auch dem Kinde gilt diese Sammlung, sollen doch die Kleidchen, Wäsche und Schuhe ihren zarten Organismus vor Auswirkungen des kommenden Winters bewahren. Nur ein schlechter und gefühlloser Mensch könnte diese Sachen für die Kinder verweigern. In erster Reihe wenden wir uns deshalb an die Frauen, die Mütter, die Leben schaffen und erneuern, und das zu geben, was ihre Kinder nicht mehr brauchen und bißchen Wärme und Lebensannehmlichkeit den armen und bedürftigen Kindern zu verschaffen vermag.

Wir sind überzeugt, daß die Frauen, die Mütter, für diese Äußerung menschlichen Gefühls das größte Verständnis haben, umgewandelt in ein Geschenk als praktische Tat. Es handelt sich um eine gemeinsame soziale Aktion, bei der auch die zur Abteilung B Gehörenden nicht untätig bleiben können. Auch um unsere jungen Leute, um unsere Kinder und Alten handelt es sich, denen in der heutigen Zeit geholfen werden muß. Wer ernten will, muß auch säen. Es gibt keine edlere Ernte ehrlicher Arbeit als diese gemeinsame Sammlung. Darum weiset das Ansuchen der auch für diese Sammlung besuchenden Mitarbeiter der Jüdischen Kultusgemeinde nicht ab! Gebet, ihr helft damit den Armen!

Zweite Veröffentlichung (Wiederholung aus Nr. 41/II. Jahrgang):

Verordnung des Reichsprotektors in Böhmen und Mähren über die Vermietung von Judenwohnungen
Nařízení Reichsprotektora in Böhmen und Mähren o pronajímání židovských bytů

Vom 7. Oktober 1940.

Auf Grund des § 1 der Verordnung über das Rechtsetzungsrecht im Protektorat Böhmen und Mähren vom 7. Juni 1939 (RGBl. I, S. 1039) wird verordnet:

§ 1

(¹) Wohnungen (Wohnräume), die an Juden (§ 6 der VO. des Reichsprotektors in Böhmen und Mähren über das jüd. Vermögen vom 21. Juli 1939 — VBlRProt. S. 45) vermietet sind, dürfen bei Auflösung des Mietvertrages nur mit Zustimmung der Zentralstelle für jüdische Auswanderung in Prag vermietet werden. Entgegen dieser Bestimmung abgeschlossene Mietverträge sind unwirksam.

(²) Diese Anordnung erstreckt sich auch auf Wohnungen (Wohnräume), die von Juden nach Auflösung des Mietverhältnisses noch innegehabt werden oder nach dem 30. Juni 1940 geräumt und noch nicht wieder bezogen wurden. Darüber abgeschlossene Mietverträge können von der Zentralstelle für jüdische Auswanderung für unwirksam erklärt werden.

(³) Die Zentralstelle für jüdische Auswanderung kann die Ausübung der ihr zustehenden Befugnisse auf die Oberlandräte übertragen.

§ 2

Durch Maßnahme nach dieser Verordnung werden Entschädigungsansprüche nicht begründet.

§ 3

Sind Wohnungen entgegen den Bestimmungen oder unter Umgehung der Bestimmungen dieser Verordnung vermietet worden, so kann die Zentralstelle für jüdische Auswanderung die Räumung der Wohnung anordnen. Nach fruchtlosem Ablauf der im Räumungsbescheid festgesetzten Frist kann die Zentralstelle für jüdische Auswanderung die Exekution durch zwangsweise Räumung bei Gericht beantragen. Die Kosten des Zwangsverfahrens sind dem Vermieter aufzuerlegen.

§ 4

Diese Verordnung tritt mit der Verkündigung in Kraft.

Prag, den 7. Oktober 1940.

Ze dne 7. října 1940.

Na základě § 1. nařízení o právu vydávati právní předpisy v Protektorátu Böhmen und Mähren ze dne 7. června 1939 (Říšský zák. I., str. 1039) se nařizuje:

§ 1.

(¹) Byty (obytné místnosti), pronajaté Židům (§ 6, nař. Reichsprotektora in Böhmen und Mähren o židovském majetku ze dne 21. července 1939 — Věstn. R. prot. str. 45.), smějí býti při zrušení nájemné smlouvy pronajaty jen se svolením Ústředny pro židovské vystěhovalectví v Praze. Nájemní smlouvy proti tomuto ustanovení uzavřené jsou neúčinné.

(²) Toto nařízení vztahuje se též na byty (obytné místnosti), které mají Židé v držení ještě po zrušení nájemného poměru nebo byly po 30. června 1940 vyklizeny a nebyly ještě znovu zaujaty. Smlouvy o tom uzavřené mohou býti Ústřednou pro židovské vystěhovalectví prohlášeny neúčinnými.

(³) Ústředna pro židovské vystěhovalectví může výkon oprávnění jí příslušejících přenésti na Oberlandraty.

§ 2.

Opatření podle tohoto nařízení nezakládají nároků na odškodnění.

§ 3.

Byly-li byty pronajaty proti ustanovením nebo za obejití ustanovení tohoto nařízení, může Ústředna pro židovské vystěhovalectví nařídit vyklizení bytu. Po bezvýsledném uplynutí lhůty stanovené ve vyklizovacím výměru může Ústředna pro židovské vystěhovalectví navrhnouti soudu exekuci nuceným vyklizením. Náklady donucovacího řízení buďtež uloženy pronajímateli.

§ 4.

Toto nařízení nabývá platnosti vyhlášením.

V Praze dne 7. října 1940.

Der Reichsprotektor in Böhmen und Mähren
In Vertretung
K. H. FRANK,
Staatssekretär.

Kampf der Wintersnot
Schenket den Armen Wärme!

Jede, noch so kleine Opfergabe ist ein Sonnenstrahl in kalten Wintertagen

Die Kleidersammlung der Jüdischen Kultusgemeinde Prag hat am 14. Oktober begonnen. Unsere Sammler werden Sie in den nächsten Tagen besuchen. Verpacken Sie, bitte, schon jetzt Ihre Opfergabe. Zögern Sie nicht — auch der Winter zögert nicht. Melden Sie Ihre Gabe an, mit Postkarte oder telefonisch.

Soziolabteilung der Jüd. Kultusgemeinde Prag V., Josefstädterstr. 5, Tel. 63151-52

Jeder Sammler ist mit einer Legitimation und Fotografie versehen. Verlangen Sie in jedem Falle deren Vorweisung.

Achter Durchführungserlaß

zur Verordnung des Reichsprotektors in Böhmen und Mähren über das jüdische Vermögen vom 21. Juni 1939 (VBlRProt. S. 45).

Vom 16. September 1940.

Auf Grund des § 11, Abs. 1, der Verordnung des Reichsprotektors in Böhmen und Mähren über das jüdische Vermögen vom 21. Juni 1939 wird bestimmt:

§ 1.

(¹) Juden, jüdische Unternehmen und jüdische Personenvereinigungen haben bis zum 15. November 1940 den in ihrem Eigentum oder Miteigentum stehenden, im Protektorat Böhmen und Mähren befindlichen Wertpapierbesitz mit Ausnahme der in § 3 des Zweiten Durchführungserlasses vom 8. Dezember 1939 (VBlRProt. S. 313) genannten Wertpapiere anzumelden.

(²) § 2 des Vierten Durchführungserlasses vom 7. Februar 1940 (VBlRProt. S. 45) findet Anwendung. Die Anmeldepflicht obliegt auch der Devisenbank, in deren Depot nach § 1 des Fünften Durchführungserlasses vom 2. März 1940 (VBlRProt. S. 81) die Wertpapiere eingelegt sind.

§ 2.

Soweit bereits nach dem Vierten Durchführungserlaß eine Anmeldung erfolgte, braucht sie nicht wiederholt zu werden.

§ 3.

Die Anmeldung erfolgt nach dem Stande vom 1. November 1940.

§ 4.

Die Anmeldung hat auf einem amtlichen Vordruck zu erfolgen, der bei den Devisenbanken in Empfang zu nehmen ist. Sie ist beim Reichsprotektor einzureichen. Soweit die Wertpapiere im Depot einer Devisenbank liegen, sind die Anmeldungen bis zum 1. November 1940 dieser zur Überprüfung und Weiterleitung einzureichen.

§ 5.

Der Anmeldepflicht unterliegen ferner Wertpapiere, die dem nichtjüdischen Ehegatten eines Juden gehören, dessen Ehe am 1. November 1940 nicht geschieden oder getrennt ist. Diese Anmeldungen sind besonders zu kennzeichnen.

§ 6.

In gleicher Weise haben Juden, jüdische Unternehmen und jüdische Personenvereinigungen sowie nichtjüdische Personen, die mit einem Juden verheiratet sind, in Zukunft jeden Eigentums- oder Miteigentumserwerb von Wertpapieren innerhalb eines Monates vom Zeitpunkt des Erwerbes an anzumelden.

§ 7.

Der Anmeldepflicht nach dem Vierten Durchführungserlaß unterliegt auch jeder nach Ablauf der Anmeldefrist jenes Erlasses erfolgte Erwerb durch Juden oder durch nichtjüdische Personen, die mit einem Juden verheiratet sind. Die Anmeldung ist innerhalb einer Frist von zwei Wochen vom Zeitpunkt des Erwerbs vorzunehmen.

Prag, den 16. September 1940.

Der Reichsprotektor in Böhmen und Mähren

Freiherr von Neurath

The world of yesterday was collapsing. One sign of this was the self-help projects introduced by the Jewish community in Prague. In the past, there had been very few welfare cases among Prague Jewry, and most of the aid projects in the city were meant for the Jews of Subcarpathian Ruthenia – the eastern, poorer part of Czechoslovakia. Now warm rooms, a heated room for children, a hostel for men who were temporarily in Prague to arrange for their emigration, were set up. At the end of 1940, there were five old age homes for Jews, two orphanages, ten children's day care centers, two hospitals, a mental hospital and an outpatient clinic. The soup kitchen expanded from day to day: before the war 150 people ate there each day; in March 1940, 2,300 meals were served there daily, including to former bank clerks, merchants and agents. A former factory owner from Reichenberg, an older man in a threadbare coat, told a *Jüdisches Nachrichtenblatt* correspondent that in past years he had visited Prague frequently and always stayed in a good hotel. "Now," he said, "I go to the soup kitchen, get some soup and a main course on a tin tray, and eat it at a long wooden table. It tastes almost as good to me as the food I ate at the good hotels. A man has to learn to adapt."[23]

In the spring of 1940, destitute emigrants were in need of clothing for their travels. In October 1940, the Jewish community of Prague launched a winter campaign to collect used clothing, underwear and shoes: "Each of us counts! Every item of clothing is important! Now, when the harsh winter months are approaching, the distress of the poor and the needy is twofold. We are sure – this time too you won't stand by idly. Contribute to the poor!"[24]

In the fall of 1941, another call for help was issued: "We are demanding sacrifice! Contribute to the clothing warehouse! We especially need warm clothes, high shoes, gloves, sweaters, warm clothing."[25] Only between the lines could one read: the transports to the East have begun.

♦

23 *Jüdisches Nachrichtenblatt*, 8.3.1940.

24 *Jüdisches Nachrichtenblatt*, 2.10.1940.

25 *Jüdisches Nachrichtenblatt*, 17.10.1041.

A few of the important laws relating to Jewish property and the exclusion of Jews from economic life were published even before *Jüdisches Nachrichtenblatt* began to appear. In April and May of 1940, the newspaper began to print, in installments, a summary of all the regulations and orders relating to the legal status of the Jews in public life, including those ordering the ousting of Jews from their employment as lawyers, public notaries, physicians and veterinarians, technicians and mine engineers. These orders were signed by the Czech puppet government.[26] From 23 October 1939, employers could terminate the work contracts of Jews by giving them discharge notices six weeks in advance, without the employees having any rights to compensation or severance pay.[27]

Orders issued by the *Reichsprotektor,* on 26 January 1940, announced the liquidation of Jewish businesses, at first in the textile, footwear and leather sectors, the main areas of commerce in which Jews engaged. The list of those businesses and trades being liquidated grew constantly. From 31 March 1940, Jews and companies belonging to Jews were forbidden to engage in the following economic spheres: retail and wholesale businesses, insurance, hotels and guest houses, travel, guiding tourists, shipping, transport and storage, transportation, banking and money changing, mortgages, guarding, collection of funds, real estate, advertising, employment agencies and matchmaking. Thus, Jews were ousted from all branches of commerce. Anyone selling their businesses or holding out-of-the-ordinary general sales up to the stated date would be punished under the law.[28]

First, the Jews and Jewish businesses had to submit a report to the national bank on all gold, silver and platinum objects, precious stones and pearls, and all the other jewelry and art works they owned. They then had to hand them over for "safekeeping" to one of the banks dealing in foreign currency commerce. The only exceptions were wedding rings, the wedding ring of a deceased spouse, a watch or silver pocket watch, two place settings of silver

26 *Jüdisches Nachrichtenblatt*, 3.5.1940.
27 *Jüdisches Nachrichtenblatt*, 4.9.1940.
28 *Jüdisches Nachrichtenblatt*, 21.1.1941.

cutlery per person, and false teeth made of a precious metal for personal use.[29] All of this was worded in official legalese: after all, it was being implemented according to the law.

From October 1940, when the lease on apartments rented to Jews expired, it was no longer possible to rent them to new Jewish tenants, except with the consent of the Center for the Emigration of Jews. Evicted Jews were permitted to move, as subtenants, only to apartments serving as dwellings for Jews.[30] The housing problems of the Jews worsened; the Germans had already expropriated many villas and apartments belonging to Jews in the better neighborhoods of the city for their own use, and their owners or tenants were evicted with only a few hours notice. The Jewish community sent surveyors to apartments still occupied by Jews to find rooms for subtenants. In a short item printed in *Jüdisches Nachrichtenblatt*, a surveyor, under the initials St.E., described the cool reception he often got from the owners of apartments. That did not deter him: "There are Jews without a roof over their heads. No one can evade helping out, even if it is at the expense of his own comfort. Nothing is achieved by giving in."[31]

These great blows, like the confiscation of property or the prohibition against working in a profession, were often staggering, but were somehow comprehensible within the framework of Nazi policy. It was the unceasing stream of the "small" prohibitions printed in nearly every issue of the weekly that was excruciating: a prohibition against entering the castle area (31 October 1940) and Wenceslas square (12 June 1941), against entering woods and forests in the Prague area (this, at the initiative of the Prague municipality on 20 September 1940). The Czech police commissioner, Chorvát, announced: "Under clauses 2 and 3, paragraph 1, of the Law Arranging Jewish Property, to take effect immediately, I forbid Jews to shop in Aryan stores, except between the hours of 11:00–13:00 and 15:00–16:30" (13 August 1940). From January 1941, the time when Jews were permitted to shop in stores and markets was

29 *Jüdisches Nachrichtenblatt*, 22.3.1940.
30 *Jüdisches Nachrichtenblatt*, 13.9.1940.
31 *Jüdisches Nachrichtenblatt*, 24.1.1941.

limited to 3–5 p.m., when almost no food was left because of the short wartime supplies.

From 1 September 1941, every Jew from the age of six had to wear the Jewish patch. "It is forbidden to appear in public without the symbol of the Jews. The symbol of the Jews is a six-pointed star, the size of a hand, made of yellow fabric, bearing the inscription *Jude* in black. It must be worn so that it is visible on the clothing, on the left side of the chest" (26 September 1941).

The humiliations and the isolation worsened, beginning with the prohibition against entering museums and exhibitions (19 December 1941), through the prohibition against borrowing books (12 September 1941) and ending with the prohibition against selling or giving as gifts fruit or vegetables, mushrooms and nuts, fresh or dried, to Jews (17 October 1941). Tobacco and its products were not to be sold to Jews (30 October 1941), then fish, wine and garlic (16 January 1942). From 1942, the Jews were forbidden to use trams, buses or trolleys from 3 p.m. on Saturday until Monday morning. On other days, Jews were allowed to use public transport only if they had a medical certificate or a paper attesting to their having been mobilized to work (23 January 1942). Later, Jews were forbidden to use dry cleaning services and a prohibition was issued against selling hats to Jews – men, boys or children (27 March 1942). Jews were also forbidden to buy or have repaired suitcases or knapsacks, items so essential for the transports (17 April 1942). The sale of German newspapers to Jews was forbidden, and then also the sale of Czech papers (1 May 1942). The use of public telephones too was forbidden to Jews (6 February 1942).

This is only a small selection of the hundreds of prohibitions and orders published in *Jüdisches Nachrichtenblatt* in the first two years of its existence. It was nearly impossible to comply with all the prohibitions, although the Jewish community constantly issued warnings:

> For the good of the individual and the community, we remind all those regarded as Jews under clause 16 of the Reichsprotektor's orders of June 21, 1939, to comply with all the instructions of the law relating to Jews. Every violation of the

> law, even if only out of negligence, has serious consequences for the individual and causes difficulties for the entire Jewish community. Every Jew, every Jewess, must be aware of their great responsibility towards this community.[32]

♦

Emigration was the main subject in the first two years of *Jüdisches Nachrichtenblatt*'s existence. On 15 December 1939, the newspaper reported on a national conference of chairmen of the Jewish communities held in Prague, whose deliberations centered on the organization of emigration. Weidmann and Edelstein presented a general survey on the issues involved in emigration and discussed with the participants all the existing possibilities of leaving the country. At the end of the deliberations, the chairmen of the communities visited the Center for the Emigration of the Jews, whose establishment, according to Weidmann, had simplified the emigration procedures. The future emigrant no longer had to dash from office to office; now, the time from submission of the application for emigration with the necessary attached documents (certificate of address, certificate of good character, confirmation of examinations of property, income tax approval, etc.) until receipt of the approval for emigration took only two weeks at the most (about the extortion, the humiliation, the abuse and the war of nerves that went on in the Center for Emigration – he wisely said nothing).

Attempts were made to place the necessity to emigrate in an historical context: "The entire history of the Jews is nothing other than eternal wandering; in the Diaspora, Jews never found rest or refuge. We need to go back to the sources, to the Jewish writings, to Jewish customs, to draw courage from them. Anyone who learns about his people and understands its history, will also bear his fate with dignity."[33]

In an item signed with the initials J.E., Jakob Edelstein, deputy

32 *Jüdisches Nachrichtenblatt*, 9.5.1941.

33 *Jüdisches Nachrichtenblatt*, 8.12.1939.

chairman of the Jewish community of Prague, in his laconic style, added his thoughts about the problem of Jewish wandering. For a long time, it was the lot of the individual, who was usually motivated by economic considerations and supported by philanthropic organizations. The second period of emigration, which he defined as "Herzlian," had different attributes: it was a well-planned, organized emigration of a large number of Jewish groups to Palestine. Now the issue of emigration was the lot of all the Jews: "Now is the time to endow a goal and direction to the strong urge of all the Jews to emigrate, whether they are people of means or penniless."[34]

This was the theory. But in practice, money was required to obtain entry visas, to buy ship tickets, and to pay bond fees abroad. On 24 January 1940, the *Jüdisches Nachrichtenblatt* published a special issue devoted entirely to the question of emigration:

> We must emigrate – that is an ironclad rule. We are dealing with emigration – that is our plan. We are nothing other than part of the great migration of the peoples, the Jewish section. A comedian – or someone who considered himself a comedian – once told the writer of these lines [whose name was not mentioned]: "To me, your newspaper looks like a huge poster with a screaming headline: "Out with us!" He isn't a comedian, but a philosopher. Without intending to, he spoke the truth. Yes, we are a poster bearing the heading: "Out with us!" because we are just an out-of-tune musical instrument, on which the authorities responsible for emigration are playing their truly sad melodies.

To dally meant taking a risk: "Better one emigration permit in hand than a thousand vain hopes." In his article, "One Year of the New Arrangement and Wandering," Singer wrote with great candor: "The obligation of general emigration has rapidly become popular, because the orders relating to Jews have given it the necessary push."[35]

34 *Jüdisches Nachrichtenblatt*, 26.7.1940.

35 *Jüdisches Nachrichtenblatt*, 26.7.1940.

Countries that in the past no Jew would have thought of were now being considered as possible destinations for a new life: Madagascar, the Dominican Republic, San Salvador, Honduras, the Philippines, Haiti, British Guyana, western India, Persia, Siam, Libya, Tangiers, Angola, Mozambique. The list of the Department for Emigration of the Jewish community in Prague contained fifty-seven countries.[36] And indeed, by the end of 1939, 20,000 Jews, i.e., twenty-five percent of the Jewish population, managed to emigrate from the area of the Protectorate.[37]

There was no lack of grandiose plans for a mass emigration: early in 1940 a plan was proposed for settlement in Bolivia, on an area of 14,000 hectares close to the estuary of the Rio Pirai and the Rio Grande. The plan was intended mainly for married farmers and tradesmen up to the age of forty, and preference was given to families with many children. Those interested were asked not to trouble the authorities for the time being or to besiege them with applications. In addition, a photograph of La Paz, the capital of Bolivia, was printed, along with an article entitled "Bolivia, the Land of the Future, and its Natural Resources," and some advice was offered: "Don't be afraid, not of snakes, not of mosquitoes."[38] Ten months later, the *Jüdisches Nachrichtenblatt* announced that the issuance of entry visas to Bolivia had been discontinued.[39]

There was talk of settlement in Alaska, a country, which in the paper's view, was suffering unjustifiably from a negative image.[40] A plan for settlement in the Virgin Islands was touted in a huge headline, but nothing further was mentioned; a project for settlement in the Philippines was abandoned due to technical considerations of transportation.[41] The grandest plan of all, written about more than any of the others, was a plan to settle one hundred thousand refugees from Europe in San Domingo. In February 1940, an item was printed with great fanfare about an agreement signed between

36 *Jüdisches Nachrichtenblatt*, 1.12.1940.
37 *Jüdisches Nachrichtenblatt*, 15.3.1940.
38 *Jüdisches Nachrichtenblatt*, 5.1.1940.
39 *Jüdisches Nachrichtenblatt*, 17.1.1940.
40 *Jüdisches Nachrichtenblatt*, 21.4.1940.
41 *Jüdisches Nachrichtenblatt*, 1.11.1940.

the President of the Dominican Republic, Rafael Trujillo, and the settlement company regarding the Sosua agricultural colony. An area of 26,000 hectares was set aside for the colony between the coast and the fertile valley of the Yasika River, and it was intended mainly for the young and the strong.[42] A year later, these hopes were dashed: "Despite the many efforts and the large sums invested in establishing the colony [which almost certainly disappeared into Trujillo's pockets], it was possible to bring only 583 settlers to San Domingo, and it is almost certain that this number will not increase considerably during this year."[43]

The most preferred country of immigration was the United States. "Nearly every Jew in Europe knows someone in the United States," the newspaper claimed. But this did not mean much. On 12 January 1940, the main headline of *Jüdisches Nachrichtenblatt* announced that in the framework of the quota for the Protectorate, 77,000 people were registered at the American Consulate in Prague (according to figures for 1 October 1939, the number of Jews living in the Protectorate then was 90,147, ten percent of them members of a different religion[44]); out of this number, 32,000 had registered by December 1938, and these too were still waiting for an entry visa. Those waiting were told that the validity of the affidavit (namely, the financial guarantee by an American resident that the new immigrant would not become a burden on the country) expired after a while. The possessor of an affidavit that was considered "weak" "must take into account that he will have to submit a new affidavit, issued within the last year, to the Consulate." Only professors, actors, singers, nurses and clergymen and possessors of a work contract approved by the American Ministry of Labor were exempt from presenting an affidavit. Only American citizens who had obtained their citizenship before 22 September 1922 were entitled to ask to bring their parents to the United States according to a quota for those with higher priorities. This depressing news

42 *Jüdisches Nachrichtenblatt*, 9.2.1940.
43 *Jüdisches Nachrichtenblatt*, 17.1.1941.
44 *Jüdisches Nachrichtenblatt*, 1.12.1939.

was accompanied by a photograph of an illuminated New York skyscraper, "The Sea of Lights of the Metropolis."[45]

Instead of gaining some relief in view of the growing hardships of their life, the Jews were faced with new obstacles: the American Consulate received instructions to be more stringent in examining the personality of those submitting an application for an entry visa: "If the Consuls cast any doubt on the applicant's chances of becoming a worthy and beneficial citizen, they refuse to grant the visa. Usually, no reason is given for the refusal."[46]

As if the obstacles placed by the United States authorities in the way of those awaiting emigration were not enough, in May 1940, following the invasion of France and the shores of western Europe, there was a new problem: getting to a ship. The newspaper did not print any direct news about the fateful events of the war, but in the items on the possibilities of emigration, it referred to new difficulties that had arisen, including the fact that all the transit visas through Switzerland had expired. The route to ships sailing from the ports of Genoa and Trieste was closed.[47] Intensive negotiations were held to find a solution to the problem of travel by land. The Department for Emigration, under the management of the untiring Hanna Steiner, concentrated all its efforts on finding a route to North America and Shanghai, which the *Jüdisches Nachrichtenblatt* called "a goal and a bridge." For some time a work contract or 400 dollars were enough to obtain a visa, but later a permit issued by the Japanese authorities was also required.[48] "Although the possibilities of transport overseas are almost nil, there is no reason to abandon the way embarked on by the emigrants, to sever all contacts and to sit idly by and accept everything passively. It will be necessary to find a way to help the emigrants get to their destinations."[49]

It was a war of nerves: the American entry visa for the emigrants was valid for only four months and was not extendable.

45 *Jüdisches Nachrichtenblatt*, 2.5.1941.
46 *Jüdisches Nachrichtenblatt*, 3.1.1941–13.6.1941.
47 *Jüdisches Nachrichtenblatt*, 12.1.1940.
48 *Jüdisches Nachrichtenblatt*, 13.12.1940.
49 *Jüdisches Nachrichtenblatt*, 31.5.1940.

Anyone who, for technical or financial reasons, was unable to leave at once, had to, once his entry visa expired, apply for a new visa and wait again.[50] The voyage by ship to the United States was possible then only via two routes: through Lisbon or through the Soviet Union and Japan. According to *Jüdisches Nachrichtenblatt*, there was still a possibility of traveling ten days through the Soviet Union to the Japanese port of Kobe, but all the ship tickets from there to North America, to Central America and South America were sold out.[51] The wait for a place on ships sailing from ports in Portugal and Spain was lengthy, and in any case the emigrant needed a Spanish and Portuguese transit visa and a way to get there by land. In October 1940, the first page of the newspaper reported on a new possibility: traveling four days by train through Berlin and Paris to San Sebastian at a cost of 400 marks and eighty-four dollars.[52] It was also possible to fly with Lufthansa or Ala Littoria airlines to Madrid (270 marks). To use either of these routes, the emigrant had to have relatives or friends abroad with means. Details could be obtained from the Department for Emigration, which outwardly showed no signs of giving up: "We cannot talk at all about the absence of any possibility of emigration... there are still routes overseas. We only need patience."[53]

Those leaving the borders of the Protectorate were permitted to take only four dollars and ten marks with them along with vouchers for 150 grams of bread per person. They were advised to take one or two thermoses of drink, a warm blanket and a small pillow.[54] They left with a sigh of relief: "We are leaving equipped with knowledge and our ability, to once again serve humanity, to contribute to the general good. Once again we will know why we are living. This will be a way to freedom," R.Fl. wrote in the section "A Small Feuilleton."[55]

50 *Jüdisches Nachrichtenblatt*, 19.1.1940.
51 *Jüdisches Nachrichtenblatt*, 25.10.1940.
52 *Jüdisches Nachrichtenblatt*, 15.11.1940.
53 *Jüdisches Nachrichtenblatt*, 9.5.1941.
54 *Jüdisches Nachrichtenblatt*, 16.5.1940.
55 *Jüdisches Nachrichtenblatt*, 13.9.1940.

On 20 June 1941, the newspaper announced the new year of American immigration quotas beginning on 1 July: the number of those registered had increased in the meantime to 86,000, while the quota for the Protectorate of Bohemia and Moravia was 2,874 a year. The thousands of applicants for immigration to the United States had only to wait patiently another ten or twenty years. There was a possibility of an interim stay in Cuba for six months: to do so one needed 2,500 dollars and a return ticket.[56] But all this was now theoretical in any case: the victories of the German army on the eastern front that opened on 22 June 1941 (not mentioned in the weekly) afforded a more effective solution to the Jewish problem than emigration. On 23 August 1941, Himmler ordered the cessation of Jewish emigration.

The question is: how many thousands of Jews would have been saved if the United States or Great Britain had shown a somewhat more humane attitude towards those attempting to flee? But questions of what might-have-been-if are painful, and will no longer help anyone.

♦

Since most of the possibilities for emigration, so long as any existed, were intended for the young and those capable of working, a large number of old and weak people remained in the area of the Protectorate, and someone had to care for them. A summary of the work undertaken in 1939–1940 by the Jewish community in Prague stated: "Yes, we often had to undertake this obligation, so that the young could emigrate. The existing old age homes were expanded and new ones established."[57] Elderly parents remained behind in the hope that their children would attempt to bring them over as soon as they were able to do so financially. An old couple, married for forty years, consoled one another: the children have already emigrated, "Hanna is in Argentina, Stella in Australia, Mitzi in Montevideo, Julia and Kurt in Africa, Pepa in Palestine. We too

56 *Jüdisches Nachrichtenblatt*, 20.6.1941.
57 *Jüdisches Nachrichtenblatt*, 26.7.1940.

will succeed in leaving safely. The ship tickets to Argentina are already on the way."[58] It would be interesting to know – did they succeed in escaping or were they stuck there like so many others? But the family name was not mentioned.

> A twenty-month old infant has to leave to join his parents. The ship ticket has been paid for, valid for all the ships from the port of Genoa. We are looking for a woman or a responsible couple to take him with them. A fee of fifty dollars will be paid when they arrive in New York.[59]

The "small notice" section, generally printed on the last page of *Jüdisches Nachrichtenblatt*, reflected the overall political and economic developments relating to the individual, the gradual decrease in expectations and demands, and the growing poverty. In the spring of 1940, elegantly furnished rooms, with a separate entrance, use of the kitchen, bathroom, telephone, sometimes with an elevator and central heating, were still offered for rent in a beautiful suburb of villas, sometimes with breakfast or all meals served. In another notice, a black fur coat was offered in exchange for a fur-lined coat in good condition. Before all the furs belonging to Jews were confiscated, a writer in the weekly advised "the elegant Jewish woman in the café, wearing a splendid fur coat and a fashionable hat" not to attract attention, not to provoke.[60]

Advertisements of cafés still open to Jews appeared: "Pelikán," "Jaro," "Tepna," "Ascherman," a garden restaurant in the Braník quarter, *pensions* outside of Prague, and the possibility of spending time in the spa of Luhačovice at the Miramar Hotel. Dr. Scheuer still offered his services in cases of premature ejaculation, sexual weakness, distress owing to a nervous condition and inferiority complexes.[61] But who did not feel distress?

One could still be choosy: in matchmaking notices, a 45-

58 *Jüdisches Nachrichtenblatt*, 15.11.1940.
59 *Jüdisches Nachrichtenblatt*, 26.1.1940.
60 *Jüdisches Nachrichtenblatt*, 19.1.1940.
61 *Jüdisches Nachrichtenblatt*, 23.2.1940.

year-old merchant, very active in his business, was looking for "a charming, educated woman, with lively spirits, from a good Jewish home, with an impeccable past, no more than thirty-five years of age."[62] Under the code name "Photograph," a 27-year-old academician was looking for an attractive woman with a nice body for the purpose of conversation.[63] And the best find of all: "A 46-year-old American wants to meet a nice young lady with means for purposes of marriage and return to the United States."[64] It's hard to understand why he needed to advertise in the paper. What was the catch?

There were also benefits to be gained from the hardships of the Jews:

- "We buy everything you don't need when you move or emigrate. Offers to 'Quick Buyer'."[65]
- "An (Aryan) physician wants to rent (buy) a clinic with all its equipment, monthly payments," appeared in the same issue that reported that all Jewish physicians were losing the right to work in their profession, along with a list of thirty Jewish physicians in the Prague area who were permitted to treat only Jewish patients.[66]
- "Purchases antique crystal glasses, also etched."[67]

The times became more and more difficult:

- "Who is prepared to give someone working in his home a bed, cupboard, sofa and chair?"
- "Looking for a generous donor, I need a clothes closet. Apply to '70-year-old.'"
- On 24 January 1941, a Czech glass worker offered marriage to a young woman or widow with an apartment of her own. "Apply to: 'A physical flaw is not a deterrent.'"
- "Can a skilled 27-year-old tradesman find a companion for

62 *Jüdisches Nachrichtenblatt*, 19.4.1940.
63 *Jüdisches Nachrichtenblatt*, 28.6.1940.
64 *Jüdisches Nachrichtenblatt*, 6.9.1940.
65 *Jüdisches Nachrichtenblatt*, 1.3.1940.
66 *Jüdisches Nachrichtenblatt*, 2.8.1940.
67 *Jüdisches Nachrichtenblatt*, 20.12.1940.

life? A simple, small woman, who cares more about inner value than outward appearance? Apply to: 'A shared path.'"

The following notice appeared on 7 November 1941, after the transports had begun. Then many people married hastily so they would not go alone to the unknown. Now the most essential items for the journey were required:

- "Looking to exchange very sturdy shoes, size 38, for a larger pair."

Jews who lost their livelihood and the right to engage in their professions sought and also found possibilities of earning a living suited to the hard times:

- "Professional, flawless black-out shades at the cheapest prices."
- "Cleaning floors, doors and windows with my own tools."
- "Dyeing stockings in all shades."
- "I repair underwear and stockings, you'll be satisfied. I pick up and deliver."
- "Removing shine from suits. Even the oldest suit will be like new after I treat it. 5 Ve-Smečkách St., door 16."
- "A Star of David as a pendant, with initials if you like, cheap and beautiful. Apply to 'Alpaca' [type of metal made of nickel silver]."
- "Shrouds sewn quickly. Call 12657 – Frank."

♦

From 1940, Jewish men born between 1891 and 1923 were mobilized for labor. Several thousand of them worked paving roads, laying railroad tracks, in forestry and in agriculture. In 1941, the work mobilization order was transferred to the labor center of the Prague community, which established work units comprised of men whose medical examinations showed they were capable of physical labor. It was compulsory to undergo the examinations and report for work: "Everyone assigned by the Prague community to remove snow must report immediately when the snowfall begins, but no later than 7.30 a.m. the following day."[68] In the first year of the occupation, the data collected and the registration of all the Jews by the Jewish community served mainly as a means of self- and mutual help; later they made it easier to assemble the transports.

The assassination of Reinhard Heydrich, the Reichsprotektor of Bohemia and Moravia, on 4 June 1942 was not mentioned at all in *Jüdisches Nachrichtenblatt*, although these events cost the lives of thousands of Jews. The main news item on 10 July 1942 merely stated:

> The death penalty will be imposed on anyone harboring in his home or giving any assistance to a person who he knows, or according to the circumstances he should assume, has any part in acts of hostility against the Reich, or anyone who fails immediately to inform the authorities of this, in particular if he knows that that person is not registered with the police as required and does not possess a lawful identity card.

The death penalty was also imposed on anyone forging identity papers or supplying forged identity papers, or acting as a middleman in obtaining them. In addition, the time period in which house or apartment owners had to notify the authorities of every new tenant was shortened from three days to 24 hours. Hundreds of Jews who had gone underground and were living with false papers were discovered in thorough house searches or lost their shelter. A punitive transport of one thousand people left Prague on 10 June 1942 headed directly eastward. Only two of the passengers remained alive: one of them jumped from the train on the way to Poland.[69]

The number of Jews in the Protectorate constantly decreased, and so did the number of pages in the weekly. From May 1941 the number of pages was reduced from sixteen to ten; from 11 July to

68 *Jüdisches Nachrichtenblatt*, 16.1.1942.

69 Zdenek Lederer, *Ghetto Theresenstadt* (London: Edward Solston & Son, 1953), p. 215.

six; a week later to four, and from 3 October 1941 until it closed down, only two pages, one sheet, remained. Its last editor was Dr. Viktor Kollek (married to a non-Jew). The newspaper, the only one the Jews could purchase, adapted to the situation, and in addition to the weekly Jewish calendar, from the fall of 1942 it published mainly notices meant for the population as a whole: the hours of blackout; the reduced hours of the postal service; ways of saving electricity, gas and water, including the prohibition against taking baths; the introduction of a new siren signal; guidelines for behavior during an air raid;[70] and the obligation to report cases of whooping cough. Here and there something "Jewish" was still printed, such as the prohibition against using linen presses, the prohibition of mixed marriages or sexual relations outside of marriage between a Jew and a non-Jewish citizen of the Protectorate, or a notice that Jews living outside the borders of the Protectorate had lost their citizenship and their property would be confiscated.[71]

The next chapter of the story is the history of the Terezin ghetto and the extermination camps.

♦

In the first two years of its existence, *Jüdisches Nachrichtenblatt – Židovské Listy* was a stubborn attempt to act logically in an insane reality, to adapt to life to a given situation, and to preserve a spark of human rights on the verge of the mechanized mass murder carried out under the aegis of the law, an extermination unprecedented in human history.

70 *Jüdisches Nachrichtenblatt*, 20.3.1942.
71 *Jüdisches Nachrichtenblatt*, 20.11.1942.

A Holocaust of Female Gender

Women in the Terezin ghetto

Zyklon B did not differentiate between men and women; the same death awaited them all. It seems ridiculous, therefore, to divide the Holocaust and its suffering by gender. If I did reconsider, however, despite my inner opposition to deal with the subject, I did so because I did not feel entitled to keep silent about the women of the Terezin ghetto. So I checked, at first for my own sake, what distinguished the lives of women there from the lives of men and how justified it is – if at all – to relate separately to the female gender, a trend that belongs to another generation, another era, to the present-day "politically correct," meant to meet contemporary needs.[1]

♦

The Terezin ghetto, Theresienstadt in German, was established in November 1941 in north Bohemia, in an eighteenth-century fortress city. For the Jews of Bohemia and Moravia, now part of the Protectorate of Bohemia and Moravia that was attached to the German Reich, the Terezin ghetto was both a rift and a continu-

When no source is noted, I relied on my memory, on my book *Elder of the Jews* (New York: Grove Press, 1989), and on my own research since 1993.

1 I approached the subject of women in the Terezin ghetto after receiving an invitation to participate in a seminar held in June 1995 at the Hebrew University in Jerusalem. My lecture at the seminar is contained in the anthology: Dalia Ofer and Leonore J. Weitzmann, eds., *Women in the Holocaust* (New Haven/London: Yale University Press, 1998), pp. 310–326.

ation. In normal times, the man was the breadwinner of the family. Married women, even if they had acquired a profession while still single, such as a teacher or secretary, became housewives or worked in the family business. Very few continued to work as self-employed or salaried professionals. But 40 percent of the women arriving at the ghetto declared they had a profession;[2] this was the result of the changes that had occurred since the German occupation on 15 March 1939, which included courses offered by the Jewish community to prepare the Jews for a life of labor in the countries they would emigrate to or for the changing conditions of their homeland. In addition, there was another practical consideration: it was better to be registered in the ghetto as having a profession, no matter how poorly qualified you were, than to be considered as having none.

In the two and a half years that they lived in the Protectorate before the deportations began, both the men and the women underwent a profound crisis, but for opposite reasons. The men had lost their ability to earn a living due to a series of laws intended to remove the Jews from economic life; they were forcibly unemployed or mobilized into forced labor, such as removing snow or paving roads, or they tried to earn a living doing odd jobs. They felt humiliated at having lost their status, their authority and their economic security. The women, on the other hand, had to cope with the ever-increasing burden of work to which they were unaccustomed. During the days of Czechoslovakia, most Jewish families had a Czech housemaid working in their home from morning to night. When the employment of Aryan workers in Jewish households was forbidden and the economic situation worsened, all the housework fell on the women's shoulders: lighting the coal stove, washing by hand (there were no washing machines), preparing meals from the meager foodstuffs allotted to Jews, knitting from unraveled wool, and sewing new clothes from old.

But it was many times more difficult to leave the comfortable home, the well-kept apartment. This often occured in two phases:

2 Hans Günther Adler, *Theresienstadt 1941–1945* (Tübingen: J.C.B. Mohr (Paul Siebeck), 1960), p. 44.

first the move from a spacious house or apartment in a neighborhood where Jews were no longer permitted to live, to a rented room in an apartment shared by several Jewish families, with all the nerve-wracking inconvenience of sharing the kitchen, bathroom and toilet; afterwards, from October 1941 and following the departure of the first five transports from the Protectorate to the Łódź ghetto, with a maximum allawance of fifty kilograms of baggage per person on a journey to the unknown. The women prepared durable rations: they baked rusks, fried *roux* that would last a long time, and made pastes of boiled milk and sugar. They sewed short or long down-lined coats, dyed white sheets to darker colors, and for days mulled over what to take. Sometimes, for the sake of a memento or an object precious to them, they would give up taking an essential item (though in the end it made no difference because at the gates of the ghetto the SS confiscated most of the supposedly permitted luggage). Some of them dared, despite the severe prohibition, to transfer belongings or even furniture from their homes to non-Jewish friends and neighbors for safekeeping. Some deliberately damaged whatever was left in the apartment; others left a neat apartment behind, in the secret hope (which took no account of the reality, since the apartments of those leaving on the transports were emptied out and their contents handed over to the Germans) that one day they would find their homes as they had left them.[3]

> I say goodbye forever, walls I loved
> My lovely bed, things so dear to me
> That faithfully were with me every day
> The door slams behind me.[4]

The trauma of taking leave of the house, of loved objects, was especially severe for married women with families, and they never got over it — even in the ghetto. While peeling potatoes, sewing or

3 Edice Svícen, *Svět bez lidských dimenzí* (Prague: Edice Svícen, 1991), pp. 72–134.

4 Trude Groag, *Poems of a Caring Nurse* (Givat Haim-Ichud: Beit Terezin, 1975), p. 9 (Hebrew).

doing other tasks in the labor force, they'd tell each other again and again about what they'd had and lost. Sometimes they held on to an object from their home – a folding alarm clock, a tiny statuette, an ivory brooch, a book of poetry, photographs – as if it were a thread that would lead them back – until in the end they were stripped of everything.[5]

Therefore the women, more than the men, tended to make their dwelling in the ghetto into a substitute home, to build a nest[6] for themselves no matter how tiny. Over time, the bunks in the ghetto barracks were built in three tiers, and then, too, the women would put covers on the mattress, hang pictures of their dear ones over the bunk, place a doily on the board at its foot and put their belongings on it, trying to keep everything clean. When they left the Terezin ghetto on their way eastward, they lost yet another home.

♦

The two construction commando units (*Aufbaukommando*) assigned to prepare the ghetto on Czech soil for all eighty thousand Jews of the Protectorate remaining often the last emigration routes were blocked in the summer of 1941 consisted of professionals – electrical engineers, water engineers, iron workers, carpenters – and laborers. Many of them were members of the Zionist youth movement *Hechalutz*, and all of them were men, in accordance with the accepted norm among both Jews and Germans. The designated elder of the new ghetto was Jakob Edelstein, formerly director of the Palestine office in Prague, an ardent Zionist who believed that pioneering meant being where the Jewish masses needed help.[7] Edelstein's staff, known in the ghetto language as "the Stab," consisted of twenty-three people, most of them his associates from the Zionist movement. They came to the ghetto on 4 De-

5 Svícen, *Svět bez lidských dimenzí*, p. 128.

6 Greta Salus, *Niemand, Nichts – ein Jude* (Darmstadt: Darmstädter Blätter, 1981), p. 11.

7 See: Ruth Bondy, *Elder of the Jews*, p. 280.

cember 1941, voluntarily, on an ordinary passenger train. The staff was also supposed to comprise only men, but in the end Edelstein agreed to include four women: his loyal secretary Peppi Steif; Erna Kahn, the secretary of his deputy, Otto Zucker; Dr. Edith Ornstein, an attorney and one of the organizers of the illegal immigration to Palestine; and Dr. Ruth Hoffe, a physician.[8] In addition to the professional knowledge of the last two and their desire to join the group, their choice was also influenced by the fact that they were the life partners of two of the staff members (the wives of the other staff members and their children arrived at Terezin ghetto at a later stage).

The leadership of the Terezin ghetto faithfully reflected the division in the past, which had been accepted as self-evident: during the three-and-a-half years of the ghetto's existence, not a single woman was appointed to the Council of Elders, the head body of the ghetto was subject to the instructions of the German command. The same was true of the management of the various administrative departments, such as the economic department, the health department, the youth department and the transport department. Even the Hamburg barracks (the barracks in the ghetto kept the German names they were given by the occupying army), intended for women's housing, were managed by a man.[9]

The only department whose management was assigned to a woman was the department for women's employment (*Frauenarbeitseinsatz*), headed by 28-year-old Dr. Edith Ornstein, whom everyone called Dittl. Contrary to the promises of the Germans that the ghetto would be ready before the mass deportation, the transports began to arrive before anything had been prepared. Dittl found the women depressed, neglected and despairing of the atrocious conditions: they were sleeping on cold, damp cement floors in the harsh Czech winter, with no heat and poor sanitation. In addition, the SS command had ordered that the men's quarters be separated from those for women and small children. As a result, the women were bitterly resentful and rebelled against Edelstein.

8 Interview with the writer, Dr. Edith Ornstein-Rueff, London, 1978.
9 Beit Terezin archives (BTA), 85.

As furious as a wasp nest, they demanded to speak directly with Dr. Siegfried Seidl, the local SS commander, but to no avail.[10] They remained shut up in their barracks without minimal facilities, and were strictly forbidden to make any contact with their families. Because of the contrast between their expectations of family life in the "Jewish city" and the actual conditions, the women sank into depression and apathy, and had no desire whatsoever to work voluntarily.[11] Only gradually was Dittl able to persuade the women to help themselves and one another, and to organize a regular work service for girls and women between the ages of fourteen and sixty, with the exception of mothers of young children and the sick. At first the newcomers, men and women separately, worked in units of one hundred (*Hundertschaften*) in all the required jobs; over time they were absorbed into a permanent workplace.

The number of ghetto residents was never static, and each week, transports came and left to what was called "the East," but whose true meaning – extermination – remained unclear. One figure remained constant: from the first deportations of the elderly from Germany and Austria in June 1942 until liberation in May 1945 – the number of women in the ghetto was larger than the number of men. This was because the men were sometimes sent to outside jobs, supposedly to establish a new camp, and also, since women lived longer, there were more older women in the ghetto than men of the same age. On 31 January 1944, the women comprised sixty percent of the overall ghetto population and their average age was 50. Eighty-five percent of them worked.[12]

The traditional division of roles continued in Terezin as well: of 11,000 mobilized for work 2,600 were auxiliary workers, mainly in cleaning (*Putzkolonne*, in the ghetto language), work that over time gave rise to a team spirit and a special sense of belonging.[13] More than 2,000 of them were nurses or caregivers in the children's houses, 1,300 were clerks, and 2,200 worked in the central laundry,

10 Dr. Edith Ornstein, Prague, 1945, BTA, 8.

11 Ibid.

12 Adler, *Theresienstadt*, p. 417.

13 Käthe Starke, *Der Führer schenkt den Juden eine Stadt* (Berlin: Haude und Spenersche Verlagsbuchhandlung, 1975), p. 47.

sewing and other workshops, or in agriculture. In April 1942, despite the opposition of some of the husbands, one thousand women were sent, for the first and last time, to work on the outside for six weeks, planting trees in the Křivoklát forests.[14]

The hard physical work – unloading cargo, transport, building an extension of the railway track from the nearby station at Bohušovice to the ghetto, sewage and water engineering, fire fighting – was done only by men. In the summer of 1942, the economic department sent the first order to the women's employment service for women to work in the central carpentry shop (*Bauhof*). This aroused a furor about employing women to do "men's work," but gradually the women began to take interest in this new branch of work, and two regular units of women were formed to carry boards and assemble bunks. Only men served in the ghetto police force, most of them formerly military men. In May 1943, as part of an operation to improve the appearance of the ghetto before a possible visit by a delegation of the International Red Cross, money was put into circulation in the ghetto, although its value was only nominal since the real means of payment was and remained food and cigarettes. But on paper, too, the salary paid to women was lower by twenty percent on average than what men earned.[15]

The division of roles between the sexes reflected not only the Jewish past, but also the German worldview: the SS command constituted only men; German women filled clerical roles. The only German uniformed women seen in the ghetto were those searching for objects the Jews were forbidden to keep – money, cigarettes, medicines, electrical appliances, and musical instruments – women known in the ghetto as "lady bugs" (*berušky*). They came from the nearby city of Leitmeritz, were on the bottom rung of the German hierarchy and were also punished for theft.[16]

This also held true for the "prominent" prisoners (*Prominenten*), who, according to the SS orders, were given somewhat better quarters than the overall ghetto population, were exempt from the

14 BTA, 85, Einsatz chapter, pp. 4, 7.

15 Adler, *Theresienstadt*, p. 418.

16 Ruth Bondy, *Elder of the Jews*.

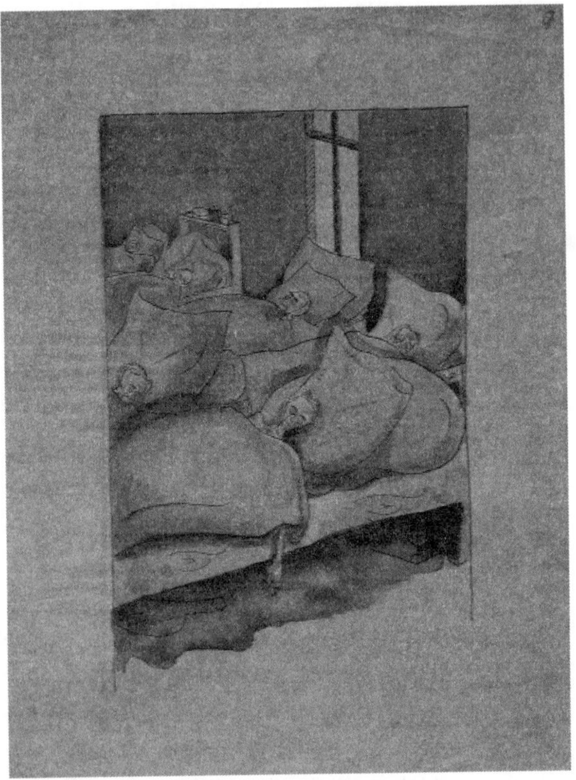

Elderly women in one of the sick wards of the Terezin ghetto, painted by Willy Groag, whose mother worked there as a nurse. Among others, she took care of Herzl's daughter Trude', who later died in the ghetto. Beit Terezin Archives (BTA).

obligation to work, and in particular were protected most of the time against deportation eastward. These were former ministers in the governments of France, Saxony, Czechoslovakia; high officers retired from the German or Austrian army; and world-renowned scientists. The women's preferred status was usually based on their husbands' status: the widow of an S.A. officer; the widow of a commander in the Danish Navy; the mother of two illegitimate children whose father was an offspring of the house of Hohenzollern; the granddaughter of Baron von Bleichröder, Bismarck's financial advisor. Although Elsa Bernstein was the mother-in-law of Gerhart Hauptmann, a well-known German playwright, she was an author in her own right.[17] However, neither Franz Kakfa's three sisters nor Sigmund Freud's four sisters enjoyed any privileged status with the Germans; they all found their death in the ghetto itself or were exterminated in the East.

Trude Neumann, the younger daughter of Herzl, the visionary of a Jewish state, died on 17 March 1943 in a nursing hospital in Terezin. The notes she wrote to the management of the ghetto ("I, the younger daughter of the deceased Zionist leader, Dr. Theodor Herzl, take the liberty of informing the local Zionists of my arrival and asking them for help"), to the nurses who cared for her ("Mrs. Neumann-Herzl can no longer endure a dirty nightgown and dirty sheets") and to herself, attested to the mental illness she suffered from many years before she arrived at the ghetto, as well as to her physical distress.[18] The notes were preserved thanks to Trude Groag, who worked as a nurse in the hospital for the elderly, and who, in her poetry, eloquently expressed the suffering of the old patients, most of whom arrived in the ghetto all alone, under the illusion that they were going to live in well-kept old-age homes. But they were always hungry, helpless and sorely missing their far-off children, and they quickly deteriorated.[19]

♦

17 Josef Polák–Karel Lagus, *Město za mřížemi* (Prague: Naše Vojsko, 1964), p. 85.

18 Central Zionist Archives (CZA), Jerusalem, H-25.

19 Groag, *Poems of a Caring Nurse*.

Although the Jews of the Protectorate arrived at Terezin with their families, the men were housed in separate barracks from the women and small children. Only members of the ghetto's leadership and the privileged were entitled to housing with their families. However, from July 1942, when the last of the non-Jewish residents were evacuated and Terezin as a whole (with the exception of the area of the German command and Czech gendarmes buildings) became a ghetto, it was possible to maintain a family life of sorts. For the first time after being closed in for six months, the inmates were permitted to walk freely in the streets and enter the housing quarters. Families and couples would meet during the few hours between the end of the workday and the nighttime curfew, which changed according to the seasons of the year and the degree of collective punishment, but usually began with nightfall – and this daily meeting was often the center of life.

The SS command, in one of its daily orders, issued an instruction requiring the women to cut their hair short like the men; men's hair was to be no longer than three millimeters, but it was not strictly enforced.[20] The same was true of the prohibition against the use of lipstick.[21] Anyone who still possessed a treasure like makeup did not hesitate to use it, frugally, especially when meeting a man she loved or was interested in. The women in the ghetto, like the men, wore clothes brought from home. Even though over time the clothes became too big because they all lost weight, and were worn out by so much use, as long as they still had the physical and mental strength the women kept up their appearance, whether for the sake of their workplace or for the family or boyfriend. Alice Hansel, a young, energetic and elegant woman, and the coordinator of one of the cleaning units, was very concerned after she had a mastectomy in the ghetto: would she ever be able to wear a bathing suit again? Would her husband be able to come to terms with the change? A

20 Polák-Lagus, *Město za mřížemi*, p. 83.

21 Egon Redlich, *Life as If: The Diary of Egon Redlich from the Theresienstadt Ghetto*, (Hebrew) (Tel Aviv: Hakibutz Hameuhad, 1983), entry dated 9.7.1943.

few days later, after Alice died, her soft wool coat was already being worn by her sister-in-law.[22]

Because of the malnutrition and the emotional shock caused by the conditions in the ghetto, at Terezin, as in all the other concentration camps, most of the women stopped menstruating, at least for some time, or their cycle was irregular. Although reports from other camps claimed that the women who stopped menstruating became anxious about their fertility in the future,[23] in my experience they were relieved: there was no cotton wool or sanitary pads; improvised pads made of fabric or folded-up rags used as substitutes chafed and were not absorbent, and it was hard to wash them and the blood-stained underpants. The disappearance of menstruation did, however, make early detection of pregnancy difficult.[24]

At first, women who were pregnant when they came to the ghetto were allowed to give birth, but in July 1943 the SS command ordered the forced termination of every pregnancy, and instructed the room heads to report any pregnancy they knew of, and also threatened that in the future, parents with infants born in the ghetto would be sent on the next transport eastward. During the three-and-a-half years of the ghetto's existence, 230 infants were born; about 25 percent were still alive in the ghetto at the end of the war[25] (one is Michael Wiener, until 1994 the Chief Medical Officer of the Israel Defense Forces). The pregnant woman and the father (who were not always legally married) were compelled to sign a consent to the termination of the pregnancy. "They're killing children in their mother's belly," Egon (Gonda) Redlich, head of the Youth Department, wrote in his diary, written mostly in Hebrew and found after the war in an attic of the former ghetto.[26] Gonda's wife Gerti, known as Bečka (from her surname, Beck), finally received, together with several other women, a special birth

22 Starke, *Der Führer schenkt*, p. 77.

23 Marlene Eve Heinemann, *Gender and Destiny: Women Writers and the Holocaust* (Connecticut: Greenwood Press, 1986), p. 7.

24 Redlich, *Life as If*, entry dated 29.10.1942.

25 Polák-Lagus, *Město za mřížemi*, p. 217.

26 Redlich, *Life as If*, entry dated 24.11.1943.

permit, after a Jewish gynecologist saved the lives of the baby and the wife of the SS officer. On 16 March 1944, Bečka gave birth to a healthy boy whom they named Dan. But seven months later, the three of them were included in a transport to Auschwitz. In exchange for food, Gonda and his wife bought a baby carriage for the trip, which ended on 23 October when they were sent straight to the gas chambers. Religious women who were pregnant chose to be sent to the East rather than undergo an abortion.[27]

In the ghetto, there was a day care center for babies and small children, most of whom were considered orphans because they had arrived at the ghetto without parents (who had been executed or imprisoned by the Gestapo). But there were also mothers who had been sent to the ghetto without their babies; these children had remained at home because they were offspring of mixed marriages. One of these women, called Fišerová, was able, despite the poor nutrition, to save the lives, at least temporarily, of the weakest infants in the center by breast-feeding them for nearly two years.[28] In contrast, Gonda writes about a young mother who suffered from a surplus of milk and preferred to feed it to her husband rather than nurse another infant.[29] The small orphans were hungrier than those who had mothers in the ghetto, who always tried to add something to their children's diet even if it was at the expense of their own nutrition.[30]

When the transports began in October 1941, hundreds of young couples in the Protectorate were married in a hasty ceremony, on the assumption that this would ensure they would be deported together.[31] In the Terezin ghetto there was no way to marry legally, but religious wedding ceremonies were performed by rabbis, and there was also a possibility, unique only to Terezin, to marry by registering as a couple at the records department, thus ensuring that they would share the same fate – either remain in the ghetto thanks to one of the couple's essential profession or fam-

27 Marian Becková, BTA, 192, p. 1.
28 Věra Hajková, BTA, 192, p. 3.
29 Redlich, *Life as If*, entry dated 24.11.1943.
30 Hajková, BTA, 192, p. 3.
31 Bondy, *Edelstein, Elder of the Jews*, p. 272.

ily ties to one of the major officeholders in the ghetto leadership, or leave together for the frightening, unknown East.

The list of protected professions changed over the years: until 1944 doctors and nurses employed in the health services were not included in the transports. Dozens of girls and young women were saved thanks to their work in agriculture. Most of the women employed in splitting feldspar (hard crystalline minerals) were also protected from deportation. The feldspar was used as insulation material in the German military industry; it was brought to the ghetto in clumps, and the women sat on backless stools and, using sharp knives, their eyes burning, they would split the layers of feldspar into thin leaves. In the last year of the ghetto's existence, the work was done on the basis of piecework, and the women were constantly afraid they would not meet their quota and thus lose their protected job.[32]

The young women made a conscious decision not to talk about food when they were hungry. But former housewives would frequently "cook" while they were working – one woman would tell another how she would prepare mushroom sauce with cream and argue about whether it was better to dilute dumpling dough with milk or soda water or with an equal mixture of the two. There were women who, out of a psychological need, wrote down recipes of dishes and baked goods whose necessary ingredients looked like greetings from another world.[33] In addition to this make-believe cooking, there was also an entire cooking industry in the ghetto. The public kitchens, located in barracks, provided every inmate of the ghetto with a coffee substitute in the morning, a thin gray liquid called lentil soup, and two or three, often rotten, potatoes cooked in their peels, with the addition of a bit of unidentifiable gravy for lunch. In the evening a daily portion of bread, about 350–370 grams, was distributed in the rooms, usually for three days at once. All of this prevented maddening hunger of the type that prevailed in the ghettos in Poland, and ensured a minimum of nutrition for every inhabitant of the ghetto each day, but never enough to satisfy anyone.

32 Gerty Spies, *Drei Jahre Theresienstadt* (Munich: Kristian Kaiser, 1984), p. 38.
33 Anoštka Kleinová, BTA, 197/9.

In addition to the public kitchens, there were warm-up kitchens (*Wärmeküchen*) in the barracks and in the women's living quarters. These had coal stoves on which the residents of the building were allowed to place a small pot or a tin can, usually to cook a soup from the meager store of foodstuffs brought from home, from pieces of potato and peels pilfered while peeling in the kitchen, and from onion stalks left in the vegetable gardens after the onions had been supplied to the SS command. For birthdays, the women would prepare a "cake" made of gray bitter bread dipped in ersatz black coffee, with the addition of a little sugar, margarine and jam, so at least its color resembled that of a chocolate cake.[34] A booklet written to mark the end of the first year of the existence of the Hamburg barracks, the main women's quarters, stated with pride that the three warm-up kitchens in the building had reached a capacity, in January 1943, of 1,800 pots per day.[35]

There was indeed a kind of pride in the work in Terezin; there was a work ethic, in the services for the general population as well, without the presence of SS men. The SS men were seen only rarely in the ghetto, and when they entered, the men had to remove their hats and women had to curtsy.[36] But this order too, was strictly enforced only in relation to the men.

In the orders for the day (*Tagesbefehle*), the sentences passed by the Jewish courts in the ghetto were regularly published – for taking bribes and other internal offenses – as well as the punishments imposed by the German command for the violation of its prohibitions, such as possessing cigarettes or money, contact with the outside world, or absence from work without permission. It turns out that the number of men who were punished far exceeded the number of women, both numerically and relatively.[37] Perhaps the Czech gendarmes, who carried out most of the searches when the inmates returned to the ghetto from their outside jobs, often turned a blind eye when a woman working in agriculture padded

34 Käthe Breslauer, Yad Vashem Archives (YVSA), 02/217.

35 BTA, 85.

36 Order of the Day, 20.10.1942 and other dates, BTA, *Tagesbefehle*.

37 According to my count of the punishments published in 200 daily orders, the ratio was approximately 1:4.

her bra with a cucumber or a cauliflower pilfered while picking produce intended for the German command; perhaps because the men had more opportunities to steal from the general property; and maybe because the men dared to smuggle more things into the ghetto and the SS treated them more severely. There were executions in the ghetto only in the beginning – and all sixteen who were hanged, in January and February of 1942, were men.[38] From then on, anyone violating the German prohibitions was thrown into the Gestapo prison in the Little Fortress near the ghetto, where the Jewish prisoners were maltreated until they died or were sent eastward in the next transport under special orders (*Sonderweisung*) of the command.

To some degree, the attitude of the Jewish men in the ghetto towards the women was often condescending and overbearing. In a booklet on the Hamburg barracks, Fritz Wohlgemut, the manager of food distribution (*Menagedienst*) in the building, wrote: "The women are not accustomed to maintaining discipline, and consequently the food services sometimes has to be educational, to make it clear to the women that they cannot come to get food whenever they feel like it, but only when it is their room's turn."[39] On the other hand, the men were quite dependent on the women: the women's living quarters (whether mother, wife, sister, daughter, or friend) were generally the meeting place of the family in the evening, because they were the ones who cooked the supplement to the food, if there was any; they repaired the men's torn socks, mended their worn-out clothes, laundered their underwear in cold water, usually without soap, and searched for lice and fleas.

It's impossible to make a sweeping generalization, but I would say that the men, who received the same number of calories, usually suffered more from hunger than the women (in the summer of 1943, the official allotment for workers was 1630 calories a day. From that you need to subtract the 10 percent supplement given to hard laborers and kitchen workers, and another 10 percent due to theft). The women, on the other hand, were more distressed by the

38 Ruth Bondy, *Elder of the Jews*.
39 Ruth Bondy, *Elder of the Jews*.

filth than the men, and suffered more from the fleas and bedbugs. Because of the terrible overcrowding, despite the enormous efforts to keep things clean, to air out the bedding and repeatedly disinfect it, the insects were the eleventh plague.[40] In all the memoirs that women wrote after the liberation (and these are more numerous than those written by men, also because there were more women among the survivors), they talk about the dirt and the insects. In the heat of summer, they were pestered by armies of bedbugs that nested in the bunks more than usual, and the women would sleep on the ground in the yard. In some of the rooms of the elderly, the residents had to wash each day from head to foot, watching over one another, and the room was swept every morning – but this did not deter the pests. Hedwig Ems, who was seventy-one when she came to the Terezin ghetto, used to wipe her bread with a napkin, at least symbolically; after all, the bread was brought from the bakery on former hearses, and had been handled by unwashed hands and held next to dirty coats.[41]

♦

The undergrounds in the Terezin ghetto – Communist, Czech-nationalist and Zionist – had no firearms nor did they make any practical preparations for the possibility of an armed revolt. But in all their regular activities – organizing cells, underground contact with the outside world, smuggling items into the ghetto, maintaining a regular system of teaching the children (forbidden by the Germans), holding secret meetings, listening secretly to the radio – the women were full partners, though the men, due to their jobs, had greater freedom of movement outside the walls of the city.

The only women's organization active in the ghetto was WIZO, the Women's International Zionist Organization; this, too, was a continuation of their former life. At the initiative of Klara Caro, a rabbi's wife from Cologne, Germany, and with Jakob Edelstein's

40 Dr. Bertha Landré, BTA, 231.

41 Hedwig Ems, BTA, pp., 12, 20.

consent, from the summer of 1942 the women of WIZO (called "Wizo-bubbes" by the members of the youth movements even if they were only forty years old) met regularly on Saturday afternoon to listen to lectures, particularly on Zionist topics. Over time, the number of participants grew from twenty to 200.[42] The leading personality among the women, and their mainstay from the time she arrived at the ghetto in July 1943, was Hanna Steiner, one of the founders of WIZO in Czechoslavakia and the director of the emigration department of the Prague community during the occupation, an extremely energetic woman with excellent organizational skills. Steiner, optimistic by nature, continued to hope even in the ghetto that she'd finally succeed in leaving with her husband for Palestine on the basis of the certificates they held. They perished in Auschwitz in the fall of 1944.[43]

Klara Caro found that good and generous people grew more so in trying times, while the small-minded petty ones became even smaller. Either thesis can be proven. From the dozens of testimonies and memories of women about the Terezin ghetto there is much evidence of sisterhood, mutual help, friendship and sacrifice among women, and an orderly communal life.[44] By the same token, one can also read about the contrary:

> It would be reasonable to assume that the life of people sharing the same tragic fate would cause them to help one another and to treat each other decently. But the opposite also happens, even though that's not always the case. The overcrowded conditions in the living quarters, the despair, the hunger, the disease, the dying all around, the cold — all of these make people bad, intolerant and domineering.[45]

The same held true for the relations between women from Germany and those from the Protectorate. Along with the claims that the Czech women, whose situation in the ghetto was somewhat better,

42 Klara Caro, YVSA, 02/224; BTA, 435.
43 Bondy, *Elder of the Jews,* p. 294–295.
44 Rose Weglein, BTA, 123.
45 Landré, BTA, 231, p. 21.

were hard and arrogant, the German women recorded memories of friendship and of devoted care by the Czech women in time of illness.[46] I dare say that the cases of close friendship among the women, even if only within a small group of those sharing the same room, working in the same unit or in a circle of friends, exceeded those marked by inconsideration and indifference towards the suffering of others.

♦

During the first months of the ghetto's existence, children under the age of twelve were housed with their mothers, but it was hard for them to live in the large sleeping halls with hundreds of women of all ages. Gradually, children's rooms were opened in the barracks, and in June-July 1942, when the last of the city's Czech residents were evacuated, children's homes were established in the vacated buildings. Mothers were not obliged to transfer their children to the homes, but most of them did so willingly, on the assumption – correct, as it turned out – that they would be better off there. The children's living conditions were easier, although in the classroom of the local school, in which thirty children had studied for five hours in the past, now the same number of children spent the entire day sleeping, studying, eating and playing. The children received some additional food, more or less regular lessons, and found friends. There were some mothers, however, who refused to part from their children, and for them day centers were set up in the barracks where the children were concentrated while the mothers were at work.

Since most of the mothers of children under twelve or thirteen perished later with their children, I found no testimonies about the effect of the separation from the children at night. There were children who missed home and who wet their beds at night. There were mothers who were not satisfied with a daily meeting in the afternoon, after work, so they looked for and found auxiliary jobs in the children's homes where they could be close to their children.

46 Spies, *Drei Jahre Theresienstadt*, p. 59.

Others obtained, usually through connections, "lucrative" work, meaning work (in agriculture or in the kitchens) where they could get their hands on some extra food for their children.

The combination of sex and Holocaust has become very saleable in today's world, which is eager for thrills. Reading some books written about the Terezin ghetto, in Czechoslovakia as well as in the United States,[47] one would think that the inmates were sex maniacs. Here I allow myself to speak from my own knowledge. I came to the ghetto at the age of eighteen and lived and worked there for a year and a half with girls of my age. The malnutrition and physical weakness certainly dampened the sexual urge. Young couples longed first and foremost for closeness, warmth, love, an embrace, consolation. With the exception of senior officeholders, who had separate rooms, the majority of the ghetto's population had no privacy. Couples had sex under a blanket on the bunks, in a lit-up hall, usually full of people. Full sexual intercourse, if it took place at all, had to be short and quiet, while the two were dressed, under conditions that did not arouse much desire. Things were different for men who received better nutrition – butchers, cooks, bakers, transport workers. Not only was their sexual drive intact, but their privileged status enabled them to obtain a private corner and also to choose the prettiest girls. It was really no different than in normal times, only that instead of money and diamonds, food was the form of great wealth. Beyond that, the fact that key officeholders were entitled to protect their families and those closest to them (up to thirty persons) from the transports eastward (until the fall of 1944, when by special order of the SS they and their families were also sent straight to the gas chambers of Auschwitz), added to their power of attraction. There was no need for paid prostitution: privileged men easily secured a young lover, even if they themselves were far from attractive, like Benjamin Murmelstein, the controversial third Elder of the Jews.[48] Immeasurably more im-

47 George E. Berkley, *Hitler's Gift: The Story of Theresienstadt* (Boston: Branden, 1993).

48 Naavah Shan, *To Be an Actress*, (Hebrew) (Tel Aviv: Hakibutz Hameuhad, 1991), p. 45.

portant than sex was love, which imbued life with strength and content, and even after the couple was separated by a transport, the hope of a reunion after the war gave them the will to hang on.[49] Lesbian relations were quite rare;[50] most of the girls, including me, did not even know what they were. We still belonged to the puritan era.

There were marriages that grew stronger under the conditions of the ghetto – perhaps, strangely enough, because of the separate living quarters, which averted the daily friction of a shared life (as a matter of fact, in his diary, Gonda Redlich referred to an opposite problem: the difficulty of living with a spouse in a small crowded room[51]) and made the brief daily meeting a mainstay of life. Also, since work in a profession, sometimes a new one, gave the women the self-confidence they had previously lacked, the relations between the spouses became more egalitarian or the reverse – the women were stronger and sustained their husbands. But the opposite also happened – some marriages, which may have been tenuous before, did not withstand the trials and tribulations of the ghetto and fell apart. The women, like the men, found a new relationship – until they were swept up in the whirlpool of the transports. The inhabitants of the ghetto wanted desperately to crowd into life everything possible, for as long as they could. They did not always remain faithful to a far-off spouse who had succeeded in fleeing in time to the free world or had been sent to another place of concentration. But neither through my own experience as an eyewitness nor through my research can I confirm definitions such as "*Bordellwirtschaft*," a brothel economy, a term used by H.G. Adler, who is considered the authority on the Terezin ghetto,[52] except in the use of the word *bordel* in Czech slang, which simply means a mess, disorder.

♦

49 Tamar Herman, "Here Too, We are Allowed to Dream, to Love," *Yalkut Moreshet* 47 (November 1989) (Hebrew), pp. 195–208.

50 Redlich, *Life as If*, 15.6.1943.

51 Ibid., entry dated 9.10.1942.

52 Adler, *Theresienstadt*, p. 678.

The nutrition, the overcrowded conditions (50,000 and more people in a place where 3,500 people and a similar number of soldiers lived before the war) and poor sanitation made the lives of most of the ghetto's inhabitants an unbroken chain of illnesses. Enteritis, meningitis, impetigo and hepatitis were Latin names[53] known to every child, but the mortality rate among the young people was relatively low. A precise record was kept of cases of death and their causes between 24 November 1941 and 31 July 1944, including a numerical breakdown between men and women (the SS command in Terezin loved statistics and used them to demonstrate to Berlin its activity, and the Jews went along willingly because it meant jobs for them). The higher proportion of women in the ghetto population is also reflected in the number of deaths: of 32,647 inmates who died, 19,878 were women. There were, however, causes of death from which a higher proportion of men died than women: intestinal cancer, asthma and bronchitis, cardiac disease (perhaps because before World War II hardly any women smoked), and kidney and urinary diseases (416 men versus 97 women).[54] In general, then, illness and death struck both genders more or less equally, and the women's greater resistance in extreme conditions was not yet so tangibly evident as it was in Auschwitz and in other extermination camps.

Although the rate of suicides in the three-and-a-half years of the ghetto's existence — 171 men, 259 women — was higher than in the general population, it was negligible considering the conditions of life there. However, in addition to active suicide — by jumping out of a window, hanging oneself, taking poison — there was passive suicide, the loss of the will to live, which was common among the elderly from Germany and Austria who were alone in the world. As long as there was someone to live for in the ghetto, as long as there was hope that someone would need them after the war, the women clung to life.[55]

The constant dread that the one remaining shred of family

53 BTA, 27.
54 BTA, 53.
55 Ems, BTA, p. 2.

life would be torn asunder by a transport to the East, and the fear of separation, loomed over the ghetto like a dark cloud. The reaction, which seemed natural, when a loved one was on a transport list was to volunteer to join them (only a husband, wife and children under the age of sixteen had the "right" to be sent together). Sons and daughters volunteered to leave with their parents, brothers with sisters,[56] unmarried young men volunteered to leave with their girlfriends and vice versa. Only a few took the long view and refused to volunteer to leave on the transport, taking their chances as to what the future might bring. And those who remained in the ghetto after their loved ones left were tormented by feelings of guilt. As the poet Ilse Weber wrote: "Tomorrow 5,000 will leave here / and we will remain, small and ashamed."[57]

The Germans cynically exploited this devotion to family during the large wave of transports in the fall of 1944. At first, they sent to the putative "new labor camp," which was none other than Auschwitz, 4,000 men of working age. The following day, the women were given the opportunity to volunteer to leave on the next transport in order to be "reunited with their husbands." Hundreds rushed to the Magdeburg barracks, where the administration was housed, to register. The women were led with their children straight to the gas chambers, including Ilse Weber and her 10-year-old son Tomas.[58] Another deportee on this transport was Fritzi Zucker, the wife of Otto Zucker, the deputy Elder of the Jews and one of the major figures in the ghetto, who was in charge of the men's transport to the "labor camp." When she was about to board the train, the camp commander Rahm said to the SS man escorting the transport: "This is Mrs. Zucker. You are responsible for seeing that tonight she'll be in her husband's arms."[59] At the time, Zucker had already become a pile of ashes, and his wife, who had been a

56 Vera Hájková, *Svět bez lidských dimenzí* (Prague: Edice Svícen, 1991), p. 181.

57 Ilse Weber, *In deinen Mauern Wohnt das Leid* (Gerlingen: Bleicher Verlag, 1991), S. 95.

58 Ludvik E. Vaclavek, "Deutsche Lyrik im Ghetto Theresienstadt," *Weimarer Beitrage: Zeitschrift für Literaturwissenschaft, Ästhetik und Kulturwissenschaften* 28:5 (1980) (Wien: Passagen Verlag), pp. 14–34.

59 Polák-Lagus, *Město za mřížemi*, p. 241.

housemother in a children's home in the ghetto, shared the same fate. Hedwig Eppstein, the wife of the second Elder of the Jews, who at the end of September 1944 had secretly been shot to death in the prison in the Little Fortress, was also sure she was going to meet her husband when she left on the transport of 28 October 1944, the last transport to be put to death at Auschwitz.[60]

After 17,000 men, women and children had left in the transports of the fall of 1944, hardly any men were left in the Terezin ghetto,[61] with the exception of most of the "prominents"[62] and all the Jews of Denmark, who were saved from deportation to the East thanks to the protection granted them by their King and their fellow countrymen. The women, tormented by sorrow and longing, undertook many of the jobs that until then had been filled by men, including hard physical labor, such as transport and unloading freight cars. In November 1944, the SS command ordered them to stand in a chain and pass from hand to hand the numbered carton boxes that contained the ashes of about 25,000 men, women and children who had died until then in the ghetto and whose bodies had been burned, and to load them on to trucks. About a third of the boxes were emptied into a mine pit; the remainder was thrown into the Ohře River, near the Terezin fortress, and the boxes were burned – to eliminate any trace.[63]

♦

The women's influence on the ghetto was first of all by their very existence – as mothers, wives, sisters, daughters, loved ones – and beyond that as workers, caring for children and the sick, in jobs that required empathy and readiness to help others, in culture and in art. Because of the separation between the men's and women's barracks, in which the Terezin ghetto differed from the ghettos in

60 Starke, *Der Führer schenkt*, p. 151.

61 Yehuda Reznicenko-Erez, ed., *Theresienstadt* (Tel Aviv: MAPAJ, 1947) (Hebrew), Memoirs, Edith Ornstein, p. 61, Memoires Grete Wiener, p. 221.

62 See the chapter, "Privileged until Further Notice."

63 Polák-Lagus, *Město za mřížemi*, pp. 243–244.

Poland, at first cultural activities were organized in the men's and women's barracks separately, out of the same psychological need. After the ghetto was opened internally in June 1942, most of the events arranged by the culture department (*Freitzeitgestaltung*, i.e., free time planning) were held jointly.

A group of talented artists, all men, found refuge in the painting room of the technical department. The women artists, some of them well known (such as Amalia Seckbach, Malvína Šálková and Charlotta Burešová), painted first of all for themselves. Friedl Dicker-Brandeis, a native of Vienna, who studied with Johannes Itten and the Bauhaus school and had a unique expressive style even before she came to the ghetto, is remembered today particularly because of the art lessons she gave children in the ghetto. Of the hundreds of children who enjoyed hours of happiness and distraction from their nightmares thanks to their painting, only a few survived. But 6,000 children's paintings and drawings were preserved, a testimony to the pedagogical and artistic vision of Friedl, who was murdered in Auschwitz at the age of forty-six.[64]

The women were an inseparable part of the rich cultural life in the ghetto, as opera and cabaret singers, actresses, directors and pianists.[65] Since the plays and rehearsals were all held after eight to ten hours of work at jobs in the ghetto, participation called for great inner strength, but it was also a source of strength for all those involved because it enabled them to appear before an audience, to forget the everyday reality, to work in their profession, and to learn from an imaginative conductor or an innovative director.

The women, like the men, wrote poems, and although sometimes these were only rhymes written for a special occasion — a birthday, anniversary, an album of mementos — they also gave expression to the reality, the absurdities of ghetto life. Hundreds of poems written by women were preserved — Gerta Spies, Ilse Weber, Trude Groag, Else Dormitzer, Ilse Blumenthal-Weiss, Ger-

64 *Friedl Dicker-Brandeis 1891–1944* (Prague: Státní Museum, 1988).

65 Inter alia: the pianists Aliza Herz-Sommer and Edith Kraus-Steiner, the singers Hedda Grab-Kernmeyer, Annie Frey and Liesl Hofer, the actress Váva Šanová — later Nava Shan — the dancer Camila Rosenbaum, the director Irena Dodalová.

trude Kantorowitz, and others. Interestingly the proportion of poems written in German, even if their writers came from Czechoslovakia, is greater than those in Czech.[66] Although, if judged severely, most of them are not on a high literary standard,[67] they give voice to an identification with the suffering of others, to the dread of what was to come. Writing poems made it easier for the women to bear the horrors of their lives; their poetry was their testimony, and sometimes it enhanced their standing among the women they lived and worked with, since reciting poetry by heart was a very popular pastime in the ghetto rooms, on the long evenings of curfew, after the enforced lights out.[68]

The strongest urge to leave behind a testimony for the coming generations speaks from the poems, in Czech, of an anonymous female poet, who before going into the gas chamber at Auschwitz, on 8 March 1944, shoved three poems into the hands of a Polish kapo to pass on to a Czech prisoner in the men's camp:

> Then skull to skull and bone to bone
> We'll mount the judgment throne
> And bring to all the fearful news:
> Lo! We, the dead, accuse![69]

66 Vaclavek, "Deutsche Lyrik," p. 25.
67 Adler, *Theresienstadt*, pp. 617–618.
68 Spies, *Drei Jahre Theresienstadt*, pp. 79–82.
69 Ota Kraus and Erich Kulka, *Death Factory: Document on Auschwitz* (Oxford: Pergamon Press, 1966), p. 210.

23. 7. 43.

10

ŠALOM NA PÁTEK

Zázračná léčivá voda v Terezíně • Sensační objevení mladého pražského badatele • Terezín bude přejmenován na ZAZRAČNÉ LÁZNĚ THERESIENBAD. •

TEREZÍN - THERESIENBAD.

Terezín, 22.VII.1943.

Mladý pražský badatel dr. B. objevil, že voda v Terezíně má léčivý, ba přímo z á z r a č n ý účinek. Vzorky vody byly prozkoumány laboratoří T.A. ing. Jos. K l e m e n t e m a Státním zdravotním ústavem v Praze. Zvláštní komise technického oddělení pracuje již na plánech pro budoucí světové lázeňské město, které má býti přejmenováno na "Z á z r a č n é l á z n ě Theresienbad".

Shalom for Friday, the humorous weekly, was produced by the staff of the technical department, who had access to paper and paints, rare in the ghetto. It appeared from April 1943 until September 1944, when all its participants were sent to Auschwitz.
YVA, 0.64, April 9, 1943.

PÁTEK
13. 8. 1943
13 STRAN

11

ŠALOM NA PÁTEK

(Š N A P)

VYCHÁZÍ V PÁTEK NA POKOJI Č. 248, BV.

KDYŽ ŠALOM, TEDY NA PÁTEK!

Die Wunderstadt Theresienbad.

68 TEREZÍN - THERESIENBAD: HRADBY. - PRAŽSKÁ BRÁNA.

Heute ist es schon kein Geheimnis mehr - heute weiss es schon die halbe Welt:

In der Nähe der Stadt Leitmeritz, im Nordwesten Böhmens, liegt THERESIENBAD, eine kleine Stadt, in welcher sich seit November 1941 - damals hiess die Stadt Terezin oder Theresienstadt - gar seltsame Dinge zugetragen haben. Anfangs konnten es sich die Gelehrten und Forscher gar nicht erklären, warum die Bewohner dieser Stadt so eigenartige Gewohnheiten haben und so sonderbare Dinge tun, ganz abweichend von der Art in der übrigen Welt.

Schon dass sie sich in dieser Stadt einschliessen und niemandem von aussen Einblick gewähren wollten, war äusserst sonderbar und begreiflicherweise wurde gerade dadurch die Aussenwelt umso

Humor as a Weapon
Songs, skits, cabaret shows, and a satirical newspaper in the Terezin ghetto

Humor is not a Molotov cocktail; you can't prepare it in advance, produce it in the underground for a defined mission, and store it in readiness for a struggle of survival. Humor stems from a profound internal personal need that serves no external purpose. First of all, humor has to exist for itself; all the rest are only byproducts. There was humor in the Terezin ghetto. The children's newspaper, the texts for cabaret shows, songs and caricatures that were preserved, memoirs written after the liberation, and especially the humoristic newspaper *Šalom na Pátek* ("Shalom for Friday") all attest to that. The newspaper appeared only in one copy between April 1943 and August 1944, and when it first started out, it informed its honorable readers that it had "no shalomistic [Zionist, in the ghetto slang], mystic or anti-shalomistic tendencies, but only a humoristic tendency."[1]

In relation to Terezin, you could argue that people were able to laugh about what was going on in the ghetto because they did not know the fate that awaited them, but this does not apply to the family camp in Birkenau.[2] There too, in the shadow of the chimneys of the crematorium, which emitted fire and smoke day and night, when the inmates understood what was in store for them

1 *Šalom na Pátek* (SNP), no. 2/11, YVSA, 0.64–64, copy BTA.

2 On the family camp, see the chapter "Games in the Shadow of the Crematoria."

(although they did not fully grasp its meaning) – humorous excerpts were included in the plays put on in the children's home. The texts were not preserved, but the few inmates who survived still remember a skit about a former prisoner who returned home and kept acting as if he were in camp, as well as a topical version of *Snow White and the Seven Dwarfs*.

The humor in the Terezin ghetto came from two deeply rooted sources – Jewish culture and Czech culture – and it is hard to determine just where one or the other exerted its influence. After all, they share a common basis: humor is the weapon of the weak. For hundreds of years, both the Jews and the Czechs contended with forces stronger than themselves that sought to erase their identity. Both were a minority in a hostile environment.

In preserved humoristic works, it is not hard to identify the influence of Czech literature: Hašek's *The Good Soldier Schweik*; the writings of Karel Čapek and Karel Poláček; and the texts of the V+W (Voskovec a Werich) satirical theater in Prague. Schweik would have felt at home in the Terezin ghetto; not only could his fans recite whole chapters of his exploits by heart for the pleasure of their audiences, but there were also innumerable situations in the ghetto that brought him to mind. Characters seemed to spring from his pages, like Theodor Janetschek, commander of the Czech gendarmes in the ghetto, a German by choice, whose round body, huge head and short legs earned him the nickname "Cauliflower":

Today he's a big shot around here
An all-powerful commander
Filling us with dread and fear
But one day he'll get a kick in the rear[3]

When Janetschek spoke to Edelstein, the first Elder of the Jews, who was witty and brave even in the eyes of his opponents, about how good the Jews in Terezin had it, since they did not have to go

3 BTA, 366.

to the front and were protected by others, Edelstein replied: "You can always convert to Judaism, Herr Hauptmann."[4]

Schweik, a symbol of Czech passive resistance to Austrian militarism, aggression and bureaucracy, would have fit into Terezin perfectly. And as a matter of fact, Josef Taussig, known as Long Pepek, an amateur author and theater critic, a fan of Hašek and Gogol, who knew *The Good Soldier Schweik* by heart, planned to write a new version of Schweik's exploits in the ghetto, and even began working on a manuscript. It was supposed to be the story of a naïve citizen of Prague who comes to City Hall to pay the dog tax, mistakenly gets in the wrong line in front of the wrong window, where his identity card is stamped with the letter J, namely Jew, and from then on is swept up in the current of the Jewish fate and arrives at the Terezin ghetto.[5]

Pepek reacted to the fall of Stalingrad in one of his "sermons," with which he would entertain his comrades at work in the transport unit:

> Today I will deliver a sermon on the words of our good soldier Schweik from the third volume, in the famous chapter on Budapest. There Schweik says: "It's no big deal to get into some place, everyone knows that. But to get out of there, that's the true art of war."[6]

In the fall of 1944 Taussig was sent to Auschwitz, and in March 1945 died in the Flossenburg camp in Germany. The Jewish Schweik died there with him.

The ghetto was good at reacting immediately to every new grotesque situation. The sham theatrical sets put up in preparation for the expected visit of a delegation of the International Red Cross (which took place in June 1944) inspired many jokes, humorous

4 Karl Löwenstein, *Aus der Hölle Minsk in das "Paradies Theresienstadt,"* (Berlin: Politik und Zeitgeschichte, 1958).

5 Norbert Frýd, *Láhvová pošta* (Prague: Československý Spisovatel, 1971), pp. 217–218.

6 Josef Bor, *Opuštěná panenka* (Prague: NPL, 1965), pp. 177–178.

pieces and songs. The inmates joked that they were going to smear the many fleas swarming in the ghetto with phosphorus paint, so the delegation would think they were fireflies.[7]

"This may be the most topical humor in the world, but it is also the most limited in its locale," wrote Pepek Taussig in his review on the subjects of the cabaret songs that were wearily repeating themselves: the bitter lentil soup, the bedbugs and lice, the "pull," the bureaucracy and the *kumbáls* (ghetto slang for separate living quarters in cubbyholes the inmates built themselves).[8] Another constantly repeated subject was the wild, often optimistic rumors that spread by word of mouth and in ghetto slang were called *bonkes* (perhaps a distortion of *bube meises*, Yiddish for old wives' tales), "news from the JPP agency" (initials of *jedna paní povídala*, meaning "one woman said"), or *latrínky*, according to the humorous Terezin dictionary: "true, verified news invented in the latrine."[9] Another subject much talked about was *šlojs*, the term used for pilfering from the general property, to distinguish it from thefts from private property which were totally unacceptable. In a long ballad, the Viennese writer of lyrics, Hans Hopper, tells how through a long series of pilfering – by the veterinarian, the butcher, the truck driver, the cook, the fire stoker and dozens of others – an entire cow shrinks into one tablespoon of chopped meat: "All that remained of the cow, what a bitter defeat/ only a sixty gram portion of chopped meat."[10]

In my view, that focus on life in Terezin was completely natural. The humor gave the inmates strength, then and there; it gave vent to their fears and eased any given situation. *Rideo, ergo sum*, I laugh, therefore I exist.

In the ghetto, there were also those who continued the humor of Karel Poláček, who drew upon the two sources, Jewish and Czech. Two novels in installments, directly influenced by

7 Josef Taussig, "Die Theresienstädter Kabarette," *Theresienstädter Studien und Dokumente* (Prague: Academia, 1994), p. 226.

8 Ibid., p. 216.

9 *SNP*, no. 9/3.

10 BTA, 366/2.

Poláček, appeared in the children's newspapers. One, "The Fate of the Meiselschwein Family in Terezin," was written by a boy (or several boys) under the pen name "Košule" and was printed in six installments in the children's newspaper *Kamarád*,[11] which came out in the Q609 children's home between October 1943 and September 1944. The second, "Men Offside in Terezin," based on Poláček's well-known novel, *Men Offside,* was printed in five installments in the children's newspaper, *Vedem*, the newspaper of the L417 children's home signed by its authors with the initials Ca-Kr.[12] The two stories have a similar plot: a stout mother and father, parents to three children in the Meiselschwein family, and two in the Načeradec family, uprooted from their tranquil petit bourgeoisie lives, experience all the ordeals of the Terezin ghetto and try to overcome them until the moment they are sent on a transport to Poland – which enabled the young authors to stop the plot when their source of inspiration dried up or their patience wore out.

At the age of fifty-one, in June 1943, Poláček himself arrived in Terezin, stooped, tired, and lacking the strength to resist even by writing. Before being deported, at the sight of the holy pictures of apathetic looking martyrs in an ancient Bible, he wrote: "In the past I assumed that the medieval painters did not know how to give expression to psychological situations like fear, astonishment, pain and the like, and that was why their saints seem to take no interest in their torments. Now I understand them better: what, after all, could they do?"[13]

The texts of lectures Karel Poláček delivered in the ghetto – "Karel Čapek," "Optimism and Pessimism," "Witnesses in the Courts," "Wealth and Poverty," "The Inhabitants of Terezin and their Leaders," and "On Patience and Impatience" – were not pre-

11 Košule (pen name), "The Fate of the Meiselschwein Family in Terezin," in *They Called It a Friend: The Children's Newspaper "Kamarád" in the Terezin Ghetto 1943–1944* (Jerusalem: Yad Vashem, 1997), issues 9–14, 24.12.1943–4.2.1944.

12 *Vedem*, the newspaper of House 1 in the children's home L417, No. 7/15, the pen name of the writer, Ca-Kr, copy in BTA.

13 Karel Poláček, *Život a dílo* (Rychnov: Židovské Muzeum Podorlicka, 1995), p. 57.

served, and they may not have been put in writing. All we have left is a comment by a young writer in the *Vedem* newspaper about Poláček's lecture in the L417 children's home on Russian literature, and what Poláček wrote on 17 September 1943, in the memoir of Miloš Salus, an engineer and former teacher in a commerce academy, and a Czech patriot involved in Czech culture, one of the central figures in the ghetto's cultural life. There Poláček wrote about the mess tin, which only a proletarian who was used to bending his back could carry:

> That is why you cannot carry your lunch standing tall, your head in the clouds, because then you'd only bring home half of the portion and you'd be hungrier than the bent-over proletarian. You have to look into your soup with the same degree of concentration as a fortune teller looks into her crystal ball when she is trying to read the future.[14]

That same tolerant humor in the face of a situation that cannot be changed, only be made easier, is reflected in dozens of feuilletons and parodies written in the ghetto by adults and children: on the loss of a food ticket, which meant the loss of at least one meal and interminable red tape until a new one was obtained; about the war against the fleas and the *Pischkolonne,* the nighttime convoy on the way to the latrine; on the pilfering of potatoes; and about other subjects from ghetto life. Humor surfaced also in articles, entitled for example "How you do what," inspired by Karel Čapek's writings.[15] Only a few sensitive souls, like Peter Ginz, the 15-year-old gifted editor of the children's paper, *Vedem,* understood that humor meant reconciling oneself, giving up: "That crazy fellow, only a few years ago/wanted to turn the world on its head."[16]

The humor of Terezin grew on the fertile soil of sorrow, so in the poetry that was preserved, the songs of pain far outnumber the humorous ones. For hundreds of years, the Jews have laughed

14 BTA, 314.

15 *They Called It a Friend,* especially pp. 24, 39, 121, 185.

16 *Vedem,* no. 7/6.

about their tragic fate. To avoid crying they laughed, like Shalom Aleichem, in spite of everything, with tears. The inmates of the ghetto expressed this worldview in many variations. In 1942, at the age of fifty-six, Emo Groag, formerly owner of a malt factory, wrote in a booklet of drawings and rhymes in German called *Abundantia*:

> We won't take things seriously
> No matter what happens, no matter what they do,
> You can be sorry about it all, cry about it all
> But you can laugh about it too.[17]

Another wrote: "Pessimists, don't make a sour face/It's far better just to laugh."[18] And similarly, the anonymous author of "Terezin Song," sung to one of the melodies of Franz Léhar's operetta, *The Countess Maritza*:

> Yes, we here in Terezin
> Take life
> Very easy
> Because otherwise it would be
> A real catastrophe.[19]

In the ghetto, Josef Lustig and Jiří Spitz established the "Stolen Theater," based on Voskovec and Werich's Liberated theater. In a cabaret they wrote, *Prinz Bettliegend*, a legend about a prince who was officially recognized as a bedridden man unfit to leave on a transport for Poland, the king says in his speech:

> Beating your head will not break down a wall,
> No good comes of curses and moaning,

17 Emo Groag, *It's Never Too Late* (Kibbutz Ma'anit: Kibbutz Ma'anit Publications, 1986), p. 46.

18 BTA, 366/19.

19 Ulrike Migdal, *Und die Musik spielt dazu* (Munich: Piper Verlag, 1986), p. 46.

As your king, my people, this I tell you all,
So strength and power may be yours,
That you may bear your trials heroically,
Have faith in yourself eternally,
And so you will endure. [20]

During the Holocaust, a normal person had plenty of reasons to go mad, even before he knew about the death factory. Sometimes humor was an attempt to remain sane, to keep from banging your head against a wall. In "Purim Song," the writer tells how he drank a toast with his happy family when their affidavit arrived, guaranteeing them the long-awaited entry visa to the United States, but before he could go through all the complicated emigration procedures and obtain the necessary approvals, he received – instead of the voyage to freedom – a call to leave on a transport to the ghetto:

Instead of going to the Yanks
We're on the way to Terezin
Instead of going to Uncle Sam
We've arrived here now.[21]

With all the irony, satire and mockery about life in the ghetto, the politically aware writers of cabaret songs of Czech origin (many of them Communists), also felt the need to end on an optimistic note, a promise of a better future. "The Song of Civilization" by Franta Kowanitz, sung to a tune by the Czech composer Jiří Ježek, enumerates the many departments established in the ghetto – for building bunks, distributing used clothes, running the warming kitchens, etc. – and concludes: "And the railway department has built a track/to facilitate our trip home when we go back."[22]

Hans Günther Adler, the severe critic who had firm opinions about the way the leadership and inmates of the ghetto behaved,

20 BTA, 366/17.
21 BTA, 366/89.
22 Bor, *Opuštěná panenka*, p. 152.

talks about "sick optimism" and "irresponsible frivolity,"[23] but in the ghetto even the pessimist believed that, "An end will come, maybe not soon, like a man who is afraid to arouse God's wrath."[24] However, even the gloomiest doomsayers did not foresee the horror of the gas chambers, perhaps because they were not, according to Karel Čapek's definition, true pessimists: "You are not a pessimist because you see the pain, stupidity, cruelty and absurdity of it all. As long as it pains you, as long as you are shocked and compassionate, you are not a pessimist."[25]

♦

The Terezin ghetto was a continuation – hard, frightening, depressing, threatening – but still a continuation, not a watershed between two eras, a reality that is one of a kind. For many generations, Jews laughed at themselves, blamed themselves, even hated themselves, just to avoid rebelling against God in His heaven who was bringing all these disasters down on their heads. In Terezin, too, it was easier to laugh at what the Jews were doing than to rebel against the evil decrees from above, which in this case too were imposed by a terrible omnipotent ruler. Obviously, the humorous pieces only referred to the Germans in allegory, in allusions, some of them quite blatant, as, for example, in the song "Decline" about the ritual of bowing down to a bull which was customary in the temples of Apis in ancient Egypt:

> Since then the rite has gone downhill,
> It's been declining fast.
> By now they're paying tribute,
> To any kind of ass.[26]

In the fifteen issues of the humoristic newspaper, *Šalom na Pátek,* I found only one undisguised slur:

23 Adler, *Theresienstadt,* p. 595.
24 Redlich, *Life as If,* entry dated 9.11.1943, p. 203.
25 Karel Čapek, *Výbor z prózy* (Prague: Státni Nakladatelství, 1946), p. 181.
26 *Vedem*, no. 23/2.

If you've got a big mouth
And your brain's not too large,
You've got what it takes
To be put in charge.[27]

The only proof in writing of humor that refers directly to an authority is a note intended for the *berušky* (the "lady bugs"), the uniformed German women in charge of searching the prisoners' living quarters and were in the habit of confiscating not only what the inmates were forbidden to keep, like money, watches, cigarettes, batteries, medicines, but also any item that caught their fancy. Emo Groag left a note on his bunk in the Sudeten barracks in case the *berušky* should visit there in his absence, which read: "Women are more attractive when they give than when they take." When he came back from work, Groag found all of his belongings scattered on the bunk, and one of the lovely ladies in green uniform had added to his note: "Women are also attractive when they take."[28]

Although the humor was only expressed in innuendo – thick in Czech, more subtle in German – the people in the ghetto must have been quite certain there would not be an informer in the audience or among their readers. In *Šalom na Pátek's* dictionary of Terezin terms there is no definition for the *Judenältester* and *Ältestenrat*, the Elder of the Jews and the Council of Elders; and where these terms should have appeared, it says: "censored," but that was meant as a joke. Everyone knew that the members of the Council of Elders were also among the newspaper's readers, and none of them would have thought of censoring a satire or a slight sneer at the Jewish leadership. The leaders preferred to act as a lightning rod that protected the community from the rage of the authorities, and they intervened only when they were apprehensive about the results of an overtly anti-Nazi satire, for example, in Karel Švenk's play, *The Last Bicycle Rider*. In a distant land, mental patients led by "her ladyship" grasped power, and whenever there was a shortage

27 *SNP*, no. 15/3.
28 Willy Groag archives, BTA 79.

or something went wrong, they blamed a dangerous element – the bicycle riders – and consequently thought it necessary to liquidate all of them.[29] But why of all people, the bicycle riders? It was based on an old Jewish joke:

- The Jews and the bicycle riders are to blame for everything.
- Why the bicycle riders?
- And why the Jews?

The name of the hero, Bořivoj Abeles (the first name a mythological Czech, the second clearly Jewish), who in the end triumphs over "her ladyship" and her rule, was already used by Švenk in a humoristic novel he had begun to write in Prague before the deportations. But he never returned, neither to his writing, nor from the camps.[30]

On more than one occasion, critics wrote disparaging remarks about the German cabarets, complaining that they wanted only to entertain and amuse, that they had no key message, were full of stupid jokes about mothers-in-law, unfaithful spouses, and physical disabilities, and were superficial and sentimental.[31] But the very ability to laugh was a liberating force. The audience, even if it couldn't explain why, felt that laughter helped, and as Frieda Rosenthal wrote in the refrain of a song thanking the Strauss Cabaret that performed in the ghetto:

The pain of hunger has gone away
And for that we thank the cabaret
The pain of longing has gone away
And for that we thank the cabaret.[32]

"And what a mood, how many jokes, how much irony and humor found refuge in the cabarets! For how many hours of relaxation

29 Eva Šormová, *Divadlo v Terezíně* (Terezin: Pamatník Terezín, 1973), p. 47.
30 BTA, 576.
31 Taussig, "Die Theresienstädter Kabarette," p. 215.
32 Migdal, *Und die Musik spielt dazu*, p. 71.

and cheer do thousands of people have to thank these improvising artists!" Professor Emil Utitz, the director of the ghetto library, wrote.[33] Even a critic as rigorous in his artistic demands as the composer Viktor Ullman, who studied with Arnold Schoenberg, expressed his gratitude to Švenk and his team for their "ironic self-awareness, for the satire, and its offspring, parody, and hence for true art."[34]

♦

Black humor – when a person laughs about something unbearable, horrible, terrifying, or laughs to avoid screaming – was far rarer in the ghetto than the optimistic, relaxing humor, but still there was some. A case of pneumonia without antibiotics meant the danger of death, but it was a temporary protection against deportation eastward. Therefore, the "happy father" says:

As the transports start to leave
Now all around is pandemonium
How lucky that our child fell ill
With a bad case of pneumonia.[35]

And the same holds true for the joke, "A visit to the doctor":

- You have to spend more time in the fresh air, to engage in sport
- But, Doctor, what sport can I engage in in Terezin?
- Maybe you could ask to be a participant in Tran-sport?[36]

I found the most direct reference to death in a 1943 caricature by Erich Lichtblau (Lesklý): before leaving on a transport eastward, an

33 Emil Utitz, *Psychologie života v Terezínském koncentračním táboře* (Prague: Děmické Nakladatelství, 1947), p. 55.

34 Viktor Ullmann, *26 Kritiken über musikalische Veranstaltungen in Theresienstadt* (Hamburg: Von Bockel Verlag, 1993), pp. 62–63.

35 *Vedem*, no. 23/2.

36 *SNP*, no. 13/16.

old man who came to the ghetto from Germany takes leave of his friends in the nursing ward, saying: "See you in the mass grave."[37]

Šalom na Pátek printed an illustrated autobiography of a Jewish doctor who, in order to earn a living, had become a good German in the past, then an ardent Czech and a member of the Czech national gymnastic organization, Sokol. Later, he became a fanatic Zionist and finally converted to Christianity, but nothing saved him from deportation to Terezin. There he fell ill with encephalitis and keratitis and all manner of other diseases, until he died and his body was burned in the local crematorium: "And so, finally, I managed to get out of the ghetto."[38]

Even in the hardest moment of all, before departing for the unknown in the East, those who were leaving tried to overcome their dread with the help of humor. When Alfred Katz and his wife Karolina were leaving on a transport to Poland, his father-in-law and friend said to him: "If you want to tell a joke on the way… remember the new one: what is the difference between the Nazis and their shoes? In the shoes, the tacks are only down below [in Czech the word for tacks, *cvoky*, also means crazy.][39]

On 15 September 1944, when 15-year-old Hanuš Hachenburg left on a cattle car going eastward, he was full of humor, and when a rumor spread that the train was not traveling to a labor camp in the Reich, as the SS men at Terezin had claimed, but to Auschwitz, he said: "Nothing can happen to me there. My mother is there." (She had been sent there straight from the Gestapo prison). However, during the selection process on the platform at Birkenau, Hanuš suddenly ran to join his friends standing on the side of those doomed to extermination.[40]

♦

37 BTA, 268.

38 *SNP*, no. 15–15/9.

39 Frýd, *Láhvová pošta*, p. 192.

40 Marie Rut Křížková, Kurt Jiří Kotouč and Zděnek Ornest, eds., *We are Children Just the Same* (Philadelphia: The Jewish Publication Society, 1995), p. 147.

In Jewish humor – unlike Czech humor – for generations there has been an undertone of self-hatred. This was perhaps due to an attempt to understand the source of the gentiles' hatred, or maybe because self-hatred also contributed to a sense of internal cohesiveness. Perhaps it helped to cope with distress, as Theodor Reik put it: "Self-deprecation and self-ridicule may be a defense mechanism that protects the Jew from an even greater danger, a sacrifice of sorts for the sake of survival."[41] Naturally, humor in Terezin was also marked by self-hatred: "Theresienstadt, Theresienstadt/The most anti-Semitic ghetto in the world."[42] And also:

> Here in Terezin where it's so nice
> It's easier to teach the lice
> To dance a polka and a mazurka
> Than to teach the Jews discipline.[43]

When, after all the ordeals of the ghetto, the father of the family, of Czech origin, is called upon to join a transport to Poland, he ends his lament on his perpetual bad luck with the words: "Look folks, see what's the latest news/They're turning us into Polish Jews."[44]

The self-hatred also resonated palpably in the feuilleton, "The Jews and their extortionism," that appeared in the children's newspaper *Vedem*, in which an outside observer of the ghetto enumerates all the sins of the Jews – exploitation, abuse, extortion, dispossession – to prove that they were also exploiting children, for example V.E. (the reference is to Valtr Eisenberg, the instructor in the children's home) "who does not hesitate to extort cultural work from them, imprisons his victims in a moldy room and does not allow them to go out into the fresh air."[45]

Another source of satire was the broken, heavily accented German spoken by the Czechs. It was immortalized in *Šalom na Pátek* in excerpts supposedly written by nine-year-old Moricek

41 Theodor Reik, *Jewish Wit* (New York: Gamut Press, 1962), p. 85.
42 Migdal, *Und die Musik spielt dazu*, p. 72.
43 *SNP*, no. 15/3.
44 *Vedem* no. 2/21/2.
45 *Vedem*, no. 43/5.

Grünbaum (but actually written by Ewald Bauer, the newspaper's "non-acting editor" as he defined himself), for example: "*vir vurdn jedevajle gevkt unt gecelt, kurc esvar zer lustyk*" instead of the proper German: "*Wir wurden jede Weile geweckt und gezählt, kurz es war sehr lustig*," namely "They woke us up every minute and counted us, in short it was very merry."[46]

Even Freud found a certain satisfaction in a feeling of superiority from the heights of his polished German in comparison to the Jewish German, that same *Mauscheln* of the East European Jews (perhaps also spoken by his father). Karel Švenk's cabaret *That Same Thing, But Different*, includes Mark Anthony's famous eulogy over Julius Caesar's body declaimed by a rabbi speaking poor Czech, peppered with expressions in Yiddish and German. As Josef Tausig wrote, it was this particular piece, performed by the actor František Miška, that evoked the most laughter from the audience.[47]

Life in the ghetto was an unbroken chain of absurd situations that made the inmates chuckle, and that amounted to a kind of declaration of independence or – in the Freudian term – protection of the integrity of the ego[48]: I am the master of my thoughts. One of the events that got a derisive response in all the extant sources was the parade of the Jewish ghetto police, organized by Dr. Karl Löwenstein, the new commander of the security services, who had a special relationship with the Nazis, to demonstrate the iron discipline of his policemen (in contrast to the lenient approach and tendency to disorder of his predecessors, the policemen of Czech origin):

> Accompanied by Tauber's band
> General Löwenstein reviews the ranks
> And onto the field comes, head uncovered
> The Elder of the Jews, Epp von Stein[49]

46 *SNP*, no. 7/1.
47 Taussig, "Die Theresienstädter Kabarette," p. 240.
48 Sigmund Freud, *Selected Essays*, I, (Hebrew) (Tel Aviv: Dvir, 1967), p. 215.
49 Dr. Otto Altenstein, BTA, 366/42.

Witnesses testified that Jakob Edelstein, who at the time no longer served as Elder of the Jews, but only as the deputy of Dr. Paul Eppstein, reacted as befitting a former traveling salesman, an occupation he engaged in when he was a refugee from Galicia at the start of his Zionist path in Czechoslovakia. Remote from all the pomp and ceremony or the demonstrated discipline, Edelstein went over to one of the policemen, all of whom were wearing new gray uniform shirts sewn from old dyed sheets, fingered the material like a textile merchant, and said: "Very nice, very nice."[50]

Šalom na Pátek reacted to the parade in "The Diary of a 17-year-old Girl": "I really liked the way they were marching in a row, waving their left arm back and forth and leaving their right arm taut, as if they were holding some secret, invisible weapon in it. And they threw their legs forward with such energy, I feared they would tear them."[51]

The joking, the jesting, the clowning around, the laughter for the sake of laughter – for the young people who grew up in Czechoslovakia these were all an inseparable part of the life they lived before the flood, and they carried on that way in Terezin, too. Rudolf Laub wrote in *Vedem* about the children's opera, *Brundibár*, which was performed more than fifty times by the children of the ghetto. After describing all the things that went wrong during the rehearsals and the stage fright during the first performances, he wrote: "Now, in the repeated performances, we already sing routinely and are only concerned that we should have lots of fun."[52] The greatest compliment that the boys he was in charge of could give Valtr Eisenberg, manager of the Shkid children's home, was that he "understands a joke." The boys' craving for jokes, mockery and tomfoolery was also an attempt to come to terms with the separation from their parents, the hunger, the longing for home and the illnesses. Hanuš Hachenburg, a sensitive boy, whose poems are among the most beautiful written in the ghetto, objected to it: "The satirical gentlemen take away all the writer's desire to write.

50 Bondy, *Elder of the Jews*, p. 351.

51 *SNP*, no. 6/5.

52 *Vedem* no. 44–45/9.

In their eyes, culture is either laughter or it is serious and then they have to make fun of it."[53]

Many humoristic texts were topical parodies written to existing melodies – folk songs, popular hits, arias from operas or songs from the W+V theater, ranging from "Old Man River" to the saccharine Czech hit, "I'd Like to Have Your Picture in a Golden Frame" – not only because of the lack of time or ability to compose new melodies, but because the texts spoke about the present, and the melodies were a link to the past. An entire medley of folk songs for which up-to-date texts were written appeared in *Vedem*. One was a parody on the favorite song of Tomáš G. Masaryk, the first president of Czechoslovakia. In the original song, a father asks his son if he has already plowed the field, and the son answers that he has plowed and plowed, but only a little, and the plough broke. The Terezin version reads:

> Oh, my son, my son, why have you come home,
> The labor office is checking to see if you worked.
> I worked, I worked, but not very much
> The work exhausted me completely.

And in another song in the medley:

> I'm a man from Kutná Hora, from Kutná Hora
> Who had to learn the shoemaking trade
> To be a manager of a bank, of a bank
> Was a completely different story.[54]

Eisenberg, who wrote the folk song medley, was a Communist, as were Taussig, Švenk and other Czech text writers. It later turned out that Communism and humor could not live under the same roof, but then, when Communism was the faith of men of good intentions, who yearned for justice and equality, there were Com-

53 *Vedem*, no. 44–45/12.

54 *Vedem*, no. 3/3–4, in Ludmila Vrkočová, *Rekviem sami sobě* (Prague: Arkýř & Artforum, 1993), pp. 152–153.

munists who knew how to laugh at themselves and their situation – Communist comedians.

There were many elements of the circus in ghetto life, and it is not surprising that it often served as a metaphor. In July 1943, when a huge tent was set up in the Terezin city square for the *Kistenproduktion,* in which inmates packed into crates parts for military vehicles on the eastern front to protect them from freezing in the winter, naturally it was called a circus. This was not only because there was a tent, but also because it was often like a performance: parts sent to Terezin from the Łódź ghetto and other places did not always arrive in an orderly fashion, and when the local command was expecting the visit of an important official at a time when production was stopped due to a lack of parts, they simply issued an order to dismantle already packed crates, and the assembly line began to move again. And like in any circus, in Terezin there were also sad clowns – in fact, all the comedians in the ghetto were sad clowns, whether they knew it or not.

> Everywhere there is always one
> Laughed at each day anew,
> Everywhere there is always one,
> Who plays the clown for you.[55]

Humor enables a sense of distance, which in turn enables humor: Everything reminiscent of Terezin as a normal city before it became a ghetto was funny, such as advertisements for a bakery, a delicatessen, a beer brewery, and other local businesses, which in the past had proclaimed: "Our mother buys coffee only from Bíček in Terezin," or "František Horvát, a delicatessen in the Terezin city square, offers its respected customers the finest of wines."[56]

A look into the future also made it possible to laugh at the humiliating present: ten years after the liberation, in a fancy restaurant, an old lady in an elegant dress goes over to a man in a tuxedo, looks at him through a monocle and asks: "Is the gentleman

55 Migdal, *Und die Musik spielt dazu,* p. 121.
56 *SNP,* no. 10/4, 13/16.

going to take the consommé?"[57] – just as every day when the bitter, gray liquid called lentil soup was handed out, old men and women asked the youngsters who did not depend only on the public distribution of food: "Is the gentleman going to take the soup?" If the reply was negative, one of them would take it and bolt it down on the spot.

And if not distance in time, then distance in place would do. To avoid further escape attempts, like those that occurred in April 1943, *Šalom na Pátek* suggested the introduction of a regular bus connection between Terezin and Prague and even printed the impressions of a prisoner upon his return to the ghetto: the inhabitants of Prague are impolite, they fail to remove their hats or curtsy before everyone in uniform as we do in Terezin, and they do not accept the ghetto currency (which was circulated to fool the International Red Cross delegation expected to visit the ghetto). A permit to go out into the street in the evening, the dream of every inmate in the ghetto, which very few ever received, made no impression on the people in Prague and, in general, the inhabitants of the city had strange customs. "Did you know, that in Prague couples live together? Oh, how queer and impractical that is!"[58] Finally, a commando unit was sent to Prague, to introduce several of the ghetto's accomplishments: huge latrines were constructed in the Old City Square, lice were imported to enable a mass disinfection, a *šlojse* (a place where the command confiscated most of the belongings of those arriving in the ghetto) was opened in the large auditorium of the Lucerna hall on Wenceslas Square, and the numbering of the rooms in all the public buildings in Prague were changed according to the outstanding example of the Magdeburg barracks, the seat of the Jewish leadership of the ghetto, to prevent anyone from finding his way around.[59]

♦

57 Taussig, "Die Theresienstädter Kabarette," p. 227.
58 *SNP*, no. 2/1–3, 4/1–3.
59 *SNP*, no. 5/3–4.

It may seem sick or warped to have a humoristic newspaper in a ghetto in which 33,000 people died and another 88,000 were sent to be exterminated. But one has to bear in mind that *Šalom na Pátek* was founded by workers in the construction department, members of the building unit, and until the fall of 1944, most of them were protected against transports eastward. Although the conditions of life in the ghetto were hard for them too – they also never had enough to eat, lived ten or more to a room, were separated from the women, and suffered from bedbugs and fleas – their lives in the ghetto were in a sense a continuation of their previous lives, from the standpoint of their occupation as architects, engineers and graphic artists, as well as in their view of the world, one of the elements of which was humor.

To correctly judge the humor of Terezin, we have to forget what we now know: that most of the writers, the illustrators, performers, comedians, as well as most of the spectators, listeners and readers, died in the gas chambers, and most of those who passed the selection died of exhaustion in one of the concentration camps in Germany or on death marches. Again and again we have to tell ourselves: they lived their daily lives in Terezin in the hope that they would survive, with the terrible dread of the transports to the East, but not with a knowledge of certain death. In humor there was consolation, a momentary victory over the reality, a touch of illusion, a trace of freedom. Humor helped the inmates hold out as long as they could, to maintain the integrity of their personalities, to cast off fear, to chuckle instead of giving in, to disguise the dread, to view the present as temporary, a bridge to tomorrow. Unfortunately, that tomorrow came too late.

Privileged until Further Notice

The status of the "Prominents" in the Terezin ghetto

Heinrich Himmler, head of the SS, may have been exaggerating in a speech delivered to his subordinates in Poznań on 4 October 1943, in an attempt to raise their morale for carrying out the difficult task of exterminating the Jewish race: "And then they come, eighty million worthy Germans, and each has his decent Jews. Of course, the others are vermin, but this one is an 'A1' Jew."[1]

It is true, however, that even high Nazi officials had a Jew somewhere who they did not want to see dead. And there were world-famous Jews whose disappearance off the face of the earth would have raised questions. These were sent to Theresienstadt, which was represented to the outside world as a "privileged ghetto;" moreover, some of them enjoyed a privileged status, or, in the language of the ghetto, were called "prominents."

In yesterday's world, a man or woman became an important, respected person due to his or her work and achievements in science, art, literature, politics or sport. In the Theresienstadt ghetto, people became VIPs by grace of the SS, sometimes thanks to a protective hand on the outside, sometimes on the basis of a written request. Nonetheless, the grade-A status of prominents in the

The dates of the transports from Terezin ghetto to the extermination camps, the dates of deaths of the inmates in the ghetto or the information about their survival until the liberation are taken from the computerized index of the Terezin ghetto inmates in the Beit Terezin Archives, Givat Chaim-Ichud.

1 Gerald Reitlinger, *The Final Solution* (London: Vallentino, Mitchell & Co, 1987), p. 297.

Terezin ghetto was far more significant than all the honors of past times, because it meant life, protection against the transports to the terrifying "East" – as it was called, since no one knew what happened there – the extermination camps in Poland. There were also grade-B VIPs in the ghetto, those for whom the Jewish leadership requested this status and obtained the approval of the German command. These were professors, people who had enjoyed privileges in the Jewish public in the past. They too were given somewhat better living conditions than the other inmates and were exempt, if they so desired, from the general obligation to work, but their status carried no guarantee that they would remain in the Terezin ghetto until the longed-for end of the war.

At the beginning of 1944, there were ninety-four grade-A prominents in the ghetto. This number is attested to by an album containing a photograph and brief biography of each of them, prepared as part of the Nazi propaganda about the "area of Jewish settlement" in preparation for the expected visit of the International Red Cross.[2] There one can find Felix Gustav Flatow, who in 1896 was a member of the German athletic team at the first Olympics in Athens, and together with his brother Viktor won five gold medals in artistic gymnastics, [3] and Eli von Bleichröder, the granddaughter of Baron Gerson Bleichröder, the financial advisor of Kaiser William I and Prince Bismarck. It also includes Ida Franziska Schneidhuber, widow of the SA officer, August Schneidhuber, whom the Nazis shot to death in June 1934, and Elsa Bernstein, an author known by the pen name Ernst Rosmer, whose father was the illegitimate son of Franz Liszt and whose daughter was married to the son of Gerhart Hauptmann, the great German playwright. All in all, a very mixed group. According to an order enforced in the Reich in August 1938, all the men in the album whose first names were not distinctly Jewish were called by an additional first name – Israel – and the women were called Sarah, in order to leave no doubt as to their Jewishness.[4]

2 BTA, 265.

3 He died in the Terezin ghetto on 29 January 1945.

4 Leni Yahil, *The Holocaust – The Fate of European Jewry 1932–1945* (New York: Oxford University Press, 1991), pp. 106–107.

In addition to the album, a folder was also preserved containing protocols and requests addressed to the Council of Elders and the SS command at Terezin, in which the submitters explained why they were entitled to the privileged status, release from the ghetto, permission to write to the outside world, or better living quarters.[5] Only thirty-three of the 148 names in the file also appear in the official album of prominents. In other words, very few of the requests were met.

The requests give voice to a variety of mental states of people fighting to survive, ranging from the dry language in the brief biography of Dr. Richard Stein, a former lecturer in ophthalmology at the German University in Prague (who immigrated to Israel in 1948 where he founded the modern eye surgery department at the Tel Hashomer hospital, now called the Sheba Medical Center);[6] or a concise list of all the positions filled by 73-year-old Dr. Alfred Meissner, who for nine years was the Czechoslovakian Minister of Justice and Minister of Welfare and served as chairman of the committee on social policy in the Czechoslovakian Parliament; to the obsequious request by Brunhilde Windehagen, an Evangelist, to be released from the ghetto since her mother had declared under oath that Brunhilde was not the daughter of her Jewish ex-husband, but of a pure Aryan.

The requests were first handed in, often through those in charge of the barracks, to the main secretariat of the Jewish leadership of the ghetto, usually to Dr. Kurt Levy, the general secretary. Dr. Levy was the one who decided whether the reasons given in the request justified an appeal to the *Dienststelle*, the authority, as the SS command was officially called, and whether it was necessary to draw up a protocol.

The protocols were recorded in the ghetto's court, and they open, as is customary in legal documents, with the words:

5 BTA, 265. Since all the requests quoted here are from the same file, this was not noted for each name.

6 Although Professor Stein did not gain privileged status, thanks to his work (he performed eye operations under the harsh conditions of the ghetto), he remained in the ghetto until liberation.

"...appears before us and declares it is true that..." Sometimes the protocol was recorded next to a sick person's bed: 84-year-old Dr. Ernst Springer testified on 29 April 1944, in the infirmary at 5 Park Street (from 1943, the streets in the ghetto, which previously were marked by letters and numbers, were given poetic sounding names, as part of the campaign to improve the appearance of the ghetto for the expected visit of the International Red Cross). The elderly Dr. Springer, formerly a senior financial advisor in Berlin, stated that on his seventieth birthday he had received greetings and a written letter of gratitude from Hindenburg, the President of the Reich. He added that his son, born of a mixed marriage, was employed in the office of Albert Speer, the Minister of Construction; his two grandchildren were soldiers at the front, and the third had been killed fighting in Russia in 1941. Five weeks later Dr. Springer's body was burned in the ghetto crematorium.

Many of the requests have a reply attached to them: "We wish to inform you that the authority has denied your request to be included in the list of prominents," was the notification given to Cecilia Wölfle, née Marx, on 5 January 1945. Mrs. Wölfle, a Catholic, had stated that her ex-husband, the graphic artist, Prof. Alfons Wölfle, who divorced her in 1934, had participated in the parade of the founders of the National-Socialist Party in 1923 and was now the arts advisor to the NSDAP leadership in Munich. Since the transports to extermination in Auschwitz were discontinued in October 1944, when the eastern front was drawing near, Mrs. Wölfle remained in the ghetto until the end of the war, although she was not considered a privileged resident.

The Nazis regarded the Theresienstadt ghetto itself as a privileged camp and that is how they represented it to the world. After all, officially, the inmates had only "changed their place of residence" to Theresienstadt, and that was the spirit in which the replies to requests for a privileged status or release from the "area of Jewish settlement" were couched. Annie Steiner, a 53-year-old single woman, whose only son Wolfgang, an army officer, had been killed on 3 February 1942 near Sevastapol, "had gladly sacrificed her son for the fatherland," and therefore was requesting permission to return to her place of residence in Austria, where she would be happy to be part of the forces mobilized to work in industry. After Annie Steiner's request was presented to Ernest Möhs, Eichmann's adjutant, who visited Terezin regularly, it was noted in the negative reply that the death of her son on the front had been taken into account in the decision to send her to Theresienstadt in the first place. The same reply was also given to Nathan Rosenberger, who claimed that the Office of Reich Security had promised him special rights considering that both of his sons, born of a mixed marriage, were serving on the front – the special treatment was already reflected in the very fact that he was in Theresienstadt.

Many of the documents bear a remark in Dr. Levy's handwriting: "To Dr. Pollenz, Transports Department, for implementation," because that was the most important thing of all. Protection against the transports eastward was ensured (until further notice) only if a remark was recorded in the index file of the transports department. Nonetheless, all the influence of the transports department was nil when orders were issued by the command: 38-year-old Dr. Pollenz himself was sent on 1 October 1944 to Birkenau and died either there or in one of the concentration camps in Germany. Dr. Kurt Levy, who served as general secretary from September 1943, met with the same fate; on 28 October 1944, he, his wife, their two children and his mother-in-law were sent on the last transport to Auschwitz, straight to the gas chambers.

♦

The status of prominents was first instituted in the fall of 1942, nearly a year after the establishment of the ghetto. Six of the ninety-four prominents included in the album in January 1944 died in the ghetto of "natural causes." In all medical matters, there was an instruction that all the documents of the prominents be marked with a capital P.[7] If one of them fell ill, the inmate in charge of the house (*Hausältester*) was to call a doctor immediately, and in the clinics they were treated without having to wait in line. Elsa Bern-

7 Hans Günther Adler, *Die Verheimlichte Wahrheit* (Tübingen: J.C.B. Mohr (Paul Siebeck), 1958), p. 210.

stein, nearly blind, was even provided with a new glass eye. Nevertheless, the status did not save anyone from death due to weakness, pneumonia or a dwindling desire to live, and in such cases, the doctors were obliged to notify the authority at once.

For some reason, unknown to this day, in the fall of 1944, nine grade-A prominents were taken to the gas chambers, together with their families. One of them was 62-year-old Johann Franz Hugo Friedländer, a faithful Catholic, formerly a senior officer (*Feldmarschalleutnant*) in the Austrian army, a recipient of prestigious medals who was wounded in World War I. However, Emil Samuel Sommer and Paul Winterstein, also high-ranking retired officers in the Austrian army, were left in the Terezin ghetto. Winterstein died on 26 May 1945, a few days after the liberation, at the age of sixty-nine.

Although they were relatively old, seventy-nine VIPs survived, namely eighty-four percent, compared to fourteen percent of the overall population of ghetto inmates and the four percent that survived out of the 88,000 sent eastward (among the older ones, the rate of survival was almost nil).[8]

Since their families were also privileged, the number of prominents reached 214, if we add up the names in the album, in the card index of the prominents kept in Prague, and the list of prominents that in June 1944 came into the hands of Ralph Oppenheim, one of the Danish Jews.[9] However, the number considered VIPs by virtue of their achievements and connections was around 120 throughout the ghetto's existence.

In addition to the file of requests, the photographs and biographies in the album, and the list and card index, there is still one more memento of the VIPs. They were immortalized in a propaganda film that the ghetto inmates ironically termed, "The Führer grants the Jews a city." Its official name was "Theresienstadt — a

8 Adler, *Theresienstadt 1941–1945*, p. 59.

9 Anna Hyndráková, Helena Krejčová, Jana Svobodová, *Prominenti v ghettu Terezín 1942–1945* (Prague: Ústav pro Soudobé Dějiny, 1996). The card index was discovered in 1993 in the archives of the Union of Jewish Communities in Prague. The list is included in Oppenheim's book, published in Danish in Copenhagen in 1945, pp. 74–77.

documentary film from the area of Jewish settlement." Friedländer, Meissner, Eli von Bleichröder, Leon Meyer, formerly a minister in the French government, and many others were compelled to serve as extras in the propaganda film. It was never publicly screened and only excerpts from it were found after the war.[10]

The privileged inmates were not housed in the large sleeping hall in barracks nor were they crowded into basements or attics, but in what were called "the houses of the prominents," former family houses: one room for one or two families, sometimes a room for one individual, sometimes three or four men or women in one room. Some of them, owing to their positions in the ghetto leadership, also received double portions of food and/or permission to receive food parcels more often – subject to them having someone to turn to. Consequently, some of the privileged inmates enjoyed better food, and some were always hungry, like the rest of the rank-and-file elderly. They had a priority right to visit what was known as a café, which was opened in the campaign to improve the appearance of the ghetto in preparation for a visit of the International Red Cross, and where visitors who produced an entry ticket were served ersatz coffee or tea to the sounds of an orchestra playing. Women in the cleaning service, the *Putzkolonne,* cleaned their rooms. They were allowed to write more than the one 30-word postcard once in several months that the other inmates were permitted. Moreover, they were exempt from waiting in lines, one of the worst plagues of the ghetto – a line for food, a line for a faucet, a line to the toilet – and they had the right to shower every day, a right that ordinary inmates could only dream about while waiting patiently for an available faucet of cold water to wash in a tin bowl.[11]

However, the improved living conditions also had some drawbacks. At times, the nerve-wracking togetherness of a few people crowded into one small room, bed next to bed, was worse than in

10 Karl Margry, "Der Nazi Film über Theresienstadt," in Miroslav Kárný, Vojtěch Blodig and Margita Karná, eds., *Theresienstadt in der Endlösung der Judenfrage* (Prague, 1992), pp. 285–305.

11 Hyndráková et al., *Prominenti v ghettu Terezín,* p. 6.

the sleeping halls where hundreds of people slept on triple-decker bunks. Nonetheless, it was the dream of many old people from Germany and Austria, who due to lack of space, were housed in attics, suffocating in the summer and freezing in the winter, to get a bed between four walls.

Dr. Kurt Unger, a disabled veteran of World War I, who was married to an Aryan woman, was sent alone from Breslau to the Terezin ghetto on 7 October 1943, where he was housed in a barracks attic and contracted lung and urinary tract disease. He asked the then Elder of the Jews, Dr. Paul Eppstein, for only one thing: a more tolerable living place for himself and his friend Fritz Proskauer who was caring for him in his illness. His request was passed on to the SS command on 29 April 1944 and rejected. Despite everything, Unger managed to survive in the ghetto until liberation. Like many others, his repeated requests were written in meticulous penmanship in Gothic script. For the command, the requests were copied on a typewriter, sometimes shortened and reworded to make them more to the point: the SS men were not blessed with forbearance.

Kaethe Wernicke also wrote her request in Gothic script and apologized for her handwriting: she was writing in the yard with the paper placed on her knees, since in the sleeping hall there was no room, no quiet, and no possibility of sitting down to write. On the basis of a long list of merits for her family rights in Germany (a photograph of the eight medals of distinction awarded to her father, Dr. Ludwig Borchert, was confiscated from her, as she noted, when she arrived in Theresienstadt), Wernicke asked of the Council of Elders only to be allotted a somewhat better place to live.

Some wrote requests addressed directly to the "Valhalla," the commandant of the camp. In September 1944, Gisela Wiese wrote to Karl Rahm, who from February of that year had been head of the SS command: "I am the widow of Friedrich Wiese, the owner of the factory for steel safes in Vienna and the President of the Ironworkers Union for many years, who is certainly known to your honor." His honor rejected her request to grant her the status of a prominent, and in a remark added that her reason was insufficient and hence disqualified.

In May 1943, Marie Glasberg, a pharmacist from Berlin, applied to the then commandant of Terezin, Dr. Siegfried Seidl, asking to be included on the list of the privileged inmates because she was a good friend of the Reichsmarshal Goering, and thanks to him had been transferred to Terezin, "although from the standpoint of my age, there was no reason for that."[12] She was given better housing and permission to write, but she did not get the status she had requested. In January 1944, Marie Glasberg tried her luck again. This time she appealed to Möhs, Eichman's adjutant, during his visit to Terezin, and he decreed her fate – no privileged status. Nonetheless, Goering's name protected Marie Glasberg until the end of the war.

Many of those who submitted requests, particularly those who came to the ghetto owing to their marriage to Aryans only in the last year of the war, relied on their connections with high-ranking Nazi figures. Simon Luis Wolf from Amsterdam, formerly the owner of a store dealing in gold and silver objects and precious stones, noted in his request that a number of well-known persons were among his customers, including Reichsmarshal Goering. Goering, Wolf added, had promised his Aryan father-in-law, who held a senior position in the Fokker aircraft plant, that he would enable Wolf and his family emigrate to Switzerland. That helped. Wolf, then seventy-one, was given the status of a grade-A prominent and remained in Terezin until the end of the war.

In the matter of Sophie Gruyters, née Schwartz, the widow of the industrialist Bernhard Karl Gruyters, a brief note read: "She is a prominent because of her late husband, who in the war [World War I] fought alongside a member of the SA headquarters, Herr Lutze, and was known for his generous support and activity on behalf of all the relief and charity institutions of the NSDAP."

Mauritus Oppenheim, who for many years was the legal advisor of the German embassy in Copenhagen, arrived in the ghetto

12 The Nazi camoflage propaganda stated that Jews were sent from Germany and Austria "to work on fortifications on the eastern front," and the elderly and incapacitated were transferred, at least for an interim period, to the Terezin ghetto.

in October 1943. He counted the minister Freiherr von Neurath among his personal friends, and added a postscript to his request: "From 1932 until my deportation, I was a member of the executive council of the Jewish community in Copenhagen and in that capacity I was presented to the King of Denmark." The protective hand of the king and the people of Denmark helped even without a personal acquaintance. All the Danish Jews remained in Terezin until the International Red Cross transferred them to Sweden in April 1945, even before the end of the war.[13]

Others relied on recommendations from former co-workers. To his request of 25 April 1943, Dr. Kurt Singer, director of the Berlin municipal opera and author of books in musicology, such as *Music and Character* and *Bruckner's Choral Works,* attached a letter from Wilhelm Furtwängler, the renowned conductor of the Berlin Philharmonic Orchestra. In February 1944, 59-year-old Singer died on a narrow bunk in the ghetto, without ever having received the status he desired.

Paul Ottenheimer, the house conductor and principal of the school of opera in Darmstadt, married to an Aryan, noted in March 1945, a month after he was sent to the ghetto, that the composer Richard Strauss and the conductor Felix von Weingarten were among his friends, and in a list of people who would champion his cause he included Winifred Wagner from Bayreuth (the great Richard's daughter-in-law, an admirer of Hitler). But he no longer needed them; liberation came two months later.

The story of the world-renowned geographer, Prof. Dr. Alfred Philippson of Bonn, was published many years ago. Overnight he went from being a neglected old man in an attic to a grade-A prominent, thanks to the direct intervention of Sven Hedin, the Swedish author and Nazi sympathizer, with Hitler.[14] Of all the things that happened to Prof. Philipson, his journeys throughout the world and the long list of his research studies, I was most impressed by his small remark that until his deportation he had lived all his life

13 Leni Yahil, "Danish Jews in Theresienstadt," (Hebrew) *Yalkut Moreshet* 4 (1965), pp. 65–87.

14 Adler, *Theresienstadt*, p. 311.

in his parents' home in Bonn, where he was born in 1864. In the shadow of the endless wandering of the Jews in the twentieth century, this detail of Prof. Philipson's life story seems no less marvelous to me than his survival. Even in the eyes of the Nazis, he was a scientist of such stature that they permitted him to receive books from the library of the geographical institute at Bonn University and continue his research in the ghetto. At the age of eighty-one he returned from the Terezin ghetto to Bonn and to his writing.

Another elderly man, the health advisor, Dr. Leo Pollnow, who was born in 1868 and was the recipient of the most distinguished medal, the Iron Cross first class, noted in his request that as an expert in eye diseases, he had had the honor of treating Miss Hindenburg, the sister of the President of Germany, and lecturing before the Empress Augusta Victoria[15] on trachoma, at her request. In his request, he mentioned several members of the nobility who could confirm the truth of his statement, but that was still not sufficient to accord him the status of a VIP. Dr. Siegmund Taussig, a Jew by race and a Catholic by religion since 1906, Chief Medical Officer in the Austrian army, noted that he had discovered the origin of papatachi fever (a disease that Israeli old-timers remember very well).

♦

Sometimes the document does not reveal the identity of the person providing protection. Flora Pollak-Parille, a widow born in Prague in 1875, a full Jewess (*Volljüdin*) who lived in Amsterdam, states in terse brevity: "I was married to a Jew, my firstborn son Franz is a result of this marriage and is a full Jew. My second son is not my husband's child, but that of an Aryan father. To the best of my knowledge, he has left Judaism, is married to an Aryan, and was active in founding the Jewish Council in Holland."[16] Based on all the

15 The name of the Empress Augusta Victoria is known in Israel because of the hospital in her name in East Jerusalem.

16 From February 1941, the Nazis placed the management of Jewish affairs in the hands of the Jewish Council in Holland.

precedents, Mrs. Pollak-Parille's request should have been denied, but that was not the case. Not only was she accorded the status of a grade-A prominent, but an order was issued stating that she was to be given medical treatment and a report on the treatment was to be submitted to the command. She was also given permission to correspond with her son without any restriction. What power that same son had was never made clear.

In the papers of Marie Margarete Nicklas from Vienna, a full Jewess and mother to four children from a mixed marriage who were considered Aryans, only this is noted: "She does not know why she was declared a prominent. Her children must have submitted a request." The countess Gabriela von Waldenfels was accorded privileged status, as was briefly noted, "On the basis of the initiative of her nephew, Count Rudolf von Waldenfels, a general in the German army, holder of the Knights Cross and the Iron Cross."

The SS was not obliged to explain its decision or reveal its considerations. Inmates submitting requests searched through their past to find what they thought would support their case. The widow Maria Wilcke, a Jew by birth but a practicing Evangelist, based her appeal on the fact that her late husband had managed a factory that produced equipment for dental clinics and had supplied the equipment for the dental clinic in Berghof at Berchtesgaden. No one dared state the name of the local resident, as if it were the forbidden name of the Divinity. The only mention of him was in Dr. Karl Löwenstein's curriculum vitae, written in the third person. In addition to all his distinctions – a lieutenant in the German Navy, recipient of an Iron Cross, first class and second class, director of the Bosse Ltd. Bank – a note said: "Transferred to Theresienstadt owing to the Fuhrer's act of mercy." That same supreme grace got Löwenstein out of the Minsk ghetto, where he was sent in a transport from Berlin in November 1941, earned him a position as commander of the "security forces," namely, the Jewish police in Terezin, and saved his life, although the ghetto's inmates regarded him with suspicion because of the extra privileges he enjoyed and because of his arrogant Prussian behavior.[17]

17 Bondy, *Elder of the Jews*, pp. 349–350.

Dr. Alice Atta, a dentist, based her request on the fact that her ex-husband, a Muslim of Turkish extraction, had treated among his patients Walther Funk, a minister in the Reich government. "With all of our appreciation for the rights your husband merits in the field of dentistry" – the central secretariat was not prepared to transfer the request to the command – "extraordinary circumstances relating to the person submitting the request himself are required."

The family tree of the Catholic Baroness Emilia Salvotti, a niece of Heinrich Heine, and daughter of Baron Heine-Geldern and widow of Baron Salvotti, was not sufficient: "We have been informed by the authorities that we cannot accede to your request to be included on the list of prominents." The central secretariat also expressed doubts about the lady's right to use the title of baroness since the Austrian republic had annulled the status of the nobility. On this question, one could have asked the opinion of Prof. Heinrich Klang, the erstwhile president of the Senate in Vienna, then a judge in the ghetto's court.[18]

Even in the ghetto, most of the privileged inmates still kept their titles. In the stairwell of their houses, they greeted one another as "Herr Baron" or "Frau Gräfin."[19] Clara Schultz, a native of St. Thomas in the West Indies, widow of a commander in the Danish Navy, was called *Kommandeurin* (Commandant) in an official document. In the case of Julia Sallinger, a singer in the Royal Prussian Opera, who was born in 1873 in Savar, Hungary, and from 1894 to 1933 sang in the Hamburg opera, five lines sufficed for her to obtain the desired status, including the sentence: "She is the mother of two illegitimate sons, Otto and Gustav, the Counts von Scholenburg." Mrs. Sallinger survived in Terezin, practicing her singing, trilling with her voice that was grating in her old age, wearing a veil on her face and a feather boa around her neck.

The requests made by the women reflect their situation in the bourgeois class between the two World Wars: most of them based their applications on the rights of a deceased (often non-Jewish) husband, an ex-husband (often compelled to divorce them), fa-

18 Starke, *Der Führer schenkt*, p. 48.
19 Ibid., p. 52.

thers, brothers or sons. They themselves were helpmates to these men, with no professions of their own, totally dependent on the world of men. One of the very few who could point to her own accomplishments was the anthropologist Dr. Stefanie Louise Martin née Oppenheim, who had been living in Utrecht, Holland. In addition to collaborating with her late husband, Rudolf Martin, a full professor at Munich University, she published her own studies, such as "The Technique of Measurements of Primates" and the "The Structure and Function of the Human Body." However, the second request of the 66-year-old anthropologist, who lived in an attic with paneless windows, slept on a mattress on the cold stone floor and voluntarily worked a full day in the youth department examining the young girls' physical structure, was denied. Nonetheless, she survived in Terezin until the end of the war, perhaps because the two stepsons she raised were Aryans, one of them an officer at the General Staff in Berlin, and the other in a key position in the Łódź Chamber of Commerce.

Shades of the empire arose from the depths of the forgotten past: Sara Nussbaum, whose late husband had for forty years been one of the heads of the German Red Cross in Kassel, noted in her request that she too had been engaged for many years in relief work for the Red Cross and as a token of appreciation had received a valuable brooch with a gold crown on it from the Empress of Germany. The command rejected her first request, submitted in November 1943, to obtain the status of a prominent. Her second request, in July 1944, to receive at least the status of a grade-B prominent or better living quarters, bore a handwritten comment by Dr. Paul Eppstein, the second Elder of the Jews of the ghetto: "Not sufficient for a prominent, not even B. Check into living quarters." There is no record of whether this comment helped or not, but fortunately for her, in February 1945, the 77-year-old Mrs. Nussbaum was placed on a transport leaving the Terezin ghetto for Switzerland.[20]

20 When registration began for a transport that the command claimed was leaving for Switzerland, many inmates assumed it was a trap and preferred to remain in the ghetto. However, the transport, a result of a deal between Himmler and the Swiss authorities, did leave the ghetto on 4 February 1945 and arrived at its destination.

In 1894, Dr. Rudolf Polak served in the garrison force in the fortress city of Theresienstadt and was later transferred to work as a pathologist and bacteriologist in the military hospital at Sarajevo (then part of the Austro-Hungarian monarchy). In July 1914, by court order, he performed an autopsy on the bodies of the Austrian crown prince Franz Ferdinand and his wife, who were murdered in Sarajevo, and embalmed their bodies under orders from Vienna. For this, Dr. Polak was awarded the Knights' Cross of the Franz Joseph order.[21] This did not suffice to grant the 70-year-old Dr. Polak the status of a prominent, but he was saved from the transports to the East.

Dr. Stefan Friedrich Prager, a 69-year-old bachelor, holder of distinguished medals from World War I, was active in advocating the re-annexation of the Saar region to Germany. In 1920, he published a book, commissioned by the government, entitled *The Solution of the Housing Shortage in England*. In light of the blitz and the rocket bombardment of England, one might wonder whether the housing problem in England was still of current interest to the authorities. Nevertheless, Prager was granted grade-A prominent status and remained in Terezin until the liberation.

Difficulties also arose when the privileged status was accorded in advance. Leon Mayer, who for twenty-two years was the mayor of Le Havre and served as the Minister of Commerce and Minister of the Merchant Navy of France, came with his wife and daughter from the Bergen-Belsen camp to the Terezin ghetto, as a prominent. However, the local command demanded a curriculum vitae. The general secretariat was uncertain about how to proceed. When 76-year-old Mayer, the holder of many medals and awards, French and otherwise, was questioned, it turned out that he was unable to recall exact dates relating to his function as a minister. "He always served as a minister until the government fell... and that happened frequently." With the help of documents he had wisely taken with him to the camps, it was possible to determine when he re-entered

21 The assassins were imprisoned in the jail in the Terezin fortress and some of them died there. The assassination of the crown prince served as a pretext for the outbreak of World War I.

the post of minister, but not when he ended his tenure. However, with the aid of a protocol and several drafts, the secretariat finally managed to compose a relevant biography. Now another problem arose: Leon Mayer asked to have his watch, which had been confiscated, returned to him. Since in the Terezin ghetto, watches were lent only to doctors and other technical professionals who needed them in their work, Dr. Eppstein was asked whether in Mayer's case he could make an exception. Only the command was authorized to return a confiscated watch, since the Jews' watches were given as gifts to wounded soldiers or to soldiers in SS and army select units. (Looking back, I don't recall that I missed a watch very much. Soap was far more essential.)

The bureaucracy of the ghetto, which at times was inflated out of the desire to survive, moved with marvelous speed compared to our own time. On 12 July 1944, Magda Polak née Bermann, a native of Gothenburg, applied to the Swedish government to get back her Swedish citizenship, which she had lost through her marriage to a Dutch citizen, Jacob Polak. Two days later, Dr. Kurt Levy asked Dr. Eppstein whether to submit Magda's request to the command or to immediately reply to her in the negative, because "such requests seem unreasonable at these times." The following day an official memorandum was submitted to the command asking for guidance on this matter. A day later, it was duly noted that Oberstrumführer Möhs had denied the request. After two days, Magda Polak received notification. The whole matter took no more than one week.

The biographies reflect the wandering of Jews from country to country. When Aharon Arkadin Rissower from Vienna, a native of Kamenka in southern Russia, was living in Odessa, he donated large sums of money to help German and Austrian prisoners of war. That sufficed for him to obtain the status of a grade-B prominent. Idel Rawinsky, the mother of two sons from mixed marriages, originally came from Kishinev, then Romania. Simon Popiel of Vienna, formerly a physician in the General Staff, grew up in Lwów in Poland and there attended the German gymnasium. Berta Levy-Lash was born in 1897 in Chicago and in 1939 her American citizenship was restored to her by law. However, she would be given her American passport only if she could present a ticket on a ship sailing to the United States. Since Berta Levy was unable to obtain the necessary foreign currency to purchase that ticket, she, her husband and their two small children, were stuck in the Protectorate. She was registered in a scheme for the exchange of citizens of the Allied countries and neutral states for German citizens through Switzerland, but before the exchange was carried out she and her family were sent to the ghetto in February 1943. Her repeated request for exchange bears the date 7 March 1944 and states: "My son, Hans Levy, transport no. Ez2000, is now in Birkenau." In September 1943, 19-year-old Hans Levy had been sent to the family camp in Birkenau.[22] On the day his mother wrote her request, he was transferred with 3,800 former Terezin inmates to a quarantine camp and the following day murdered with all the other inmates there in the gas chambers.

Although the prominents were exempt from the obligation to work that applied to the inmates of the ghetto aged 14–65, and in any case most of them were over-age, many who were not sick or frail nevertheless tried to find employment – to shorten the day, to be among people, or to avoid sinking into despair. Dr. Georg Stöhr, formerly chief physician of the Vienna police headquarters, who was given privileged status owing to his service in World War I and after it as an officer on active duty, became a librarian in the ghetto library. The director of the library was Prof. Emil Utitz, accorded the status of a prominent because in the past he had been a professor at the German University in Prague and was a member of scientific societies in philosophy, psychology and aesthetics. According to Utitz, most of the prominents were too old and sick to be of much use: "A society of shadows with a glorious past hovering in the present like ghosts."[23]

♦

22 See chapter "Games in the Shadow of the Crematoria."

23 Emil Utitz, *Psychologie des Lebens im Konzentrationslager Theresienstadt* (Vienna: Verlag A. Sexl, 1948), p. 67.

Not all those who thought they were entitled to privileged status were prepared to accept the criteria for determining that status, which apparently gave preference to scientists and academics. In his request, 67-year-old Dr. Edmund Hadra set out his rights as a brigadier doctor in World War I on the western and eastern front, his wounds and the medals he received. He concluded with the words: "And now the main point: in these wartime actions, I served not only the country I was born in and in which my forefathers lived for 150 years, as is documented, but to the same extent Judaism as well. For in my unit, I always stressed the fact that I am a member of the Jewish people. Perhaps these wartime actions will carry at least the same weight as thick volumes written by learned professors."

The status of the prominent, based as it was on personal achievements, usually stemmed from accomplishments in the intellectual domain rather than from financial achievements. That does not mean that the SS considered finance to be less important. But, after all, the very wealthy had succeeded in fleeing in time to the free world; they had the means to acquire entry visas to countries overseas and to pay for the trip with foreign currency. And the property of those who did not manage to escape fell into the hands of the German Reich in any case, and therefore was no longer of any benefit to its former owners.

One of the few important industrialists on the list of prominents was the engineer Emil Pick, who, until their transfer to Aryan hands, owned the Cosmos plants in Čáslav (the largest factory for oil, margarine and soap in Czechoslovakia), a factory for alcohol and yeast in Trenčín in Slovakia, and a large farm. Pick also held a large number of honorary positions, and in addition, as he noted in his biography, had built a public swimming pool in Čáslav. Eighty-year-old Pick survived in the ghetto until the end of the war.

The German Reich was very wasteful. It thoughtlessly squandered such a vast reservoir of talent, preferring to exterminate it or make no use of it. The biographies of those requesting privileged status attest to only a tiny fragment of the large human treasure that was wasted. The 55-year-old engineer, Prof. Hein Watermann from Holland, invented a sophisticated method to examine oil drills and was a professional advisor in the Royal Shell group. The protocol relating to the engineer Josef Tauber, born in 1873, takes up more than two typewritten pages: "I carried out the mechanization and modernization of the telephone and telegraph system in Czechoslovakia. My picture is on display in the technical museum in Prague." Dr. Leo Löwenstein from Berlin, manager of plants in the chemical and electrochemical industry, and author of scientific works on electrolytic processes, invented a method to measure the distance of a sound, of special importance in World War I, and which "even today plays an important role in the artillery." He also invented, among others, a method of exterminating pests[24] and a new method of protection against fires in mines, and had 190 patents registered in his name in Germany and elsewhere in the world.

The achievements in the field of medicine of candidates for the privileged status were no less impressive. Richard Werner, a bachelor born in 1875, director of the Institute for Cancer Research in Heidelberg, inventor of innovative methods of stomach and intestinal surgery, and author of many scientific works in chemotherapy and the biological treatment of cancer, wrote in his curriculum vitae that he had "rejected offers of a position in the South American universities." God, but why? How many times did he regret that decision? Professor Werner died in the Terezin ghetto on 15 February 1945. Professor Felix Schleissner was the director of a children's clinic at the German University in Prague, and published seventy-five research studies on pediatrics, particularly contagious diseases. He did receive the status of a prominent, but died in the ghetto in November 1944 at the age of sixty-five. Dr. Robert Salus, a professor at the German University in Prague, was the director of the university's eye clinic and the ophthalmologist of the Schwarzenberg nobility. "I wrote more than one hundred scientific works,

24 For the industrial extermination of the Jews, the Nazis used a different pesticide, also an invention of a Jewish chemist, Dr. Emil Poláček. In the 1930s, Poláček invented a new method of producing pure cyanide acid. The material was produced in Kolín, Bohemia, and marketed in tin cans. Its trade name was Zyklon B., BTA, 483/56.

including an ophthalmology textbook... my work on changes in the blood vessels of the retina produced important theoretical and practical results whose significance can only be evaluated after the war," 66-year-old Salus wrote, with great optimism, in his request. He gained life.

Objectively, I should feel sorry about every privileged status that was granted and relief about each refusal. After all, the transports that went eastward to extermination camps had to contain the precise number of people the command had ordered – 1,000, 2,000, 2,500 – and in place of each person who was protected against the transports, another one, unprotected, doubtless younger, left. But the biographies removed the writers of the requests from the statistics and anonymity and turned them into individuals. I can see them in front of me: emaciated, wearing suits and shirts now too large for them, their faces gray from malnutrition, reciting their past history to the people recording the protocols, similar to them in appearance – both of them hoping again and again to hold out – somehow – until the end of the war.

♦

Sometimes it is hard to summon up enough understanding of the mental anguish of those inmates of the ghetto, Jews under the Nuremberg racial laws but Catholics or Protestants by religion, deeply rooted – as they emphasized in their requests – in the German or Austrian Aryan world, who suddenly found themselves in a Jewish ghetto. In March 1944, the nearly blind 78-year-old Elisa Hagemeister appealed to the camp commandant Rahm, asking for his protection and help; misfortune had brought her to Theresienstadt, although she had always felt herself to be Aryan, despite her mother's dubious Jewish origin. We can understand how distressed she was when her two sons volunteered twice for military service and were rejected because they were the offspring of a mixed marriage; we can understand the pride they would have felt "if they had been given the chance to serve their homeland as soldiers"; but even today it is hard to forgive her for signing her letter "*mit deutschem Gruss*" ("with German greetings").

Elisa Hagemeister and others like her did not ask for privileged status, but rather for absolute liberation from the ghetto. The reasons for their requests were varied: In 1917 Margareta Weintraub married Marten Gunar, a Swedish citizen, and gave birth to a daughter who was living in Sweden. Although they divorced in 1920, thanks to her ex-husband's efforts her Swedish citizenship, which she lost with her second marriage, was restored to her. She learned this, however, only after her arrival in Terezin in February 1943. "Since I am a Swedish citizen, I don't belong in the ghetto," she wrote. Sarah Perlborg, a native of London, asked to be recognized as a British citizen and transferred with her 22-year-old son Günther to the detention camp for the British, and to be included in the exchange operation.

Most of them, however, related to the injustice they suffered because their Aryan origin was not recognized. "Although the son, born a Catholic, has been serving since 1940 on the eastern front..." or "although I lived in one household with children considered Aryans..." Hildegard Schörgenhümer, divorced from her Aryan husband and brought to the ghetto by order of the Gestapo in Graz, left two children at home, aged nine and twelve, and asked to return to them. Möhs denied her request.

In March 1944, Margarete Pedde, widow of an Aryan police officer from Mühleim on the Rhine, asked to be released from the ghetto because her 17-year-old daughter, Inge, engaged to a sailor in the Navy, had given birth to a baby girl in 1942, but was transferred to Katowice to serve as a clerk there and had to leave her infant daughter in Germany. "They are putting pressure on Inge to give her daughter up [for adoption], but she loves her and doesn't want to give her up." Margarete Pedde wanted to help the two of them. That same day her letter was transferred to the Elder of the Jews, but the authorities decided that the circumstances described in it did not justify the submission of an official request for release from the ghetto. Alize Schwarzländer's son was only twelve when his mother was brought to Terezin in the spring of 1944, although at the time Jewish mothers of children under the age of fourteen of mixed marriages were protected against transports. The general secretariat tried to help – but in vain. In June, Mrs. Schwarzländer came to the conclusion, as Levy wrote to Eppstein, that "her ex-husband had apparently initiated her premature transfer to Theresienstadt." Levy was able to obtain for her at least permission to write to her son.

Jorgen Wulff, a native of Copenhagen, married since 1942 to an Aryan Danish citizen, was brought to the ghetto in October 1943. Immediately upon his arrival, he protested: there has been a mistake, even in Germany, in the case of a valid marriage between a Jew and an Aryan, the Jewish spouse is protected from deportation. Indeed, Wulff was right, but Möhs decided otherwise. In June 1944, on the basis of a second appeal, a note was made in Wulff's file that he and his family were to be housed in preferred quarters, and since he was a Danish citizen, even though he did not enjoy a personal privileged status, Wulff was protected from transports to the East.

Handwritten comments in the margins or questions addressed to Eppstein were added to many of the documents. "Do you agree?" Levy asked his opinion on 23 April 1944, regarding the matter of Dr. Alice Meyer, the widow of Professor Hans Meyer, formerly director of a laboratory in the German University of Prague. "No!" Eppstein ruled.

Although those requesting release from the ghetto on the basis of humane considerations or because they believed they were sent there by mistake were quite naïve, in some instances, inmates of the ghetto were released, but their exact number is unknown. In his book *Theresienstadt 1941–1945*, Adler enumerates thirty-one cases of fortunate people released from the ghetto in the three-and-a-half years of its existence.[25]

When inmates submitted requests based only on their actions for the sake of Jews, which were not sufficient reasons for transferring these requests to the SS authority, the Jewish leadership sometimes acted without asking the command. This happened in the case of Laura Singer, the widow of Dr. Ludwig Singer, a member of the Czechoslovakian parliament for the Jewish National Party and President of the Jewish community in Prague (his grave in the

25 Adler, *Theresienstadt*, p. 47.

new, 100-year-old Jewish cemetery is located in a very prominent place). In her request, Mrs. Singer relied on Robert Stricker and Otto Zucker, members of the ghetto's Council of Elders, both Zionist leaders. On 9 August 1944, Zucker informed Dr. Benjamin Murmelstein, the third Elder of the Jews: "The leadership has decided to issue instructions for better living quarters for Mrs. Singer without an order from the SS authority." Seven weeks later, Zucker himself was sent to his death in Auschwitz.

♦

The file contains documents relating to only a third of the people who were granted the status of grade-A prominent. It is not clear, therefore, whether the Terezin command received orders regarding some of them in advance from a higher instance, so that there was no need for a protocol or biography, or perhaps there was another file that was not preserved. The first assumption is supported, for example, by a comment by the command (*Aktenvermerk*, in the ghetto language) L/320a, dated 28 January 1944, relating to Benjamin Wolff of Amsterdam, regarding whose grade-A status the Council of Elders had received orders even before the man himself arrived in the ghetto.[26] But it is countered by the biographies of people who almost certainly arrived in the ghetto with prominent status, for example, Dr. Georg Gradanauer, author and editor, born in 1886, who in 1918 was elected Prime Minister of Saxony, was Minister of the Interior, Saxony's representative to the Reich Council and representative of the Social Democratic faction in the Reichstag. The second assumption is supported by the fact that not a single document bears the signature of Jakob Edelstein, the first Elder of the Jews, who was shot to death in June 1944 in Auschwitz, or of Leo Janowitz, the first general secretary, who was also killed in Auschwitz in March 1944. But it is countered by the fact that the documents bear dates from 17 April 1943 (when Janowitz was still general secretary) up to 31 March 1945. Several of the written comments seem to be clarifications of the privileged status of in-

26 Hyndráková et al., *Prominenti v ghettu Terezín*, p. 292.

mates decided on in advance by the SS, as in the case of Maria von Plónnies: "Her husband was an Aryan, the children were raised as Evangelists, the entire family was close to the National Socialist movement even before it rose to power."

The biographies and requests of 147 people in the file do not reflect a true picture of the inmates of Terezin ghetto in general. Full Jews, lacking any connections with influential people in Germany or outside of it, with no claim to citizenship in a neutral state or country overseas, and with no impressive title – did not even think of requesting a privileged status, and if they tried to apply for one, they were rejected out of hand, even before their request was submitted in writing. I myself did not even know about the existence of the prominent status: I was in the ghetto from July 1942 to December 1943, and never even heard the word "Prominent," and certainly never met a single one of them. You would go out to work in the morning, return exhausted in the afternoon, and hurry to meet family and friends. These stories are exceptions.

In a certain sense, it was easier for the masses of ordinary Jews. They felt they were Jews, they did not agonize about where they belonged, they just wanted to remain alive. "I always thought it was a blessing that the Nuremberg laws did not demand any patriotism on the part of the Jews. The lines were clearly drawn," Professor Utitz wrote.[27]

Even in the ghetto there were some German Jews who were unable to wrest themselves free of their full identification with the Third Reich. Dr. Fritz Rathenau, a cousin of Walter Rathenau, the German Foreign Minister, who was murdered in 1922, was employed from 1899 by the Prussian government and was, among other positions, in charge of the regions of eastern Prussian and the policy relating to minorities in the Prussian Interior Ministry. In his request for prominent status, Rathenau saw fit to note: "Early on, I took note of Poland's subversive policy and vigorously cautioned against it in writing and orally."

Eugen Schlesinger, a journalist and author until 1934, had been head of the Society of Austrian Artists. Now seventy, recently

27 Utitz, *Psychologie des Lebens*, p. 44.

released from hospital and suffering from a heart condition, he requested the status of a prominent so that he could live with his wife, since he needed her constant care. As a German living in Bosnia with close contacts in the German consulate in Sarajevo, during World War I, he donated 25,000 gulden to rescue several German crew members of a submarine commanded by Fritz von Papen, who had been taken prisoner. Schlesinger wisely took all the relevant documents with him to the ghetto, apparently keeping them on his body or else they would have been confiscated upon his arrival. But before the Elder of the Jews could transfer the protocol to the SS authority, Schlesinger and his wife were included on a transport to the East. In reply to Dr. Pollenz' handwritten question about how to proceed in that case, Rudolph Prochnik , secretary to Murmelstein, the third Elder of the Jews wrote: "Leave [them] on the transport." On May 14, Schlesinger was sent to the family camp in Birkenau and most likely early in July led to the gas chambers, if he hadn't died of hunger or weakness before then. The official rejection of his request bears the date of August 1944. It could no longer hurt him.

Although far more terrible things occurred during those years, there were cases that seem really appalling if we look at them from the point of view of Germany. Rudolph Stiassnie from Vienna was interned in the ghetto (at least he was left there until liberation) although two of his sons from his first marriage fell in the war, one in France, and one in Russia. Ida Praska from Linz was sent to the ghetto after her Aryan husband was killed on the eastern front in September 1942. The five grandchildren of 79-year-old Lina Schönfluss from Rosenberg in western Prussia went to the war, "two of them are already amputees." In August 1943, a month after her arrival in the ghetto, the elderly lady whose address was "an attic on 9 Bahnhof Street," requested permission to return to her homeland. Her request was denied.

Leopold Anton Frost, the son of a mixed marriage from Vienna, served from September 1939 to August 1941 on active duty in the German war fleet and was sent on leave after being wounded, but not released. Frost only requested permission to write. According to an entry written by the SS authority marked E180, his request was denied. Lina Schmal, who arrived in the ghetto only in February 1945, with the last arrivals who were immediate family members of Aryans, asked only for permission to write more frequently to her 14-year-old illegitimate son, who had been left alone.

Some of the requests and applications submitted to the authority via Benjamin Murmelstein, the last Elder of the Jews, were written in March 1945, several weeks before the end of the war. The German bureaucracy and the methodical extermination of former Terezin inmates on death marches did not cease until the end of the Reich.

The Miracle of the Loaves
Heinz Prossnitz' package aid

In May 1945, when it turned out that Heinz Prossnitz had not survived, Erika Wolf and Edith Březina, the last of his friends to remain in Prague after all the rest were deported to the Terezin ghetto and the extermination camps, wrote a brief survey in place of a eulogy:

4,400 kilograms of foodstuffs directly to Theresienstadt
830 kilograms of foodstuffs to Birkenau and the Łódź ghetto
600 kilograms of clothing and foodstuffs to Sachsenhausen
and Hamburg
Without any public means
Without any public support
At his own initiative
At his own risk
During the economic control
And restrictions on the Jews
Under the Damocles sword of the Gestapo.[1]

1 I wrote the story of Heinz Prossnitz' amazing project mainly because I wanted the public at large, and not only a few researchers, to know about it. Therefore, I decided to limit the number of notes, to avoid interrupting the flow of the text. The greater part of the material on which this study is based is in Heinz Prossnitz's archive kept in two cartons in the Yad Vashem archives, and labeled 0.7.cz/301–311, and it would be tedious to keep noting that in connection with every postcard, note and piece of paper mentioned here. Copies of some of the material in the Prossniz collection and in Yad Vashem are kept in file no. 356 in the Beit Terezin archives in Kibbutz Givat Chaim-Ichud (BTA). For details about Heinz' personality, about the social life in Maccabi Hatzair,

In our own time, these numbers mean hardly anything, but the worth of one loaf of bread I received from Heinz in the Birkenau camp in February 1944 cannot be assessed either in money or in words. It didn't only mean some added calories, more strength, a brief feeling of satiety; it also meant greetings from another world beyond the mountains of darkness. The bread arrived in the name of the recipient, a name from the past, which seemed to have been completely expunged as soon as the Auschwitz number was tattooed on his or her arm. After my return from the camps, I wanted to thank Heinz Prossnitz, whom I had never met personally, but he had vanished. It turned out that on 28 October 1944, he was sent with his parents in the last group of employees of the Prague Council of Jews directly to the Birkenau gas chambers. The following day, the death factory there ceased its operation.

To properly appreciate Heinz Prossnitz' endeavor, I must start from the beginning. But where is that? Perhaps in the family tree of the Prossnitz family, whose forefathers came to Prague in the seventeenth century from the city of Prossnitz (Prostějov in Czech) in Moravia. In the *Familiantenbuch* (book of families, listing the Jews of Prague entitled to establish a family, whose number was limited and determined by law), the Prossnitz family included a button maker, a jeweler and a lemon merchant. Heinz' father, Fritz Prossnitz, born in 1897, was a bank clerk, then considered a respectable occupation that promised a comfortable bourgeois life. However, on 15 March 1939, with the German occupation, suddenly everything was turned upside down. The Jewish bank clerks were among the first to lose their source of livelihood. Fritz Prossnitz began to work in the financial department of the Prague Jewish community, which until then had been an institution of

and the joint work in gardening, I was helped by the written and oral memoirs of his friends, which were collected in 1998: Mordechai Livni (Maxi Lieben), Kiryat Tivon; Yaacov Tzur (Kurt Cierer), Kibbutz Naan; Lenka Krummholz (Polesi), Montreal; Edith Rosen (Naomi Březina), Kfar Saba; Dr. Edith Ramon (Dita Bondy), Jerusalem. The data on birthdates, dates of transports to the Terezin ghetto and from there to the extermination camps, and the dates of death originated in the computerized index of the Terezin ghetto inmates, Beit Terezin, Kibbutz Givat Chaim-Ichud.

scarce importance in the lives of most of the city's Jews, and now suddenly carried tremendous weight. In October 1941, when the first deportations from Prague to the East, or more precisely, to the Łódź ghetto, began, Fritz Prossnitz already had a key management position in the financial department, which also promised him protection from future transports.

Like many other Jewish youngsters, after the conquest of Czechoslovakia and its partition into a Protectorate in the West and a fascist Slovakian republic in the East, Heinz, born in 1926, joined a Zionist youth movement – a milieu where Jewish youth could still feel equal and have a sense of belonging. They could preserve their self-respect vis-à-vis the hostile world outside, which gradually ousted the Jews from its midst. The Zionist youth movements – *Maccabi Hatzair, Tekhelet-Lavan, Hashomer Hatzair, El-Al, Bnei Akiva* – were connected to the various kibbutz movements in Palestine and adhered to different ideologies. But it was not the ideology that decided whether a young Jew would join one or another movement; it was more a matter of chance: a friend brought a friend, an acquaintance recommended it, the local branch of the movement was close to where you lived. What 14- or 15-year-old was interested in the ideological nuances of the socialist worldview or in the differences between the various collective forms of settlement in Palestine? The point was to spend time together, here and now, and to share a goal – to become pioneers in the Promised Land. Some of the fresh Zionists chose a new Hebrew name: Jindra became Avri; Willy, Zeev; Paul, Dov; Edith, Naomi. Others stuck to their old names or their names stuck to them.

Heinz joined the Maccabi Hatzair movement and, with eight or ten young people of his age, set up a group that took the name *Havlagah* (Hebrew for restraint). The name definitely did not reflect the nature of the group of youngsters so avidly hungry for life, but in any case most of them did not know what it meant or that it derived from the policy of the Jewish Yishuv during the Arab riots in 1936–1939. The counselor of the Havlagah group was Fredy Hirsch, born in 1916, a refugee from Aachen in Germany and a physical education teacher by profession. Fredy was adored not only by his group, but by most of the youngsters, first of all because of his appearance. He was tall, erect, athletic, sure of himself, and faithful to the ideal of the new Jew who would emerge in the Land of Israel (the other counselors called him "Apollo with a Jewish nose," somewhat derisively, because in their view the intellect was the most important feature).[2] Heinz was nothing like Fredy. He was a redhead, of medium height, with skinny legs and a slight lisp, but he was very intelligent, quick-minded, resourceful and always ready to laugh. Heinz had great ambitions, but he suffered from a sense of inferiority, especially in the company of girls. He was also captivated by Fredy, who emphasized discipline, physical fitness and inner strength. On 11 February 1940, Fredy's birthday, the youngsters in the group had a tree planted in his name in the Jewish National Fund (JNF) forests in Palestine, and composed a poem for him, probably written by Heinz, expressing their wish that he'd lead them for many days to come and that some day a whole forest in Palestine would bear his name:

> Although our parents may object
> And sometimes they get mad,
> Because our studies we neglect
> And our grades are very bad,
> We're with you now, in the future too,
> We'll always stick with you.

But even as a member of the youth movement, Heinz was rebuked in July 1940; two months earlier he had been given seven JNF boxes to distribute, but although he'd been reminded several times he still hadn't reported on his actions to the offices of the foundation. Such negligence was apt to lead to an unpleasant outcome, and the leadership of Maccabi Hatzair was duly notified. Although the letter from the JNF was written in Czech, Heinz replied in German, probably because the letter was also meant for Fredy who was not fluent in Czech. Heinz admitted that he had received the

2 Willy Groag, Ma'anit, in a conversation with the author. On Fredy Hirsch, see also chapters "The History of the Closing Gates" and "Games in the Shadow of the Crematoria."

seven boxes on 1 May, but had managed to find a place for only one of them. He had reported to the JNF office only on 3 July, because he assumed there was no urgency and he was busy with his schoolwork.

Discipline was strict in the Zionist youth movement, and in Fredy's case, doubly so. Avri Ullman, a member of Havlagah, was severely punished for inappropriate behavior: he was forbidden to wear the Maccabi Hatzair badge or take part in the group's activity for three days, and for one week he was forbidden all contact with the members of the group, with the exception of one person that he could choose. Speaking the whole truth, even if it might lead to punishment, was one of Fredy's ironclad principles. Heinz was also caught lying; under the heading "Top Secret," he wrote in German (and that means it was for Fredy) a list of eight offenses: he had failed to attend a gym class on the pretext that he had something important to do, but in fact had gone to have his photo taken; he once said at home that he had to go out on an important matter, but had gone to the den of Maccabi Hatzair; he had claimed he had a record of *Mignon* at home, which wasn't true… and similar sins of the age of innocence. There's no record of what punishment Heinz received.

Until the end of the 1939–1940 school year, the Jewish pupils attended the general schools. Heinz Prossnitz was a student at the science-oriented high school (officially called the Czech Real Gymnasium) of the "Society for Individual Education," which was opposed to the prevailing mechanical, boring approach in most of the schools that ignored the student as an individual. This school held weekly hikes in the vicinity of Prague, regular meetings with parents (hardly known in the other schools), and joint summer camps. According to a report to Heinz' parents by his teachers in the third grade of the gymnasium (after five years of elementary school), he was a gifted, extremely intelligent student, one of the best in the class. He was weak in geometry and art, but excelled in German, history and geography, and lately also in physics and Latin. His behavior was satisfactory, although he sometimes talked to his friends in class or his attention wavered, probably due to his excess energy. His parents were warned that Heinz was busy with too many activities outside of school, and although in principle the school was not opposed to such activities, in the Scout movement, for example, these might have a negative effect on his schoolwork, although that had not yet happened. They recommended that his parents curtail these activities as much as possible.

Heinz, however, did not get into any trouble in the gymnasium because from the school year 1940–1941 the Jewish pupils were forbidden to attend the general schools. From then on, most of them studied underground, in small groups and in private circles, with Jewish teachers who had also been ousted from the educational system. Some of the Zionist youngsters went to the Youth Aliya school in Prague, whose establishment was approved by the German authorities because officially it was intended to prepare them for emigration to Palestine. According to the lesson plans, the students in Ju-Al, the abbreviated name of the school, had to reply to weighty questions such as, "Why is Zionism the solution to the Jewish problem?" and to note the difference between Keren Hayesod and Keren Kayemet.

If Heinz Prossnitz's activity seemed too frenetic in the Real Gymnasium, his life became even more hectic in the Ju-Al school. His schedule showed that in addition to his morning studies, he took craft classes twice a week in the afternoon (in preparation for his emigration to Palestine). He also had private lessons in English (twice a week) and in Hebrew (once a week). In addition, there were gym classes, daily meetings of the group, individual homework from eight to ten in the evening, which included Hebrew, scouting, geography of Palestine and the history of Zionism, and finally reading. All that in five weekdays; Saturdays were devoted to the movement. On Sundays, the Havlagah group would usually go out with the Rachel group, a sister-group of girls, to hike around Prague, marching in formation, singing marching songs, playing scout games, sitting around a bonfire, roasting hot dogs and potatoes and laughing a lot. On rainy days, the group would occasionally meet in the home of one of the members and listen to recordings of classical music.

As the Jews became increasingly isolated, the groups in the Zionist youth movements grew like living cells; they increased, split, merged. Some of the boys in Havlagah left the group and were replaced by five girls from the Rachel group. No one remembers the name of the new group. Heinz fell in love at first sight with a beautiful girl, Liesl Winternitz, nicknamed *cvoček* (little crazy girl). Dita Bondy, another girl in the group, in whom Heinz confided about his love, advised him to get over her because Liesl did not feel the same about him.[3] In the meantime, Fredy Hirsch had been appointed to take charge of the physical education of all the Zionist youth movements in Prague, whose activity was centered at the sports field of the Hagibor organization in Strašnice, a suburb in the eastern part of the city. The group's new counselor, replacing Fredy, was Dov (Pal) Revesz, a 20-year-old native Hungarian and the young man who had won Liesl's heart.

The focus of all of Maccabi Hatzair's activities was the den on Na Zderaze Street, which housed all the leaders of the movement who were not from Prague (Fredy Hirsch, Zeev Scheck, Egon Redlich and others). A few of the Ju-Al students from the provinces also shared the apartment there, and some of their classmates who lived in Prague envied them because they were free of parental supervision. Fritz and Marie (nicknamed Mitzi) Prossnitz had high expectations of their only son Heinz, which he often felt he was not meeting. On 30 July 1941, apparently after an argument with his parents when they threatened to send him away from home, he wrote: "If I am allowed to live for a month with my parents, I will do all I can to meet their expectations, namely, to examine all my shortcomings and wrongdoings, for which they are rebuking me, and then I will consistently behave properly." In keeping with his character, Heinz added a timetable to his declaration of intent, which began with rising at 7 a.m., included half a day's work, two hours of study (biology, ancient Roman history, Czech literature, etc.), two hours of reading a book in the evening, and ended at 10 p.m. with brushing his teeth. "P.S. In every condition, I will observe the orders of the house 100%."

The life of the group changed totally in the summer of 1941.

3 Dita Bondy's letter to Heinz, 12.8.1940, Yad Vashem Archives (YVA), 0.7.cz/302.

The authorities blocked emigration, the activity of Zionist youth movements was forbidden, and the Ju-Al school was closed down. From now on, the youngsters could only meet in small groups in private apartments. The situation grew considerably worse in September 1941, when the Jews were obliged to wear a yellow Star of David that at one glance set them apart from the general population. On the first page of his pocket diary, next to his name and address, Heinz drew a Star of David and wrote next to it: "Beware, a Jew!"

But still worse was to come. In October 1941, the deportations eastward began. Some members of the Jewish community may have known what to expect, but that information did not reach the public at large, and the transports were a sudden blow to them. In any case, anyone who did know, knew only for a short time: on 17 September 1941, Hitler expressed his desire to purge the Reich and the Protectorate of Jews. At the end of September, Reinhard Heydrich arrived in Prague as Acting Reichsprotektor, and on 28 September held a press conference at which, under an order of absolute secrecy, he disclosed to the German journalists and the collaborators among the Czech journalists that within a short time 5,000 Jews would be expelled, although he did not mention what their destination would be.[4] On 2 October, the second registration of Jews (the first was in 1939) had already begun.

On 4 October, Jakob Edelstein, deputy chairman of the Jewish community, met with six representatives of the Zionist youth movements in his apartment on Bilkova Street in the Old City. The meeting was attended by Fredy Hirsch, head of the physical education department; Seppl Lichtenstern, head of the youth department in the Jewish community; Gonda Redlich and Dr. Heini Klein, heads of professional retraining courses for youth (formerly the Ju-Al school), as well as Jenda Kaufmann and Zeev Scheck, representatives of the joint leadership of the youth movements. Everyone expected Edelstein to give them some important news. But Yekef, as his friends called him, maintained his usual tone of a friendly chat and began describing at length his trip to Poland

4 Bondy, *Elder of the Jews*, pp. 228–229.

in the fall of 1939 (as part of Eichmann's failed plan to establish a Jewish area of settlement near Nisko, on the new border between Germany and the Soviet Union). He asked the others, in passing, how they would react to different circumstances of deportation. When they left Edelstein's apartment, five of them guessed that deportations were on the way, and one of them, Fredy, already knew that they were.[5]

Two days later, Edelstein summoned the six young men to his home again and strongly advised them to set up a youth center in which all the youth institutions would be represented. A few days later, Fredy told the same forum (which had been joined by Dov Revesz) that the following day, Friday, the first transport of one thousand persons would leave Prague, its destination still unknown, but the assumption was that it was in the direction of Łódź. At that ill-fated hour, all those present decided to establish a service to aid those leaving on the transports and to call on all young people aged 14–25 to participate. The purpose of the service was to look after the children and teenagers while their parents were busy preparing for the transport, to help them pack their suitcases and knapsacks and to carry the luggage to the assembly point in the former commercial fairground in the Holešovice quarter. Fredy Hirsch was chosen to run the center, and Seppl Lichtenstern undertook to be the liaison between the Jewish community and the assembly point. Dov Revesz was in charge of assigning tasks on behalf of the aid service.[6]

Looking back, now that the fate of the deported Jews is known, one might ask whether the first reaction of the leadership of the youth movements to the start of the deportations should really have been to set up aid services for the transports. But since no one knew what awaited the deportees, providing help to those leaving seemed the most natural, essential and humane thing to do.

The first deportees were given only twenty-four hours notice to prepare: what to put in the fifty kilograms of luggage each per-

5 Zeev Scheck on the meeting with Edelstein and the establishment of the aid services, recorded after the liberation, BTA, 571/17.

6 Zeev Scheck's testimony on the aid service recorded after the end of the war (n.d.), BTA, 571/17.

son was permitted to take, how, in a time of such strict rationing, to get hold of the most essential objects – a warm coat (furs and fur lining belonging to Jews had been confiscated long before), sturdy shoes, non-perishable foodstuffs? And in fact, after the deportees arrived in Łódź, it turned out that many of them were not equipped with what they needed for the harsh Polish winter; they had not taken enough warm clothing and underwear, and had no down quilts or no cooking utensils. They were missing the most essential items for life in the ghetto.

It was more than obvious that the members of the former Havlagah group would pitch in to work energetically in the aid service. Not only were two of their counselors running the service, but some of their friends – Karel Abeles, Honza Körner, Lenka Polesi – and their families were leaving on the first transports to Łódź. The group set up a joint fund. The members who worked – in factories, workshops, gardening – gave part of their wages; those who got pocket money from their parents gave most of it to the fund. Some of the girls worked in the Jewish community's workshop where duvets were sewn, more comfortable for the trip than quilts: it was exhausting work in a thick cloud of feather dust. In the days of the first deportations, between 16 October and 3 November 1941 (and even afterwards), they all reported to the center at 33 Dlouhá Street set up to provide aid to the transports. From Fredy and Dov they received instructions and addresses of those summoned to the transport, agitated and helpless when it came to packing and in need of help. Since those leaving were forbidden to take any money with them, here and there, the young people, whenever they thought it appropriate, asked for a contribution to their aid fund, instead of letting the money fall into the hands of the Germans. Heinz undertook to manage the fund. That was the beginning of his life endeavor.

Friends in Łódź

A short time later, the first postcards began arriving from the deportees in Łódź: "We're fine, we're healthy," they usually wrote.

They didn't specifically ask for help, but they did hint that they were lacking some basic needs. Those arriving in Łódź did in fact face a difficult situation: the 20,000 deportees from the Reich, as well as from Vienna, Prague and Luxembourg arrived in the ghetto when it was already intolerably overcrowded, with more than 168,000 inhabitants. Not only that, but the new, inexperienced arrivals were at a total loss when faced with the unexpected conditions of the ghetto, compared to the local residents who, since the establishment of the ghetto in February 1940, had learned to manage, knew how to find things on the black market and how to use "pull" and bribes. But all of them, the old-timers and the newcomers, suffered from severe malnutrition, from the freezing cold, from the chaotic supply of food and the shortage of coal. Years later, historians found that starvation was worse in the Łódź ghetto than in most of the other ghettos.

In the first twenty months, only checks could be sent to the Łódź ghetto. Sums of twenty, twenty-five and thirty German marks were sent regularly from the joint fund to friends in Łódź. It later turned out that only a fraction of that money ever reached its destination. Ten percent was deducted "to cover expenses" and up to sixty percent was expropriated "for the general good." Often, out of ten marks, only three were left, but even that was enough to buy a loaf of bread – and that was a lot. To buy food, people from Prague in the Łódź ghetto sold everything they had brought with them, except for the most essential items, but even that was not enough to keep them alive. Karel Abeles' parents and brother died one after another, and Karel fell ill with a bad case of hepatitis. Shortly afterwards, Heinz' first food packages began to arrive. They put Karel back on his feet and afterwards helped him pass the selection at Auschwitz.[7] The other members of Maccabi Hatzair also received packages, as did their families and anyone else who turned to Heinz. According to the reckoning that Heinz made in the summer of 1944, when he thought he was about to be sent to the Terezin ghetto, 40,000 marks from the joint fund had been transferred to the Łódź ghetto, as well as another 15,000 from what

7 Karl Brožík's (Abeles) letter, Frankfurt, 1986, BTA, 356/31.

he called in Hebrew the "Poland fund" – funds that apparently arrived through underground routes from other countries, mainly Switzerland.

It is difficult to determine how much of this money actually reached the people it was intended for. Clearly, what did arrive could not save them from the epidemics and the gas chambers of Chelmno and Auschwitz. But in July 1944, with the encouragement of his friends in the Łódź ghetto, Dr. Oskar Singer, the erstwhile editor of the *Prager Tagblatt*, appealed to Fritz Prossnitz for urgent help. In May 1944, Hans Körner and his sister Hanka also confirmed receipt of a "gift," thanked Heinz and expressed the hope that he would not forget them in the future. They wrote that they were working hard and that Lenka Polesi and Karel Abeles were with them too. At the end of 1943 or the beginning of 1944, when Lenka received the first package from Heinz – overjoyed, she danced the whole way from the distribution point to her parents.[8] Lenka, Karel and Honza were among the last 65,000 Jews left in the Łódź ghetto. They were brought to Auschwitz only in August and September of 1944, and the money and packages they received from Prague unquestionably helped them pass the selection.

Out of fear that the epidemics from the overcrowded ghetto, which lacked a central sewage system, might spread to the Aryan surroundings, the transports from Central Europe to Łódź were discontinued in November 1941. Of the 5,002 Prague Jews deported to Łódź, only 276 were alive by the end of the war, four of them recipients of the aid sent by Heinz and his friends.

The angel of death is lurking

A replacement for Łódź was needed. As an interim solution for the "problem of the Jews of the Protectorate," a ghetto was established in the fortress city of Theresienstadt – Terezin as the Czechs called it – in northern Bohemia. The first establishment unit arrived there on 24 November 1941. Although the short trip to Terezin

8 Lenka Polesi's testimony, Montreal.

did not arouse the same dread as deportation to the unknown in Poland, for many months the inmates of the ghetto were forbidden any contact with the outside world, and several young men paid with their lives when they were caught sending an illegal letter. To their dread, already in early 1942, the Jews learned that Terezin was not a final refuge until Hitler's defeat, as they had hoped, but only a way station on the road eastward.

From Terezin and Poland, Heinz received news through the underground that included appeals for help. Heinz (Avri) Ullman, a member of the Havlagah group, who was sent on 24 April 1942 from Prague to Terezin and only four days later was deported to the East, wrote on 5 May from Komarów, east of Lublin: "I've been here twelve days with my parents; the friends from Prague are far from here." Three days later, Avri sent another letter in which he said he was recovering from an inflammation of the middle ear; that he and his parents were living with two other families – twelve people in a cold, windy room – and that he often thinks of "choleh" [sick in Hebrew] and that Johnny (namely himself, Jenda in Czech, Heinz in German, John in English) sends regards to Fritz "Lechem' [bread] (the two words were originally written in Hebrew, in Latin letters). Heinz and his friends immediately filled Avri's request, but never heard from him again. In August and September of 1942, Heinz sent two telegrams to the Jewish self-aid organization in Lublin asking for information about the whereabouts of Heinz Ullman and Paul Levy. The reply stated: "The addresses of the people you are looking for and the destination of their transfer from Komarów are unknown." No trace of them was ever found. They were sixteen years old.

In Heinz Prossnitz' archives there is a note written in Czech on a receipt in Polish. The note reads: "I am taking the first opportunity to write to you. I've been in a concentration camp from the beginning. I don't know where Mother is. My uncle is here. Send something. Trust me, it will be handed over. Regards and kisses to everyone." The signature is not legible, but the contents of the letter indicate that it was sent by one of Heinz' friends who left on a transport from Prague directly to the East, without an interim stay in the Terezin ghetto. This was the penal transport that left Prague on 10 June 1942, after the assassination attempt on Reinhard Heydrich and his subsequent death. This suggests that the letter was written by Kurt Lederer, a member of Havlagah who was included in that transport designated as Aah. This assumption is supported by a postcard sent to Heinz on 17 August 1942 by a Polish Jew called Israel Isser Hartmeir. The sender's address was SS Camp 783, Lublin, Lipowa 7. The postcard mentions Kurt, Heinz' friend, and confirms receipt of the postcard and the letter. But the ten marks that were supposed to be in the letter never arrived, nor did the packages that Heinz refers to in his letter. Hartmeir writes that he is working as a locksmith and therefore has access to various places without a guard. The postcard, written in Polish, includes several Hebrew expressions written in Latin letters such as "shomer" (guard), "asur ledaber" (forbidden to talk) and "malakh hamavet" (the angel of death): "The angel of death has been waiting for me every day, but he hasn't caught me." Moreover, Hartmeir had made contact with Kurt, and as far as possible would try to receive the packages for him: "Kurt is healthy and is not far from me… about the place I am in there is no need to write."

In a postcard dated 3 September 1942, Hartmeir confirms receipt of three packages and states that Heinz' friend is well for the time being, thank God, but no one knows what will happen later, because where he is there is also a "tanur esh" (an oven of fire) and "malakh hamavet" (both words in Hebrew). Sixteen-year-old Kurt died only six days later, on 9 September 1942, in the Majdanek extermination camp near Lublin. Of the one thousand deportees in the Aah transport, only two survived.

Terezin awaits everyone

Fredy Hirsch was the first of Heinz's friends to be sent to Terezin. He arrived in December 1941, with the second building unit (AK2). Throughout 1942, most of the members of Maccabi Hatzair and other youth movements active in the aid service to the transports were gradually sent to the Terezin ghetto, generally with their parents. Despite the strict prohibition effective until September 1942 against any written contact with ghetto inmates, Heinz Prossnitz sent letters and packages to his friends in Terezin with those who left later. Moreover, with the consent of Eichmann's office, the Center for Jewish Emigration (*Zentralstelle für jüdische Auswanderung*), the Jewish community in Prague regularly sent various goods – mattresses, furniture, books – to Terezin, and anyone with the right connections, like Heinz, was able to smuggle in personal packages as well. Egon Redlich writes in his diary about a suitcase full of food that arrived that way to the Hechalutz leadership, and the discussions as to who should enjoy its contents.[9]

In addition to Heinz, the only other members of youth movements his age to remain in Prague in early 1943 were Maxi Lieben and Kurt Cierer, both because of their fathers' work in the Jewish community that protected them for a time from the deportations. Also still in Prague were Zeev Scheck, Heinz Schuster and Lazar (Leizer) Moldavan, members of the Hechalutz leadership who worked for the Jewish community and were still able to stay in touch with the free world. On 20 May 1943, through an emissary from Switzerland who secretly brought them 30,000 marks, Heinz Schuster and Lazar Moldavan sent a letter to a representative of Hechalutz in Geneva: "We will use them [the marks] to provide our friends with Jakob [in Terezin] the most essential items, because that is permitted." The letter contains hints about the situation in the Protectorate: "We are now only a handful of Jews, many of whom who did not belong to us in the past [Jews under the racial laws who had a non-Jewish spouse]. With Jakob, only a few of the locals remain, most of them were forced to continue on the trip to Geller [Poland]. We are unable to receive any news of them. But what we hear saddens us greatly." The letter also hinted: "We heard that you can send us some food, and that makes us very happy, because we are complying with orders that forbid us to buy meat, milk, white flour and baked goods, eggs, fruit, vegetables, fish, cheese, candy and jam."[10]

9 Redlich, *Life as If*, entry dated 4.4.1992, p. 73.
10 BTA, 351/18.

But a short time later, in July 1943, most of the employees of the community still remaining in Prague were sent to the Terezin ghetto with their families, including Maxi Lieben, Kurt Cierer, Zeev Scheck, Lazar Moldavan and Heinz Schuster. Heinz Prossnitz assumed that it was also his turn to be sent to Terezin, so he prepared lists of all the receipts of packages and money in the ghettos and camps, as well as postcards to all the liaison people outside of Prague and the country, notifying them that he would soon be leaving Prague, but omitting the date for the time being. For his successors, he listed all the addresses in other countries, including the address of the German Red Cross in Ettal, Upper Bavaria. For himself he wrote down dozens of messages from family members and friends to give to the ghetto inmates and packed books and gifts for his friends.

On 7 July 1943, however, there was a new development. In the midst of his preparations for the transport, the German authorities instructed Fritz Prossnitz to remain in Prague with his wife and son. In a letter smuggled to Fredy Hirsch and his other friends in Terezin, Heinz expressed his disappointment; he was all ready to go to Terezin, in his thoughts he was already living there, glad to be reunited with his friends and to renew their work together. Now he was completely alone, without one good friend, and with no social life:

> It's all bad except for the fact that I can continue sending money to Łódź and packages to you, and that for a few more weeks I'll be able to sleep in my own bed and eat better than I could at Terezin… I hope I can go on working in the garden outside of Prague, which is empty of Jews. Then I'll get five kronen an hour and extra food stamps. Otherwise I won't be able to get everything for Łódź on my own.[11]

Until his deportation, Heinz worked with a group of friends in the suburb of Hloubětín in the vegetable garden of what used to be a Jewish hospital for the mentally ill, and was now empty. In reply

11 BTA, 356/409/19.

to a letter from a friend, Sonia Roubíček, who wrote that she was working in agriculture in Terezin, Heinz said his only consolation while working with a shovel was the thought that Sonia, Suska and his other friends in Terezin were doing the very same work, and then he immediately felt closer to them. To the smuggled letter in German to Fredy and his other friends, Heinz added in Czech: "I just learned that packages can be sent to you only against stamps sent by you. Divide among yourselves. You can send me 30 stamps a month. Start right away!"[12]

He was referring to the permit stamps to receive a package that ghetto inmates could obtain when their turn came once in several months, on condition that they still had someone outside the ghetto to whom they could send the stamps. But very few still had Jewish relatives or friends outside the ghetto, and they were absolutely forbidden to contact any Aryans. The transports from Prague only exempted Jews who were validly married to an Aryan spouse (like Franz Friedmann, the chairman of the Prague Council of Elders, as the community was now called), people of different categories of mixed race, and a few "full Jews" who the Center for Jewish Emigration considered essential for the time being. One of these was Fritz Prossnitz, head of the finance department, his wife Mitzi and their son Heinz. I don't know of any official document that defined this essential status, but it is reasonable to assume it involved managing the financial accounts of Jewish assets that had become German property after their owners were deported. Nor did I find a document written by Fritz and Mitzi Prossnitz that could attest to their attitude towards the aid project that their son had undertaken.

In his last personal entry, in June 1944, Heinz describes his parents' fury at his "evil behavior" because he sold his shoes (a word he wrote in English) to obtain money to buy margarine on the black market for his packages.

> My parents are angry, and rightly so, because I lie, cheat, steal and do not show any consideration for them, and all

12 BTA, 356/409/19.

> I think about is the parcels [written in English] that I send to the most inappropriate people, and afterwards they don't have *kesef* [money in Hebrew] for the most urgent circumstances. Again, I promised myself to change the situation and to change myself too. But I didn't lie and I didn't do anything bad. I am not talking about thoughts; I've had quite a few bad thoughts. After lunch, again I packed parcels, and Mother is completely right when she says that I am doing it just to be popular.

It would be a mistake to conclude from this that Fritz and Mitzi Prossnitz were completely opposed to their son's efforts to help the deportees. Although Fritz was known to be strict and pedantic, some also characterized him as a coward. He may have been afraid that his son's actions, in particular his connections with black market dealers, would endanger the family. After all, in that time of strict rationing, the punishment for trading on the black market – both for the seller and the buyer – was imprisonment in a Gestapo prison, internment in a concentration camp, or death by hanging. However, many postcards from Terezin and Birkenau, in particular from former employees of the Prague community, were not addressed to Heinz, but to his parents, and dozens of packages were sent in their name. In one of his entries, Heinz enumerates his financial sources: alongside the Havlagah fund and the Maccabi Hatzair fund, he also wrote "contribution by parents." When Heinz found himself in financial difficulties, he did not hesitate to state bluntly: "I urgently need 1,000 kronen," as he wrote to Pavel (Salus) and to Čulda (Jirka Altmann).[13]

The package network

In the fall of 1943, only two of Heinz' partners in the aid service remained in Prague: Erika (Eka) Wolf, whose mother was an Aryan German, and Edith Březina, whose Hebrew name was Naomi. Her

13 BTA, 356/9.

father, an Aryan, had left the family when Edith was still a baby, but she was never registered as a Jew and did not wear the yellow Star of David. The two girls were blond and blue-eyed, considered a typical Aryan appearance. Since the Jews of Prague were permitted to use only one post office, and only at a certain time, Naomi would carry the heavy packages to the post office; sometimes she and Heinz would walk arm in arm so that her elbow covered the Star of David on his coat.[14]

Erika's mother also undertook many tasks: she brought the foodstuffs to the Wolf family's apartment and then carried the heavy packages to the post office.[15] The packages generally contained potatoes and bread, and sometimes also a little margarine and sugar. Although it was risky, one day Naomi traveled to the village of Dačice where her grandparents' furniture was stored, and sold it in exchange for food. Fortunately, neither she, nor Erika or Heinz, were ever caught trading on the black market.

Not only was food in scarce supply during the war, but also the items needed to make the parcels – wrapping paper, boxes and rope – although Heinz found a supplier for everything he needed. A whole network was established: friends, relatives or Aryans with whom deportees had left money. The Aryans were forbidden to have any direct contact with Jews, but they secretly brought Heinz food, money or food stamps so he could send packages in his name. There were also half-Jews and other "Aryan relatives" who were permitted to have contact with Jews, but since they were as frightened of such contact as if it were the plague, they secretly brought Heinz packages so they could remain anonymous. Someone sent Heinz a typewritten list of the contents of a large package that he should send on to Terezin. In addition to food, the list also included a salve for wounds, toothpaste and toilet paper – extremely rare items in the ghetto, as well as a small birthday cake with seven tiny candles on which "Míšenka" was written in icing.

To supply all the growing needs and to expand his aid project, instead of sending some packages directly to Terezin, Heinz sent

14 Edith Rosen's testimony.
15 A letter from Dr. Rudolph Wolf, Eching, Germany, to the author, 18.5.1989.

them through Germany, mostly via Paul Israel Roth of Breslau (a Jew, as indicated by the middle name he was forced to take) who apparently had a non-Jewish wife, and via Hans Bauer of Dresden. I was unable to clarify who these two men were. In one of his postcards, Heinz asked: "Have you received regards from cousin Roth?" but that means nothing. The use of a term for a relative – uncle, aunt, cousin, nephew – was often meant to mislead the censor.

I do not know who Hans Bauer, owner of the Johann Bauer Company, at Wallstrasse 19, Dresden, to whom packages were sent, was, or why he was prepared to take the risk. In one of his letters of confirmation, Hans Bauer mentions Pauli, the name that Dov Revesz was known by in his family, and he may be the connecting link. In any case, in one of his letters Bauer says explicitly: "I do not want any money." Bauer asked Heinz not to send him too many packages in one day, to make sure that the individual packages inside the one large package were the correct weight, because 100 grams of excess weight would cause problems at the post office. He also wrote to Heinz that one of the packages was not properly wrapped and had been torn in the mail. Heinz apologized, and explained that the wrapping paper obtainable in Prague was of a poor quality and tore easily. Heinz would number the packages he sent to Bauer, who would then confirm their arrival. In this way, more than 800 kilos of food were sent, in addition to the 4,000 kilos that Heinz and his parents sent directly. The Heinz Prossnitz archives contain thirty-four postal receipts on Roth's name and 204 on Bauer's name.

The permit stamp was sent from the Terezin ghetto to the Council of Elders in the Prague community, which then notified the addressee: "The above-mentioned sent you a stamp. Please come personally to receive it, on the basis of this notification, in our offices in Prague 5, Josefstädtergasse 5, on the ground floor, between 09:00–11:30 and 15:00–17:30." The notification bore the stamp: "Come to get it within eight days."

Along with the package sent in exchange for the permit stamp through the Council of Elders in Prague, a printed postcard was also sent to the addressee. It read: "On the basis of your permit stamp, I have sent you a package today. Please confirm its receipt."

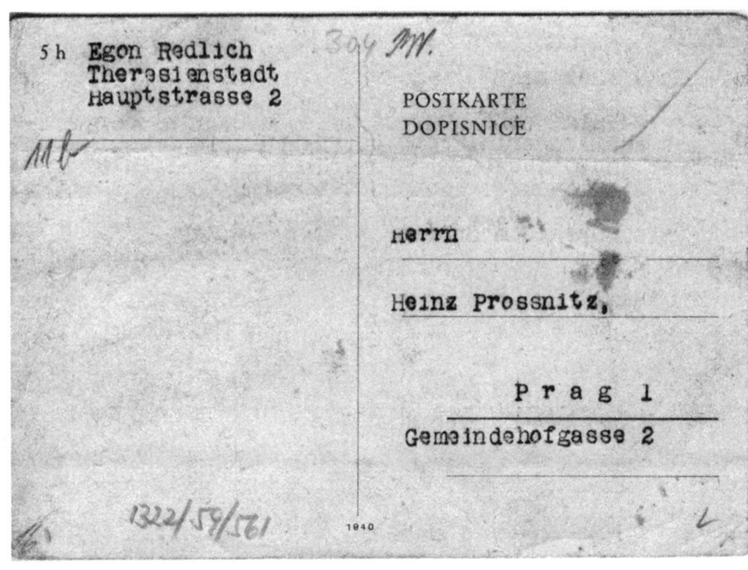
5 h Egon Redlich
Theresienstadt
Hauptstrasse 2

POSTKARTE
DOPISNICE

Herrn

Heinz Prossnitz,

Prag 1

Gemeindehofgasse 2

1940

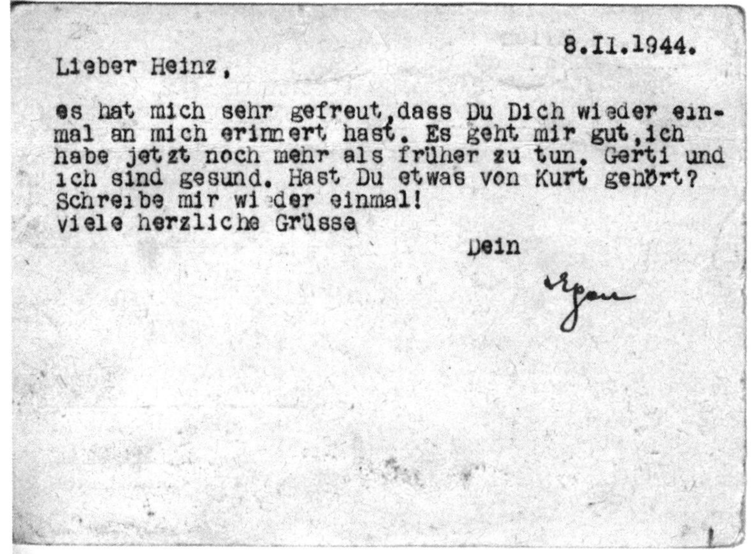
8.II.1944.

Lieber Heinz,

es hat mich sehr gefreut, dass Du Dich wieder einmal an mich erinnert hast. Es geht mir gut, ich habe jetzt noch mehr als früher zu tun. Gerti und ich sind gesund. Hast Du etwas von Kurt gehört? Schreibe mir wieder einmal!
viele herzliche Grüsse

Dein

Egon

One of the hundreds of postcards sent from Terezin and other ghettos and camps to Heinz Prossnitz, who had remained in Prague thanks to his father's job, and who organized an entire help network, sending the prisoners large amounts of food and money. BTA.

The place for the date, name and signature remained blank, and there Heinz could add at least "dear Liesl" (in a package to Alice Winternitz). The recipient of the package was also allowed to send a confirmation form which stated: "I confirm with thanks receipt of your package from… a letter will follow" (which was not true). The happy recipients of the packages could add at least "my dear" or "dear Heinz" at the top of the form or "yours" to the signature, as Fredy Hirsch did on 24 July 1943.

The myth of Terezin as a "model ghetto" has become deeply rooted in the history of the Holocaust, and people tend to forget that more than 33,000 inmates died there, the majority from weakness and disease caused by malnutrition or spread because of it. It is true that compared to other ghettos and the extermination camps, the hunger was not as life threatening, children were not bloated from starvation and starved skeletons were not lying around in the streets, but hunger gnawed at the inmates, young and old, weakened them and led to vitamin deficiencies and a long list of diseases and illnesses. The food packages (and not many inmates were among the fortunate recipients) strengthened those who received them both physically and mentally, gave them a few hours of happiness, and provided them with hope. Among the recipients of the packages sent by Heinz and his parents were all the members of the Zionist leadership: the first Elder of the Jews, Jakob Edelstein; his deputy Otto Zucker; the general secretary Leo Janowitz; Egon (Gonda) Redlich, the head of the youth department; members of the Maccabi Hatzair leadership; and of course all of Heinz' friends and relatives – altogether about one hundred persons. The postcards sent to Heinz and his parents, written as required in German, usually start with thanks for the gift packages, or state: "I have taken the liberty of sending you my permit stamp"; and sometimes hinted: "Karl Kopecký would also be happy to hear from you."

Heinz Prossnitz also served as a clearinghouse for news. Through him, messages and greetings from the free or relatively free world arrived (to Dov Revesz from his parents in Hungary, to Hans Gärtner from his mother in Davos, Switzerland, from Palestine through Nathan Schwalb in Geneva). He had connections with Istanbul and Ankara, Bolivia and Sweden. Signs of life from the Łódź ghetto or Birkenau were passed on to family members in the Terezin ghetto; news about Terezin inmates was transmitted to Aryan friends and helpers. Here and there, the writers used Hebrew expressions in the German text or hints that any Gestapo man, even a beginner, could easily decipher. "I rarely hear from Aunt Artsia [a reference to Eretz Israel]," Heinz wrote to Zeev Scheck; "I often think about Nathan [in Switzerland] and about Moshe B` [Moshe Baumgarten, in Palestine]," Zeev wrote to Heinz.[16] Crumbs of news about Palestine were like the pieces of bread Hansel and Gretel scattered in the dark forest: they were signposts marking the way back to freedom.

Some sent postcards asking Heinz to find out why they still hadn't received a sign of life from family or friends to whom they had sent permit stamps. Others complained to Heinz: "Why haven't I heard from you for so long?" or "Why don't you write more often?" Many times Heinz tried to introduce some order into his widespread correspondence, to record on sheets of paper, in school copybooks and notebooks, who wrote to him, when and from where, to whom and when he had replied, and the dates of the packages he sent. But this attempt was short-lived; in addition to his gardening work, he had too much to do in too little time. Recorded in his notebooks are the birthdays of all his friends, lists of medications and their destination, addresses of relatives and friends of inmates outside the country and in the Protectorate – all sincere efforts to be methodical, to maintain some order.

Although the major content of the 580 postcards sent from the Terezin ghetto to Heinz and his parents at the well-known address in Prague, 2 Biskupský Dvůr (in German Gemeindehofgasse) was technical in nature – what had arrived, to whom to pass on greetings – they portray a distorted picture. The inmates wrote the routine wording, "I'm fine and healthy," not only because of the censor, but because they were trying for their own sake and the sake of their loved ones outside the ghetto to find points of light in life in the ghetto. They wrote about their work as a so-

16 BTA, 356/409/22.

cial worker (Dita Bondy), in agriculture (Renate Kraus), in youth guidance (Zeev Scheck) and in leveling the soil as pleasant work in the fresh air (Beda Alter). Hana Ehrlich describes her work as a kindergarten teacher: "I spend the whole day outside with the children… there are lovely playgrounds here." They wrote about football games, concerts, theater shows, a lecture on the poetry of the German poet Christian Morgenstern, daily meetings or living quarters shared with friends. "It's hard to describe the work that's being done here, especially for the youth," Zeev Scheck wrote.[17] Despite the order requiring all pregnancies to be terminated, in the ghetto Heinz Schuster became the father of a baby daughter called Dina, and he joyfully reported to Heinz that she was developing nicely and was delighted by every picture book. In one of his packages, Heinz sent a pair of baby shoes to Dina. From the ghetto, greetings were sent to Heinz on his birthday and for the New Year. All of this gave rise to an illusion of normalcy, of life going on as usual, as if the dread of transports to the East did not exist.

However, Heinz knew that despite all the threads connecting him to Terezin, he did not have a true picture of life in the ghetto, as he wrote to Alice Ehrmann, Zeev Scheck's girlfriend (and later his wife):

> You can imagine that I'd like to know more about the life, the work, the cultural life and the people. Have they changed, and if so, how? I sometimes think of each one of those close to me alone, about how they'd react to one thing or another, would we understand one another after such a long separation, in our thinking and in every other aspect. Although I live in Prague, that's only in the sense of the place I reside in. I am not actually here, nor there. But neither do I know what to wish for. All in all, I'm just truly miserable. It's impossible to help the way a person would like to and as much as is necessary, etc., etc.[18]

17 Ibid.
18 BTA, 356/409/33.

Heinz did feel lonely, but in the few postcards and letters of his that remained (most were destroyed, like their recipients), I found no sign that he was growing weary, that the burden was too much for him, or that the aid project had grown beyond his strength. Instead – only repeated pleas to his friends: "Send stamps!"

In the postcards his friends sent from the ghetto, there was rarely any mention of illness. "Father's confined to bed all the time," Maxi Lieben wrote; "Father's been in the hospital for months (intestinal illness)," wrote Peter Berger. "Father's been operated on (appendicitis)," wrote Renate Kraus. Most of these fathers, about whom their children were so concerned, were not yet fifty years old, but in the ghetto and the camps old age came early. Inmates of the ghetto knew that those left outside did not have an easy time either. "I hope you won't forget me in the future," said everything. The fifty postcards sent from the Birkenau extermination camp to the Prossnitz family and later preserved show how misleading the news from "there" was.

In the shadow of the crematoria

On 6 September 1943, two transports – 5,007 men, women and children – left Terezin. Leo Janowitz, his wife Trude and Fredy Hirsch were at the head of the list that was going, so they said in the ghetto, to set up a new work camp in the East. They all arrived without undergoing selection at a camp in the Auschwitz-Birkenau complex officially designated B/2/b and generally called "the family camp."[19] In contrast to all the other camps, the inmates were not beaten to death and the sick were not sent to the gas chambers, but the hunger, the long hours standing for roll call, the freezing cold, the dreadful living conditions – all these were the same. When they arrived at the "Birkenau work camp near Neuberun," the inmates were given postcards, on which they were permitted to write thirty words to their relatives and friends in the Terezin ghetto and outside it.

19 See also the chapter, "Games in the Shadow of the Crematoria."

Heinz Prossnitz received some of these postcards, too. On 13 October 1943, he wrote to the National Federation of Jews in Germany, through which all the mail to the family camp was channeled, asking about instructions for writing to Birkenau. The Federation replied from Berlin that the nine postcards Heinz had enclosed with his letter had been sent on to Birkenau, even though they were not written in block letters or typewritten, as required. He was also informed that every person may send three postcards a month to the camp. The postcards from Birkenau were rigorously censored, so the inmates resorted to hints. "I meet Sonia every day and other friends, particularly Raev [the Hebrew word for hungry]," Hans Freund, born in 1922, wrote. "I am very worried about the engineer Sladký [sweet in Czech] and Uncle Odkolek [a well-known bakery in Prague], they should write every week." One sent regards to Mr. Zelený [green in Czech], another asked to send regards to "my sweet nephew" or sent "sweet kisses." Another mentioned "Aunt Chema [butter in Hebrew]" or "Aunt Jičinská" [a large bakery in Prague].

On 9 January 1944, Malka Kartagener, a girl from a religious home who was one of the last youngsters sent to Terezin from Prague, notified Heinz that she had arrived at the family camp with her parents and sister and with Uncle Sladký [sweet], who sends thanks for the daily shipment of bread. Since Malka arrived in the family camp only in the second half of December 1943 and this was her first postcard, her thanks probably do not refer to the past, but to the future. When the hints alluding to the gnawing hunger were too obvious, the censor deleted single words in the text with a black marker.

Here and there, in addition to the usual closing, "Don't forget me" or "I am waiting to hear from you soon," the writers mentioned the name of a fellow inmate in the family camp. Kurt Cierer, known as Ceres, mentioned his friend Dita's sister (namely, me), and by that he meant: send to her, too. And Heinz did indeed send me a loaf of bread as he did to many others. According to Cierer's confirmation, the packages arrived safely.

Ruth Barber, who came to the family camp early in September 1943, wrote to Heinz on 9 October: "I have no words to tell you how overjoyed I was by your gift packages. You are the only one who thinks of me and I'll never forget that… Don't forget me." In another postcard Ruth again thanked him for the gift packages that arrived regularly: "I was especially glad for the bread and the sweets." Here too it is not clear whether this isn't a suggestion for the future, since the inmates in the camp had no possibility of cooking, and needed foodstuffs that could be eaten immediately, because there was no safe place to keep them.

Kurt Levy confirmed the receipt of six loaves of bread and two packages. Peter Winternitz, Liesl's brother, confirmed receipt of the packages, including the large ones, without noting how many there were. Miriam Edelstein, wife of the first Elder of the Jews, who was brought to Birkenau in December 1943, thanked Fritz Prossnitz, in the name of her mother and son as well, for the packages he sent, and she too does not mention their number. In another postcard, Miriam writes that she is concerned about Jakob, because she doesn't know where or how he is. Miriam did not know that Jakob Edelstein, who was arrested in the Terezin ghetto in November 1943, was imprisoned not far from her, in the penal barracks of the main camp in Auschwitz. She also did not guess why the inmates were ordered to write the date 25 March 1944 on their postcards, although they wrote them at the beginning of the month.

Trude, the wife of Leo Janowitz who was appointed manager of the *Schreibstube*, the camp office ("my husband is working in his profession," Trude wrote), also confirmed the receipt of packages several times without mentioning their number. As part of the preparations for the anticipated visit of the Red Cross delegation to the Terezin ghetto and perhaps also to a camp in the East, as well as to prove that the "Birkenau labor camp near Neuberun" was what its name stated, Leo Janowitz was given permission, as soon as he arrived, to write to Switzerland, to his friend Dr. Fritz Ullman, the liaison in Geneva.[20] On 9 January 1944, Trude Janowitz wrote to Fritz Prossnitz that she had received news from Ulli, as Ullman was called by his friends. All those greetings, those signs of life, from the family camp, created the illusion in Terezin, Prague and

20 CZA, A 320/208.

other places that it was a place of some permanence, a continuation of life.

On 16 June 1944, Hermine Janowitz, Leo's mother, wrote to Prague from the Terezin ghetto: "I was very happy to hear that Leo is well and I hope for the very best in the future too." This is what she wrote three months after all that was left of Leo and Trude, Fredy Hirsch, Heini and Tula Klein, Ruth Barber, Peter Winternitz and all the others from the September transport was a small pile of ashes.

Only a few tried to include hints in their postcards to Heinz about the real situation in Birkenau-Auschwitz. One who did was 32-year-old Herman Reach, who thanked him for the package he sent and added: "We are very worried about Chaim [life in Hebrew]." And 18-year-old Sonia Hecht wrote a postcard on 20 December 1943: "We think about you a lot, with Mrs. Mandel Hauch" (an allusion to the odor of almonds typical of cyanide gas). But no one understood the real meaning of the allusion.

However, news about the fate of the September transport began slowly to seep outside. On 20 May 1944, Heinz wrote to Fritz Ullman in Geneva: "Have you heard anything lately from Seppl's [Lichtenstein who came to Birkenau in December 1943] family? Mavet [death in Hebrew] came there and will stay there for a long time." In his reply, Ullman asked Heinz to write again, "also if anyone hears anything about Robert Mavet."[21]

Heinz did not give up. According to his records, in the nine months of the family camp's existence, 25–36 loaves of bread and about ten packages per person were sent to his friends there (Suse Heller, Ruth Barber, Sonia Roubíček, Peter Winternitz, Hans Gärtner, Trude Janowitz, Miriam and Arye Edelstein and others). All of Rothschild's wealth was nothing compared to these packages. A survey that Heinz prepared on 2 June 1944, when he assumed

21 A letter from Leo Janowitz and other news received from the family camp that led Gerhard Riegner, the Jewish Agency representative in Switzerland, to send a cable to London regarding possible help. Riegner notes that the address in Birkenau is according to the name of the recipient and his birthdate and not the name of the street (!) or the block number (Adler, *Die Verheimlichte Wahrheit*, pp. 307–308).

he would soon be transferred to Terezin, shows that by then he had sent 1,492 kilograms of bread and 293 food packages worth 56,000 kronen. It is hard for me to assess the value of this sum in today's terms, but the miracle of the loaves can easily be assessed: added strength, happy days, a spark of hope and faith in man in the shadow of the crematoria.

Early in July 1944, the Birkenau family camp was liquidated. Some 3,000 young men and women passed the selection and were sent to work in Germany; all the remaining inmates were put to death in the gas chambers. Of the fifty or so who received packages from Heinz in the family camp, about ten survived.

"Heinz saved my life through his help and sacrifice," Honza Gärtner wrote in 1949, when he suggested that a forest or a street in Israel be named after Heinz Prossnitz. "He was a true hero!"[22]

Summing up a life

For years, the Jews of Prague had been forbidden to leave their homes in the evening. Heinz read a lot. The long list of books he read includes, among others, *Boccacio's Tales* (five volumes), *Goethe* by Emil Ludwig, Dubnow's *History of the Jews*, *An American Tragedy* by Dreiser, *Bambi* by Felix Salten; and works by Rilke, Dostoevsky, Zola, Turgenev, Hamsun, Voltaire (his collected works), Tagore, and Buber. Another list featured Freud's *Introduction to Psychoanalysis*, *Edward VII* by Maurois and *What Next, Little Man*? by Fallada. He read all of these books in German; Somerset Maugham he read in English.

In a letter dated 3 March 1944 to Doris Mannheimer smuggled into Terezin, Heinz laments all those things that had totally disappeared: the joint work in the garden, the endless talks, the lively arguments, the friends, all those people who shared opinions and interests. "Everything is empty, everything has disappeared." He hints to Doris that he too will be coming there soon. To Zeev Scheck, he wrote: "The Prerau [the name of a city near the city

22 Honza Gärtner's letter to Zeev Scheck, Prague, 9.1.1949, BTA, 356/24.

of Prossnitz] family will soon be coming to little Dina [the name of Heinz Schuster's daughter who was born in the ghetto]." In the summer of 1944, he repeated all the preparations for the transport. He prepared postcards announcing his imminent journey and left only the date open.

On 9 July 1944, Heinz Prossnitz celebrated his eighteenth birthday. Naomi Březina, now his closest friend, gave him a leather portfolio as a gift and added a humorous poem in German, describing him with an indulgent smile. In part it read:

> You've got a big mouth,
> Poke your nose in constantly,
> Lots of people, commotion and talk,
> Are just your cup of tea.
> If you've got an idea, then without any doubt,
> Right here and now, you must carry it out.
> At packing parcels you're an expert, that's true
> No one can do it better than you.
> And even if doors close time after time,
> You always find a hole through which you can climb.[23]

Heinz himself wrote on 11 June 1944, in Czech:

> During the war and several times before then, I planned to write a diary, but for one reason or another I never carried out that plan. When I think of the last years, my heart clenches with sorrow because I never wrote about one thing or another, about some event, because so many things, some beautiful and others less beautiful, were erased from my memory. Yesterday when I celebrated my 18th birthday, I had the idea of writing a novel of my life, with an ongoing plot or in several parts in the form of short novellas. I've already started working on it, and in writing this diary I wish occasionally to go back into the past.

23 Private archives, Edith Rosen, Kfar Saba.

The previous evening, his parents had gone to their neighbors to listen to a concert on records (the gramophones belonging to Jews had been confiscated long before), but Heinz remained at home, although he longed for company, because at the last concert he had behaved, as he put it, "shamefully," and had nearly fallen asleep during *Aida*.

> So last night, after my parents were asleep, I began writing the first novella. I think it's very weak. In this vein, I was thinking about my future profession. God knows what will come of me. After all, I want to immigrate to Eretz Israel and to take part, body and soul, in establishing our state. But the climate?
>
> It seems to me I'm mainly interested in power, money and influence, that I want to be a personality. As a Jew, a politician, a researcher, an industrialist or an artist. Who knows. I won't get very far in any Communist regime. But what good will all this do since I'm 18 and still have no general or specific knowledge and no life experience? But never mind that, all of that is very sad. If at least the war would end and we'd get through it safely in Prague, then we'll see what's next, depending on how the overall political conditions and the Jewish question in Palestine develop. I don't think I'll be much of a chalutz [pioneer]. I'm too much of an individualist. I wouldn't be happy in a group and the group wouldn't be happy with me. But it would be wrong to draw any premature conclusions; everything will end differently later.

In keeping with his character, and sticking to his good intentions, Heinz also prepared a program for his studies and reading: "My life plan, which I sketched along general lines, has made me very happy… goodnight!" Nothing more was preserved.

In the fall of 1944, the end of the war seemed imminent. France was free, and the Allied armies were drawing close to Germany from the East and the West. On 27 October 1944, when the Prossnitz family received a call to leave on a transport in a group of eighteen people, employees of the Council of Prague Jews and their families, they all assumed that their journey would bring them to the Terezin ghetto. Fritz and Marie Prossnitz left their personal details in Prague along with instructions about who to contact with regard to sending packages to them. Heinz prepared a map of the city of Terezin so he could arrange a secret meeting place with Naomi, whenever that would be possible. He handed over the cash box, the keys and the addresses to her, and noted to whom to write in German, and to whom in Czech.

Ironically enough, at that very time the connection between Prague and Switzerland (and through there to Palestine) improved. While the Prossnitzes were busy packing, two Swedes came to their home, sent by Nathan Schwalb, the Hechalutz representative in Geneva, bringing 25,000 dollars with them. Fritz Prossnitz was afraid they were provocateurs and showed them the door. Naomi wrote to Nathan about this and expressed the hope that one of the emissaries would return soon. The correspondence with Switzerland was peppered with Hebrew code words: Naomi wrote about the constant "mora" [dread] in which Franz Friedmann, head of the Council of Jews in Prague, lived, and hence was not prepared to help in the exchange of the small "kaspi" [money] (Friedman himself sent a message to Switzerland, through the underground, that there was no need of funds). Naomi informed Nathan that Seppl (Lichtenstern) was now in "Kuf-Zadeh" (KZ, a concentration camp) and that Fredy, Leo (Janowitz) and his wife and Heini (Klein) and his wife are now living with the "Mavet" [death] family.[24]

The Prossnitz family did arrive in Terezin, but their friends in the ghetto did not even know about it. They only came in order to join a transport of one thousand deportees leaving for Auschwitz on 28 October 1944. On the station platform at Birkenau a selection was carried out as usual, and the young and strong were sent to work in Germany. However, the group of eighteen from Prague, including Heinz, his parents and members of the ghetto leadership who arrived in a special car on that train, all went straight to the

24 Ibid.

gas chambers, without any selection. The following day the factory of death was shut down. The Red Army was approaching.

The project goes on without him

After Heinz left, Naomi and Eka continued his work according to his instructions. Postcards and expressions of gratitude to him kept arriving. Malka Kartagener, a recipient of his packages at the Birkenau family camp, was one of the 600 young women who passed the selection and had been sent in early July 1944 to Hamburg, to clear the debris after the heavy Allied bombing raids on the city. Compared to the horrors of Auschwitz, without the crematoria chimneys and the odor of scorched flesh, life in Hamburg was tolerable, although there, too, the prisoners suffered from hunger and the daily bombardments (even if the latter gladdened them, since they brought the end of the war closer).

Although they were strictly forbidden to write, several of the young women did succeed, with the help of foreign forced laborers or a German foreman, in secretly sending letters to friends and acquaintances in the Protectorate. Eighteen-year-old Malka appealed to Heinz to send her, her mother and sister bread and other foodstuffs. Heinz was still in Prague and sent her a package along with a letter to the address of a foreign worker The package contained bread, barley, oatmeal, sugar, jam, margarine, a honey cake, onions and pears, and Malka was in seventh heaven: how well Heinz knew how to put together a package that had everything one could possibly wish for! "I am especially encouraged by the knowledge that there is someone I can turn to and who is glad to get some news of me." She regrets that she cannot answer Heinz's many questions: "Uncle "Sof" [end in Hebrew] will make everything clear to you." To my sorrow, the heavy fears were justified. In her letter of thanks, Malka asks Heinz to send her, if possible, a pair of old trousers, warm clothing, a candle and a fine-toothed comb (against lice). "Sometimes I tell myself I have no right to burden you so much. But everything is so hard that a person forgets about consideration for others. I hope you understand and forgive me."

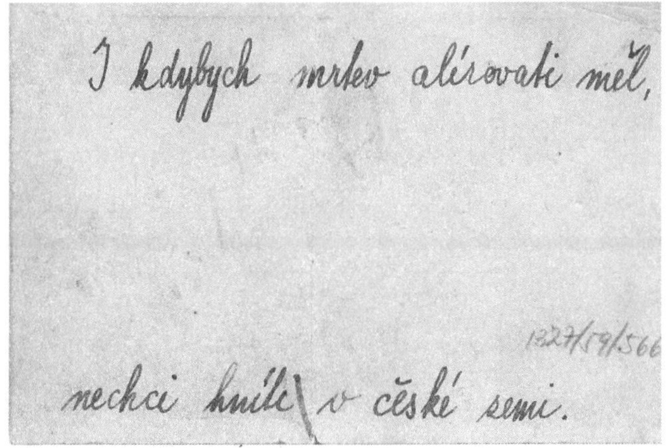
I kdybych mrtev alijovati měl,

1327/59/566

nechci hníti v české zemi.

Testament of Heinz Prossnitz, which included the emblem of his Zionist youth movement Maccabi Hatzair and a portrait of Theodor Herzl: "Even if I should make the *aliya* dead, I do not wish to rot in Czech soil." He was killed, aged 18, in October 1944 in Auschwitz. BTA.

Naomi sent Malka another package and a letter via Mr. Gosmann from Hamburg-Billstedt telling her that Heinz and his parents had "changed their address." Malka replies sadly: "We so much hoped that he would be spared the Via Dolorosa." She expressed the hope that God in His heaven would look after Heinz. This time, too, God was disappointing.

Most of the young men who passed the selection in the Birkenau family camp were sent to Schwarzheide, a sub-camp of Sachsenhausen, to work there in the Brabag synthetic fuel plants, which were severely damaged in the air raids. Unlike the women in Hamburg, they were permitted to write a letter once every two months and to receive an unlimited number of packages, but very few gave any sign of life. One was Seppl Lichtenstern, who asked for warm clothing and food. Naomi wrote to Nathan Schwalb in Geneva that Seppl had almost nothing to wear or to eat and that she was doing her best to help him. But even Naomi's packages could not save Seppl; on 22 April 1945, in the last days of the war, he died in a death march, at the age of thirty.

The hundreds of letters, postcards and notes, and the confirmations sent to Heinz Prossnitz, now preserved in the Yad Vashem archives, are often the last sign of life left by their writers.

The end of the story

Heinz's legacy contains an envelope bearing the instruction: "To be opened if I ever disappear forever." The envelope contained an emblem of Maccabi Hatzair in Prague; a postcard with a picture of a ship, the coast of Palestine, and a portrait of Herzl with the words: If you will it, it is no dream; and a note that read: "Even if I have to arrive in Eretz Israel dead, I do not want to rot in the earth of Czechoslovakia." His ashes fertilized the soil of Poland.

Is there a moral to Heinz Prossnitz's story? The first conclusion is that in the kingdom of absolute evil, human love is also crushed. But the opposite conclusion is also possible: one should never give up, not even in the face of overwhelming odds. A person should never say to himself: What can I, a helpless cog in the wheel, do? Yes, Heinz was overcome, most of those who received his packages did not survive, but a loaf of bread, as in some of Magritte's paintings, hovers over the pitiless skies of Poland as a symbol of identification with the suffering of others.

Erika Wolf and Naomi Březina immigrated to Israel after the war. Erika died several years ago in Beer Sheva. Naomi, now Edith Rosen, lives in Kfar Saba and looks after homeless cats and dogs; human beings disappointed her. Only one sole recipient of packages, Kurt Cierer, thanked her immediately after the end of the war.[25] The few who survived tried first of all to rebuild their lives from the ruins. They dispersed all over the world and found new homes in Israel, the United States, Canada, Venezuela and Germany. The debt to Heinz Prossnitz was never repaid.

25 A letter from Yaacov Tzur (Kurt Cierer), Hamburg, 10.6.1945, E. Rosen's archive.

Games in the Shadow of the Crematoria

The children's barracks in the Birkenau family camp (September 1943–July 1944)

For more than twenty years, the history of the Birkenau family camp has been thoroughly researched, in particular by the Czech historian, Miroslav Kárný.[1] In this chapter, I should like to discuss only one of the aspects of the family camp, one that is both admirable and horrible – the children's barracks in the very heart of the Auschwitz-Birkenau complex. I will begin with a brief general background.

The Terezin ghetto in northern Bohemia was established in November 1941, and during the first year of its existence its inmates were sent eastward to their extermination in transports of 1,000–2,000 people, mainly to Izbica, Zamość, Maly Trostinets, Treblinka and other places. The first transport from the Terezin ghetto to Auschwitz left the ghetto on 26 October 1942. The arrivals underwent a selection on the train platform, and very few of them – men and women who looked fit for physical work – sur-

1 Among other studies: Miroslav Kárný, "Terezínský rodinný tábor v Birkenau," *Sborník historický* sv. 26 (1979), pp. 229–304; "Das Theresienstädter Familienlager in Birkenau," *Judaica Bohemiae* XV (1979), pp. 2–3. In March 1994, a conference of historians was held in Prague devoted to the subject of the family camps in Auschwitz-Birkenau. One of the papers printed in the proceedings of the conference (*Terezínský rodinný tábor v Osvětimi-Birkenau*, Terezínská Iniciativa – Melantrich Praha, 1994) was by Miroslav Kárný on "The family camp of Terezin Inmates as 'the Final Solution'." The data in this introduction are based on it and on my own research on the subject.

vived. Children and the elderly were sent straight to the gas chambers. The inmates of the Terezin ghetto knew only that the destination of the transports was a nebulous place known as the "East."

However, in September 1943, the situation changed. On 6 September, 5,007 men, women and children left the ghetto in two transports. They were told they were going to set up a new work camp in the East, and hence two key members of the ghetto leadership were placed at the head of the group: Dr. Leo Janowitz, until then secretary of the Council of Elders, and Fredy Hirsch, deputy head of the youth department. This time, too, the real destination was Auschwitz, but for the first time in the history of the Jewish transports, none of the arrivals underwent a selection: no one was sent to the gas chambers. All of them, from infants to the old, remained alive, their heads were not shaved, which was customary at Auschwitz, and they were not forced to wear the blue and grey striped clothing of inmates but were allowed to keep the clothes they were wearing on the transport or were given "civilian" clothing left behind by earlier arrivals who had been exterminated. They were all transferred to an empty camp not yet completely constructed, bearing the designation B/2/b, that everyone called the *Familienlager*, the family camp.

There was only one other family camp in the Auschwitz-Birkenau complex, and that was the gypsy camp. Although the two camps had different histories, they both ended in the same way – extermination. The establishment of the gypsy camp is documented in a December 1942 letter by Himmler and in a February 1943 implementation order. Until today, no German document relating to the family camp of the Terezin inmates has been found that explains why it was established or what purpose it was meant to serve in the plans of the SS.

One supposition is that the camp's establishment was connected with a planned visit by an International Red Cross delegation to the Terezin ghetto: what if members of the delegation should ask about the Terezin inmates sent to "work in the East"? Most of them had already been exterminated, and if the Red Cross delegation should insist on visiting a camp of Terezin inmates in the East, then it had to exist.

This supposition seems illogical. Why set up a camp for show in the very heart of the foul-smelling extermination complex, in the shadow of the crematoria chimneys that spout fire and smoke day and night? It would have been possible, of course, to halt the death industry for some time prior to the delegation's arrival; it would have been possible to explain that the crematoria chimneys belong to factories that employ the prisoners. But the harsh conditions, the hunger and the disease in the camp would not have supported this theory. Within six months, nearly a quarter of the prisoners who arrived in September 1943 had died of "natural causes," from weakness and disease, and the appearance of those who remained spoke for itself.

The second supposition is linked to rumors that began to reach the Terezin ghetto about mass killings in the East. The family camp was perhaps established to reassure future victims and to refute the news of mass extermination that had begun to trickle into the free world as well, especially by way of Switzerland. A few days after their arrival, the prisoners of the family camp were permitted to send thirty-word postcards from "Birkenau labor camp near Neuberun" to their families and friends in the Terezin ghetto, and to the few Jews who still remained outside the camps and the ghettos (mainly because they were married to non-Jews). Leo Janowitz was also permitted to send a letter to Switzerland, to his friend Fritz Ullman in Geneva, a Jewish Agency man, who was the liaison between Palestine and the free world and Czech Jews in the German-occupied areas. In his letter, Janowitz informed Ullman about the establishment of the new camp where he was working together with Fredy Hirsch.

The family camp may have been established for both of these reasons. Thus far, we can see some logic. But how can one explain the fact that in the card index of prisoners in the main camp at Auschwitz, next to the names of the people from the September transport there was the notation "SB [the initials of *Sonderbehandlung*, special handling, the code name for killing without a trial] after six months." The length of time they would remain alive was determined in advance, unrelated to the date of the planned visit of the International Red Cross delegation to the Terezin ghetto, which had not yet been finally fixed. Until the end of February 1944, the prisoners of the family camp knew nothing about the notation of "special handling." They assumed the Germans needed them for purposes of show and hoped to hang on until the end of the war, which always seemed so close.

However, on 8 March 1944, exactly six months after their arrival at Auschwitz, in one night the 3,792 survivors of the September transport were taken to the gas chambers and killed.

In the family camp, 5,007 prisoners from the two transports of December 1943 remained. They were joined in May 1944 by another 7,500 prisoners from the Terezin ghetto. Their arrival can also be explained logically. At the time, 46,000 people in the Terezin ghetto were crowded into an area of less than 800 square meters. In anticipation of the impending visit of the International Red Cross delegation, it was essential to thin out the population. Indeed, in May 1944 Himmler permitted representatives of the International Red Cross to visit the Terezin ghetto and one of the labor camps, without noting its name.

The family camp no longer served a useful purpose after the visit of the Red Cross delegation to the Terezin ghetto on 23 June 1944, a visit that from the standpoint of the SS apparatus was a great success. Immediately after the visit, the head of the delegation, Dr. Morris Rossel, wrote a glowing report on the Terezin ghetto, describing it as a city in almost every respect. Its inmates, according to him, lacked nothing except cigarettes and alcohol. Dr. Rossel defined the ghetto as a final destination, and hence the members of the delegation did not express a wish to see a labor camp in the East, nor did they ask about the tens of thousands of inmates (52,000) removed by then from the ghetto.

In the last days of June 1944, a series of selections were carried out in the family camp. About 3,500 young men and women were sent to work in camps in Germany (only a third of them survived the war). The remaining inmates, some 6,500 men, women and children, were exterminated by gas between 10–12 July 1944.

The children's barracks[2]

> As we plodded along the snow-covered path between the barbed wire fences from the showers to the family camp, groups of women came towards us, and upon seeing the many children in our procession, they called out in Polish: "Children, children!" and burst into sobs. And we did not know why.

The children's barracks in the family camp, that same bizarre and amazing enclave inside the Auschwitz-Birkenau complex, never existed at all – if one relies, as exacting historians do, only on written documentation. There are only the testimonies of the prisoners who survived, memoirs written relatively soon after the liberation and interviews recorded twenty years later,[3] and in all these, human memory played tricks even with the basic facts. All the witnesses agree on one thing, and that is the role played by Fredy Hirsch in establishing a children's barracks in Block 31 at the edge of the B/2/b camp, and that is where I should begin.

From the 1940–1941 school year, Jewish students in the Protectorate of Bohemia and Moravia were forbidden to attend the general schools, both Czech and German. The school network in the Terezin ghetto was a natural continuation of the educational frameworks established in the Jewish communities owing to this

2 The description of life in the children's barracks is based on written and oral testimonies, some detailed, some brief, of about 30 boys and counselors who survived. When the testimonies overlapped more or less, I did not note the names of the individuals in the notes. I noted the source when the information it contained was unique. I also relied on my own memory (which is sometimes erratic) and on my research for the biography, *Elder of the Jews*.

3 Memories of Hanka Fischel in Rezniczenko-Erez, ed., *Theresienstadt,* pp. 175–218, pp. 175–218; Gershon Ben David, ed., *The Educational and Cultural Activity in the Terezin ghetto and in the* family camp, Oral Testimonies nrs. 376–379, the Institute for Oral Documentation, the Hebrew University, Jerusalem, 1965. The following testified about the children's barracks: Sinai Adler, Avraham Ophir (Avi Fischer), Eli Bachner, Yehudah Bakon, Dov Barnea (Honza Brammer), Esther Milo (Zdenka Miller), Hanka Fischel, Ota B. Kraus, Otto Dov Kulka, Arye Karny (Harry Kraus) and Yaakov Rachman (Rejšik).

prohibition. The children's barracks in the family camp was a consistent, less natural continuation of the educational project in the ghetto.

By the same token, the endeavor of Alfred Hirsch, known to everyone as Fredy, was a continuation, both the idea and deed. In an article he wrote at the start of the German occupation in *Jüdisches Nachrichtenblatt,* the newspaper of the Prague community,[4] as well as his words on the occasion of the first anniversary of the children's barracks L-417 in the Terezin ghetto,[5] Fredy reiterated the basic concept that grew out of his Zionist faith: the urgent need to toughen the body for the sake of reviving the Jewish people, the need to save the Jewish youth under Nazi rule from the erosion of all the values taking place around them, the duty to achieve self-control in body and spirit. This was the concept he tried to inculcate in his charges in the Maccabi Hatzair Zionist youth movement: "Whatever toughens me is beneficial; whatever does not destroy us, strengthens us; everything is possible, if there is a will."[6] In practice, this belief was expressed in physical exercise and in scout activities on the Hagibor sport field in Prague, in transforming surfaces on the thick walls of the Terezin fortress into playing grounds for the youth, in cleanliness checks in the children's homes that were so strict that the children called them "one of the plagues of the ghetto,"[7] and in maintaining discipline, first and foremost self-discipline.

In marked contrast to the absolute rupture between the world of yesterday and the reality of Auschwitz-Birkenau, and to the change that occurred with the expulsion from home to the Terezin ghetto not only in standard of living, in quantity and quality, but in the very essence of the person, there was one constant. Fredy in Birkenau was no different than Fredy in Prague, where he had arrived as a refugee from Germany in 1935. The immacu-

4 On Fredy Hirsch, see also the chapter "The History of the Closing Gates"; Fredy Hirsch, "Die Vorbereitungen zur Auswanderung," *Jüdisches Nachrichtenblatt*, Prague, 15.12.1939.

5 BTA, 99/29.

6 Herbert T. Mandl, *Der Held und sein Geheimnis* (Langwaden, 1991), p. 15.

7 Ota Klein, *Životní styl a moderní civilizace* (Prague: Symposium, 1969), p. 72.

lately combed hair, the polished boots, the erect stature, the energetic movements, the Prussian discipline – and the whistle. There was no outward sign of a disruption. Undoubtedly his appearance helped him in his contacts with the Germans. There was a similarity in dress, in behavior, in diction.[8]

There is no direct testimony about the establishment of the children's block in Birkenau. The counselors from the two transports that left the Terezin ghetto on 6 September 1943 and were the first to arrive at the family camp told their friends about it, friends who came to the camp in December of that year (and only some of those, including myself, survived). They said that Fredy and Leo Janowitz, the general secretary of the Council of Jews in the Terezin ghetto and the first on the list of the September transport, who were supposed to head what was called the "new labor camp in the East," applied to the camp commandant a few days after their arrival.[9] They stated that the presence of children in the barracks interfered with the work of the adults and the maintenance of discipline in the camp, especially during roll call, and suggested that during the daytime hours, the children, most of whom spoke only Czech, be gathered separately in a barracks (a "block" in camp language) where they'd be taught first of all to understand the German commands that were necessary for life in the camp. It is not clear at what level of the SS command the establishment of the barracks was approved or to what extent that approval was part of the preparations for the planned visit of a delegation of the International Red Cross to the Terezin ghetto in 1944. From the powerful position of camp kapo (*Lagerkapo*) that he was given upon his arrival to Birkenau, Fredy transferred to head the children's barracks, becoming the *Blockältester*, the official title for that post. This move was consistent with the policy laid down by Jakob Edelstein, the first Elder of the Jews of the Terezin ghetto, immediately after the

8 Testimony of Michael Honey (Honigwachs) in: John Freund, ed., *After Those Fifty Years – Memoirs of the Birkenau Boys* (Toronto: John Freud, 1992), p. 118.

9 Rezniczenko-Erez, ed., *Theresienstadt*, p. 193 (the name of the commandant is not mentioned).

10 Bondy, *Elder of the Jews*, p. 119.

occupation of the western part of Czechoslovakia and its conversion into a German Protectorate in March 1939: to exploit the interests of the Germans for the sake of saving Jews, in particular the youth, the seeds from which the future generations of Jews would grow.[10]

With the 5,007 inmates of Terezin who left for Birkenau in two transports (designated Dl-Dm) on 6 September 1943, there were 274 children under the age of fourteen,[11] most of whom, with the exception of infants and sick children, were taken into the children's barracks. The number 600 and at times 700 that the survivors of the barracks speak about relates to January-February 1944, after the arrival in December of two more transports in which there were 353 children.

Fredy selected the workers for the children's barracks – about twenty – on the basis of his personal acquaintance with teachers from the Jewish schools in Prague and Brno, and counselors and women who took care of children from Prague and the Terezin ghetto. As housemother he appointed Hanka Epstein, formerly head of the Jewish infants' home in the Vinohrady quarter of Prague. In Birkenau, 38-year-old Hanka, who never married and whose whole life centered on the homeless children in her care, retained her agility, energy and resourcefulness. She taught the counselors to make knitting needles from chips of wood and to repair articles of clothing using threads removed from the prisoners' coarse blankets.

Fredy chose some more counselors from among the additional 5,007 people who arrived in December, and they are the ones who testified about the way the children's barracks were run, because the September counselors were all killed. Fredy probably decided on the procedures for the barracks in the first days of its existence, and they did not change much after his death. While in Prague and in the Terezin ghetto, the maintenance of physical health was an important part of the education of Jewish youth, here it was the main existential objective. Fredy forced the children to wash with the murky water of Birkenau, even on cold winter days, when six

11 Shimon Adler, Block 31: *History of the Children in the Birkenau family camp* (Hebrew) (Jerusalem, unpublished Master Thesis, 1993).

or eight of them had only one rag between them as a towel, and the counselors had to check to see if their hands, neck and crotch were clean to prevent the spread of lice and infectious diseases, as well as to check the cleanliness of their bunks and eating utensils.[12]

These were children who had just experienced the long, traumatic journey from Terezin to Auschwitz in overcrowded cattle cars, without drinking water and with one pail that everyone used as a toilet in front of all the others. They had experienced the rushed exit from the cars into the bright light of projectors, accompanied by shouts, threats and barking dogs. For the first time in their lives, they saw their grandparents naked, humiliated and helpless. In the commotion of the first days, some of them were, temporarily, torn away from their parents. They all lost their most precious belongings from their home and the ghetto, and remained only with the clothes on their backs. Within a few days, they grew years older – and nonetheless remained children hungry for company, for activity, games, study.

The girls and small boys slept in barracks with their mothers, and the older boys in barracks with their fathers or their counselors. After the morning wakeup, the counselors and their helpers brought the children to the latrines – rows and rows of round holes in long concrete benches – and to the washing barracks that contained rows of faucets under which there was a wooden trough and a filthy, slippery floor.

Just before 8 a.m., they all went into the children's barracks. For roll call held by the SS men twice a day, in the morning and the early afternoon,[13] the children reported in the children's barracks. That was a huge relief, particularly in the cold winter months of Poland, when the temperature fell to 20 degrees below zero and standing outside in thin clothing without moving was for many prison-

12 I have no idea how we, children and counselors, managed to stay clean without soap, without the possibility of changing our clothes. Perhaps this was mainly thanks to a psychological influence, but I don't remember a sense of being personally dirty in the family camp. And no one can remember any more how we managed without paper in the latrines.

13 According to several testimonies, the children's roll call took place only in the afternoon. Perhaps this varied in different time periods.

ers a greater torment than the hunger. In the children's barracks, the SS men did not abuse the children or their counselors, and the few slaps they handed out were usually related to the counting, in fives, that did not match their records (in one case a boy sleeping under a blanket had been forgotten).[14] If human life was of no value in itself, it had a value as a number – dead or alive, the number had to be accurate. The children knew how important it was for the roll call to be correct and quick, especially as far as Fredy was concerned, and they were disciplined, first and foremost for his sake.

The children's barracks was in an ordinary camp block, without windows except for air openings under the ceiling. Like the other blocks, it had originally been a surplus stable left over from Rommel's African campaign. It was divided by beams into nine stalls (for nine horses) on each side, without any partitions between them, and a concrete covered heating pipe one meter high and 60 centimeters wide that passed through the middle of the block from one end to the other, and served as a platform or a stage. The children were divided into groups by age, between ten and fifteen in a group, and sat in circles on low wooden stools (no one knows who ordered these stools or where they were made). The small children, namely kindergarten and first grade age, sat near the entrance to the block, the older children behind them on both sides, probably also for safety considerations in case of a surprise visit by SS men. The activities of the little ones – singing, games, stories – did not violate the prohibition against studies so the SS could not find anything wrong in them. The groups sat very close to one another, and the pupils could hear the lessons in at least the two adjacent groups.

The parents and the other camp inhabitants were forbidden to enter the children's barracks, because there was no room and also to maintain cleanliness and preserve the meager possessions of the

14 Dov Barnea, in Ben David, ed., *The Educational Activity*, testimony No. 379; Trude Bártková writes that Reportführer Buntrock murdered two-year-old Ivošek during a roll call in the children's barracks (Trude Bártková, *Osvětimský slabikář*, Uherské Hradiště, 1979). There is no other testimony about such small children in the barracks nor about the murder of a child during a roll call.

barracks. The prisoners who worked in other kommandos or did not work at all and had no children or small siblings had no contact with it. On the other hand, the children's barracks attracted artisans from the men's camp who, as part of their job, were allowed to move between the camps. Although the survival instinct of the prisoners in the extermination camp prohibited any longings for the past, here they seemed to get a whiff of distant days, when they too had a home and family, and sometimes they brought a gift for the children: paper, a pencil, an article of clothing, a toy. SS men also visited the barracks, perhaps out of a spark of humanity, brief and fleeting.

The children's barrack was naturally the meeting place between Rottenführer Pestek and the beautiful Renée Neumann, with whom he fell in love (he paid for it with his life), as well as the center of the underground. There was little chance of an informer in the children's barrack and, also, it was located at the far end of the camp so there was enough time to warn anyone of approaching danger. The children saw all those who went into and came out of Fredy's small room, and never wondered about it: to them Fredy was the most important person in the camp – and from this standpoint, the testimonies of the survivors completely distort the situation. Leo Janowitz, as head of the camp office, the *Schreibstube,* held a higher position, as did the elders of the blocks and the various kapos, who made decisions affecting the lives of the thousands of prisoners in the family camp outside the children's barracks. One of these was Ada Fischer, looking like the hunchback of Notre Dame, who had served as executioner in the Terezin ghetto at the two executions carried out there in January and February of 1942. Although he loved children, caressed them and helped them, the children recoiled from him.[15]

Fredy made the rules: the children ate the daily soup in the barracks. The soup was brought in casks from the kitchen at the front of the camp[16] and was thicker and hotter than the soup the

15 Eli Bachner, "Theresienstadt and the family camp in Auschwitz," *Yalkut Moreshet,* 25 (Hebrew) (November, 1976), p. 85.

16 According to other testimonies, the kitchen of the gypsy camp. Here, too, this may refer to different time periods.

ordinary prisoners got, as well as the food supplements Fredy obtained for them — ersatz coffee with a little milk, noodles cooked in milk, white bread, a slice of cake, soup cooked from the contents of packages whose addressees had died in the meantime and which were brought to the barracks in a wagon from the main camp in Auschwitz.[17] These supplements came in tiny portions, and not every day, but that little bit added strength and joy. The children's health was in fact much better than that of the other inhabitants of the camp. During the six-month stay of the September transport prisoners in the family camp, the general mortality rate from "natural causes" stemming from the camp conditions was as high as 22 percent, and among the December people even higher, while among the children in their barracks I only recall one case of a death, a girl of about fourteen who died from encephalitis.

At first the parents, especially those with very small children, were apprehensive. They feared that while the older children would know how to make sure they got their share of the food when it was distributed, the counselors might steal from the smaller ones. Over time, however, they learned to trust them. Fredy forbade the counselors to even taste any of the children's food and punished offenders by ousting them from the children's barracks. The prohibition was usually adhered to even after Fredy's death;[18] at most a counselor would allow himself to clean the bowl with his finger after the food was handed out, and then feel a little ashamed. Fredy also forbade the counselors from accepting a gift of a spoon of thick soup from their charges. One night Avi Fischer, counselor of a group of older boys, tied himself to a boy who was feverish to prevent him from falling out of his bunk. When the boys in the group wanted to give him a prize for this — in the form of a spoon of soup from each one — they had to get Fredy's permission.[19] There were groups of

17 The testimony of Honza Gärtner, BTA 99/5; according to him, the packages were transferred to the family camp at the initiative of the woman who ran the postal service in the women's camp, who fell in love with Fredy Hirsch.

18 According to Yaacov Rachman, "The counselors also enjoyed the children's food," in Ben David, ed., *The Educational Activity*, testimony No. 395.

19 Avraham Ophir, in Ben David, ed., *The Educational Activity*, testimony No. 394.

older children in which each day they all gave one spoon of soup to one of them, in turn, so that each would feel relatively full one day, at least once in two weeks. A birthday gift would be an additional portion of soup or "cake," made of bitter bread dipped in a brown liquid called coffee, sweetened with beet jam, and the birthday boy or girl would share it with all the others in the group.

In the children's barracks, in marked contrast to its surroundings, there were no thefts, no cursing, no acts of violence by the strong against the weak. Discipline among the children was maintained during their studies and other activities, not by threats or punishments, but almost by itself. All of the children had been through the Terezin ghetto; most of them had been in the children's homes there and were used to living in a group and having to consider others. And yet, there were exceptions, especially among the older children. As there were among the adults, among the boys too, in Birkenau, there were those who were resourceful and marvelously adept at adjusting, who knew how to get along, to trade, to obtain extra food, to find a niche for themselves. Under normal conditions, they'd be the ones to earn their first million in the stock market before the age of twenty-five – and here too they knew the ins and outs of the stock exchange, of bread and cigarettes. Kapos from the general clothing storeroom, the *Kleiderkammer*, supplied the barracks with some clothes for children whose old clothing was all torn, but there were children who sold the clothing they received in exchange for bread, and the following day appeared in the same torn clothing they had worn before.[20] Some of the 14-year-old boys worked as runners, servants of the kapos, acted as their pimps, obtaining girls for them from among the female prisoners, witnessed parties in their rooms, ate enough to fill their bellies, and wore warm clothes and good boots. They thought themselves superior to their hungry, poorly dressed counselors, who had no authority over them, also because they knew better than they did what was happening in Birkenau.[21]

20 Klein, *Životní styl*, Rezniczenko-Erez, ed., *Theresienstadt*, p. 149; John Freund, ed., *After Those Fifty Years*, p. 20.

21 Testimony of Michael Honey (Honigwachs) in: Freund, ed., *After Those Fifty Years*, p.119.

During Fredy's time, the children exercised every morning under his instruction. At the noon break, after three hours of group work and the distribution of soup, the children went to the blocks, to their parents: to their mothers, some of whom dragged the heavy casks of soup from the kitchen to the blocks just to get another portion of soup for their children; to their fathers, some of whom shrank more with each passing day, even though they were not yet fifty. There the children heard stories about home, huddled with them under one blanket, and would return to their barracks for another two hours of activity and the afternoon roll call.

Their studies were not studies in the usual sense of the word, nor were they the same as those held in the underground in the Terezin ghetto. There were no staff meetings with Fredy to discuss the curriculum, because that would have been pointless. Everything depended on the counselor and his ability to improvise, his skill at keeping his charges busy, interesting them and holding their attention, teaching them without any teaching aids except his own memory. There was a "library" in the barracks, containing about a dozen books collected randomly (including Wells' *The History of the World*, a Bible, a Russian grammar book, and Freud's *Introduction to Psychology*).[22] There was also a librarian, or to be more exact, a guard over the books, a girl, one of the youngsters too old to be entitled to be in the children's barracks. To enable these boys and girls to be there, Fredy and his successors employed them in odd jobs such as keeping the stove lit, bringing food from the kitchen, or cleaning the barracks. The counselors themselves served as a kind of lending library: at length, and in installments, they told the children the contents of books they had read in the past, and would move from group to group in order to expand the inventory of oral books. The boys' favorite stories were those about heroes, Indians, Eskimos, athletes, and victories in battle. Some counselors, drawing on their past experience, played scouting games with their group (including one good deed a day and a day of silence), and kept them busy with social games like guessing

22 Avraham Ophir, in Ben David, ed., *The Educational Activity*, testimony No. 394, p. 20.

the names of famous people by asking questions. Sometimes one of the children would give a lecture on something he knew or that interested him.

To relieve the overcrowded conditions after the arrival of the December transport and to increase the number of children in the barracks, Fredy applied to Dr. Josef Mengele, who was in charge of Block 31 and the infirmary barracks opposite it, which was also part of his fiefdom, to allocate another block to the children's barracks. Perhaps in pressing his request, he gained support from the SS men's satisfaction with the performance of *Snow White and the Seven Dwarfs* that was put on in the children's barracks in January 1944.[23] The play, in German, was an adaptation of the Walt Disney film, with token costumes, singing, dancing and murals, performed in the presence of head of the camp Böhm and other SS men,[24] who did not conceal their delight.

So at the end of January or in early February, the neighboring Block 29 began to serve as a barracks for very young children. There were no toys, no teaching aids, only some old wrapping paper, sometimes a precious pencil. The children sang Czech and Hebrew children's songs, such as "Šla Naninka do zelí" or "Glidati hachi tovah" ("My ice cream is best"), listened to stories and legends, and made handicrafts from waste that the mothers brought from the workshops where they were employed. The children of Block 29 also invented their own games, drawn from camp life, the only reality they knew: the roll call game, and the game of corpses (that they saw piled up behind the barracks or on carts). They did not know what a flower, an apple, or a cow looked like. Even the older children sometimes had a hard time understanding the details of stories from another world: there was one about the two Koželuh brothers, well-known Czech athletes, who came from such a poor family that they subsisted only on bread and potatoes — in Birkenau those were signs of the greatest wealth imaginable.

23 The exact date of the play is not clear. Hanka Fischel, who arrived in Birkenau in December 1943, talks about many weeks of preparation; others speak about a play for Christmas.

24 I did not succeed in finding out who exactly was present at the performance of the play.

On Friday evening and Saturday, the entire children's barracks had a joint party, and each group was entitled to prepare a five-minute show. The work of writing the scripts (usually on used paper, with charred sticks instead of pencils), learning the text and songs, preparing the token costumes from the little available in the block – all of this occupied the groups for many hours. With the exception of *Snow White and the Seven Dwarfs*, meant to justify the existence of the children's barracks to the SS, the plays were put on in Czech. Among these was *Robinson Crusoe*, with Friday, sailors and monkeys, and a song of hope for their homecoming; excerpts from the play *Manon Lescaut* in the poetic adaptation by the Czech poet Vitězslav Nezval; and ballads by Francois Villon – all drawn from the memories of the counselors, members of a generation that were still avid readers of poetry. The children wrote poems, too. Fairy tales were performed for the young children in a puppet theater with puppet heads made of potatoes. Drawings of Indians, Eskimos, black children, a palm tree and monkeys – the work of Marianne Hermann, known as Mausi – were later added to illustrations from Snow White drawn on the walls of the block by Dina Gotlieb.

Once, when Avi Fischer was putting on a pantomime act, showing how all kinds of people – a traveler in a train, an old grandmother – read a newspaper, a piece of wrapping paper serving as a substitute for a newspaper, several SS men entered the barracks in a good mood, and one of them handed Avi a real newspaper from the same day (the likes of which the prisoners hadn't seen for years).[25] On 11 February 1944, the barracks prepared a surprise party for Fredy marking his twenty-eighth birthday. The small children sang a song of thanks to him, to the melody of a Czech children's song: "We are little musicians/and now we can come/to the barracks/to congratulate Fredy."[26]

During one Friday night party, 12-year-old Štěpán showed what it would be like to return to normal life. Instead of paying

25 Avraham Ophir, in Ben David, ed., *The Educational Activity*, testimony No. 394.

26 Bártková, *Osvětimský slabikář*, p. 23.

with money, the released prisoner insists on paying with bread and cigarettes, the currency of the camp, and when the shopkeeper thinks him crazy and calls an ambulance, he refuses to get in it and yells: "No, no, only on foot!" All of them, the children and their counselors, understood the allusion – in Birkenau an ambulance or a truck meant being taken to the gas chambers – and they all burst into laughter.[27]

From the edge of the camp, where Block 31 was located, the railway platform was visible not far away, and you could see the daily arrival of transports, and the people lining up for the selection. And on the right, somewhat further away, were the chimneys of the crematoria emitting flames and thick, foul-smelling smoke day and night. So what did the children know about the mass extermination? Fredy forbade the counselors to talk to the children about death, about gas chambers and crematoria. And in fact, until the extermination of the September transport on the night of 8 March 1944, it was still possible to maintain that pretense. There was still hope that the family camp, with its special conditions, was meant for show and would survive until the end of the war, which early in 1944 seemed very close. Although Fredy's order to maintain silence remained in force even after his death and the counselors' answers to the children's questions about extermination were evasive, the gas chamber murder of the September transport, including the children of the barracks and their counselors, made it impossible to hide from the children that certain death was awaiting them all. Even the little ones would say: "We'll go out through the chimney," without understanding how that was practically feasible. When the smoke from the chimneys was thick and black, the older ones would joke: "Today they're burning the fat ones." They spoke openly about the expected death, although they were unable to completely grasp its meaning. After all, the counselors too, aged 20–22, only a few years older than their charges, who knew about the fate of the September transport and the remark "SB [special treatment] after a stay of six months" noted as well on their cards

27 Avraham Ophir, in Ben David, ed., *The Educational Activity*, testimony No. 394, p. 22.

in the political department of the main camp, even if they had no illusions, still were incapable of accepting that the end of life was unavoidable.

From early March 1944, the children were aware of an increased number of visits by prisoners from the other camps to Fredy's small room. The older boys prepared a party for 6 March, the date when their home in the Terezin ghetto was established. When one of them, Yehudah Bakon, went to invite Fredy, he found him agitated and deep in thought. Fredy asked the boys' forgiveness but said he couldn't attend the party.[28] If, in fact, the possibility of a revolt was being discussed in Fredy's room, the counselors of the December transport – and only a few of them survived – knew nothing first hand. They only sensed that something was about to happen. Rumor had it that the September people were going to be transferred to another camp.

Two days before the September transport left for its official destination, the Heidebreck camp, which camp commandant Schwarzhuber had talked about, Fredy Hirsch appointed 29-year-old Seppl Lichtenstern as head of the children's barracks and 26-year-old Honza (Jan) Brammer as his deputy.[29] Seppl came from the Sudeten region and his mother tongue was German. He was a member of the leadership of the Tekhelet-Laven youth movement and of Hechalutz, and during the German occupation in Prague he organized illegal immigration at the Palestine Office. Honza's cultural background was Czech; he was a member of the Czech-speaking youth movement El-Al, was experienced at counseling and practical work with youth, and in the Terezin ghetto had been head of the youth employment department. The two divided the functions between them: Seppl represented the children's barracks externally, namely, vis-à-vis the Germans and the other officeholders, and was responsible for the children's studies. Honza dealt with the ongoing organizational side. Seppl, whose behavior was restrained and quiet, was closer to the counselors than Fredy, who

28 Yehudah Bakon, in Ben David, ed., *The Educational Activity*, testimony No. 378.

29 Dov Barnea, in Ben David, ed., *The Educational Activity*, testimony No. 379.

kept a certain distance, had been. He did not intimidate them as Fredy had, but neither did he project Fredy's brand of authority and resolve.

When saying goodbye, the older boys asked the housemother, Hanka Epstein, to write and send them regards from Heidebreck. She replied: "The day after tomorrow look at the chimney, I'll wave my apron at you to say hello."[30] She was replaced by her assistant, Miriam, the wife of Jakob Edelstein, who was brought to Auschwitz in a separate carriage in the same train that brought his family (his wife, only son and his mother-in-law), and was then in the punitive block in the main camp without Miriam knowing his whereabouts. Their 14-year-old son Arye was one of the youngsters in the children's barracks.

Fredy took leave of the counselors in a pessimistic tone, and asked them to give his regards to his friends in Palestine. He took with him his famous whistle, and on 7 March 1944 went with all the rest to the neighboring detention camp (B/2/a). The following day, news came over the fence that Fredy did not feel well, and Miriam Edelstein was asked to prepare a pudding for him, which is what they called the gruel cooked from old cookie crumbs taken from the packages of the deceased. One of the older boys passed the bowl with the pudding under the fence,[31] a daring act because of the danger of touching the electrified wire (objects were usually transferred from camp to camp by being thrown over the fence). Afterwards news came to the children's barracks that Fredy had committed suicide by swallowing luminal pills. No one will ever know for sure whether Fredy only asked the doctors for tranquillizers and they deliberately gave him a higher dose, to preclude any possibility of an uprising that would have endangered their return to the family camp, as Dr. Mengele had promised them (and indeed kept that promise), or whether Fredy was unable to confront the terrible dilemma and choose to see his charges massacred in the event of a revolt (and it was clear that none of the children would be saved) or go to their death in the gas chambers despite

30 Bondy, *Elder of the Jews,* p. 412.

31 Rezniczenko-Erez, ed., *Theresienstadt,* p. 204.

his struggle to gain their survival. I reject the assumption, even though it appears in the guise of a novel,[32] that Fredy despaired because Eichmann did not keep his promise to reward him for his actions by saving his life. First of all, even those less experienced than Fredy,[33] in contacts with the Germans, did not believe Eichmann (when he first appeared in February 1944 in the family camp, Leo Janowitz said: "Eichmann means trouble"). Second, and primarily, if indeed someone had offered to save Fredy's life, as some people claimed in their testimonies,[34] I believe that his personal fate was not the overriding consideration. I say this from my own knowledge and on the basis of my research. The driving force in Fredy's life was his inner pride, his desire to serve as a personal example and to take responsibility for the lives of the children, and he would never have agreed to be saved alone and then, safe and sound, face those remaining in the children's barracks the day after his charges were exterminated.

On the night of 8 March, a strict curfew was imposed on the family camp. Those remaining heard shouts and the din of trucks coming and going – and in the morning the neighboring camp was empty. Thick smoke poured out of the crematoria chimneys. Hanka Epstein waved her black apron from up high.

The first day or two after that dreadful night, when news began to arrive about the death of the people from the September transport, the children's barracks was like a house of mourning. They were all stunned, spoke in whispers; no songs or laughter were heard. But very quickly, the hunger for life took over. Jobs became available, there was more room on the bunks in the blocks, good blankets were left over from those who were gone. The chil-

32 Ota Kraus, *The Painted Wall* (Tel Aviv: Yarom Golan, 1997), p. 29.

33 According to Esther Milo, in Ben David, ed., *The Educational Activity*, testimony No. 393, a postcard arrived in Terezin from Fredy Hirsch in Birkenau, in which he wrote: "Tante Mavet ist mit uns," namely "Aunt Death is with us."

34 Rezniczenko-Erez, ed., *Theresienstadt*, p. 203. From a conversation with Trude Janowitz before the September transport left, I know that one of the SS men offered to allow her to stay in the family camp. Trude decided to go with her husband Leo and all the other prisoners.

dren's barracks went back to its old routine. Since the number of children was reduced by half, there was no longer any need for the neighboring block that served as a kindergarten, and it became a residence block for mothers with small children and the women who took care of them. Honza Brammer interviewed new counselors to fill the approved number of twenty – and there was no lack of candidates. He selected them on the basis of their experience in teaching and counseling, as well as their personality.[35] Most of the counselors, like Fredy, came from the ranks of the Zionist youth movements; some of them had a high school education, often only partial, but there were also professional teachers among them, as well as active Communists like Hugo Lengsfeld and Jiří Franěk.[36] Although Fredy or one or another of the counselors would occasionally talk to their charges about Eretz Israel, they mainly occupied the children with what they had read, learned, remembered and whatever was close to their hearts. Here, in contrast to the Terezin ghetto, worldviews played a negligible role in the teaching and did not adversely affect the friendly relations between the counselors. It was no longer a matter of educating the children for a life of freedom, but rather of occupying them, strengthening them, helping them forget. The aim was to enable the children to pass the time more or less pleasantly, one more day and then one more day until the zero hour at the end of their six-month stay in Birkenau.

The children loved to be in their barracks, and that was enough. The counselors did not ask themselves why, when death was lurking at the door, they were teaching them the alphabet or geometry, why they had them memorize the Czech rules of grammar or learn about the force of gravity of the earth. They needed their counseling work no less than the children did. For them too, driven by the compulsion to live each day that remained, this was a way of forgetting. Moreover, unlike Terezin, where the care of the children was not one of the economically "profitable" jobs like

35 Dov Barnea, in Ben David, ed., *The Educational Activity*, testimony No. 379.

36 The testimony of Pavel Lenek (Hugo Lengsfeld) as recorded by Miroslav Kárný in Prague in 1975, BTA 44/37; Avraham Ophir, in Ben David. ed., *The Educational Activity*, testimony No. 394.

working in the kitchen or agriculture, here, in the family camp, it had many advantages: a heated barracks far from the abusive kapos, the closeness of friends, a roll call without standing in the rain and the cold, small pleasures – a Friday night get-together, the possibility of mending a torn item of clothing in the small sewing shop at the front of the barracks, a conversation among friends and the sense of a refuge.

The children's favorite song during the sing-along hour was "Alouette," a French-Canadian folk song with a merry melody, accompanied by gestures that Avi Fischer had taught them. Neither the children nor the counselors paid attention to the sharp contrast between the merry tune and the gloomy words about the beautiful lark whose feathers, wings, feet and head were being plucked off. "Alouette" was not only the hymn of the children's barracks, it also remained a symbol.

In the meantime, the hard winter passed, and spring came. A small fruit tree, the only one in the camp, began to blossom next to Block 31, and it was an attraction for the kindergarten children, like the crow that the cooks kept in a cage next to the kitchen at the entrance to the camp. Now, after the snow had melted and the roads were dry, the kindergarten children could file out in a row to walk along the camp road up to the crow's cage. They could play in the yard between the two last blocks, carefully so that neither they nor their improvised ball touched the electrified fence – the children had witnessed suicides and accidents and had seen the scorched corpses that remained hanging on the wires for hours.

In May 1944, another 7,500 prisoners arrived from the Terezin ghetto, and the overcrowded conditions in the camp became terrible again. Although many of the May children were taken into the children's barracks and new counselors were accepted, also for activity with the teenagers who remained in the blocks, the time between the arrival of the newcomers and the expected extermination of the December arrivals was too short to enable them to become a cohesive group. The older children often ran away from the children's barracks and wandered around the camp or went to their parents. This time too, as they did when the December transport arrived, the old-timers, children and adults alike, tried to open the eyes of the newcomers and mercilessly make them aware of the cruel reality – from here no one leaves alive.

18 and 19 June marked the end of the six-month grace period for the December transportees before the anticipated "special treatment," but nothing happened. On 20 June, Arye, the son of Jakob Edelstein, was taken from the children's barracks by order of the SS. Miriam was then lying ill with diphtheria in the infirmary block, and was taken from there on a stretcher despite the doctors' opposition. Neither of them was ever seen again. Only a few days later did the counselors of the barracks learn from Zosek, a Polish roofer, that the Edelstein family – Jakob, Miriam, her mother and Arye – had all been shot to death at the wall of death in the main camp of Auschwitz.[37]

Towards the end of June, typists from the woman's camp began to appear in the camp to prepare the prisoners' records, and Dr. Mengele paid frequent visits to the children's barracks. Selections were announced, for men and women separately, and those aged 16–45 were entitled to report for them. Mothers of small children were also permitted to report, but it was clear that if any mothers passed the selection, that would mean they'd leave their children to their fate. The mothers hesitated, discussed it with one another, and asked the counselors for their advice. Mothers of children in my group, a group of 5- to 6-year-olds, also asked me what I would do if I were in their place. I tried to be evasive: "I have no children of my own." But they pressured me. Finally, I said, "I think that if I had a small child, I would stay with him." They nodded; that's what they had decided anyway, they just wanted me to confirm that they'd made the right decision. Only two, maybe three, mothers of smaller children did report for the selection and left Auschwitz. All the others knowingly chose to remain with their children – and there were hardly any illusions about what they could all expect.[38]

37 Bondy, *The Elder of the Jews*, p. 441; J. Franěk, quoted in Kraus and Kulka, *The Death Factory in Auschwitz*, p. 166.

38 Bachner, "Theresienstadt and the family camp in Auschwitz," p. 87.

A selection was conducted in the children's barracks in the presence of Dr. Mengele and other SS men, women and men separately. Like the others, the female counselors and the young girls were also ordered to undress and skip naked over the heating pipe and do exercises on it to prove their physical fitness. When asked their profession, many of the women thought it best to say gardener or seamstress. At the advice of their counselors, the older children lied about their age, adding a few years. Some of them passed the selection, and some who failed the first time secretly got back into line and passed the second. Some of the boys and girls were not prepared to leave their parents who had failed. When I said goodbye to the children in my group and their mothers, before leaving for the as-yet-unknown destination, I felt, like the other counselors who had passed the selection, terribly despondent at having abandoned them when they needed me. If I had been prepared to remain with the children in my group, it is possible – as one of the mothers told me in our hour of indecision – that some of the women might have left because they had so much faith in me. But my drive to live was stronger.

During the discussions at meetings of the survivors in Israel about the education of the children in the Terezin ghetto and in the family camp, while many expressed a favorable view of what had been done, there were also dissenting opinions. There were some who believed that instead of educating the children to values, friendship, decency and consideration for others, the counselors should have taught them to steal, to cheat and to rob. The experience of the family camp does not bear out this approach. The children in the barracks knew many hours of joy, laughter and shared experiences, and in the face of the gas chambers not even Fagin's school would have helped them.

Moreover, on 6 July 1944, after the men and women fit for work left the family camp, Dr. Mengele conducted another selection, for boys aged 14–16, but among the ninty to ninety-six boys selected there were younger ones who had lied about their age. All the boys were transferred to the men's camp to serve as runners, servants of the kapos, or in other jobs. About half of them survived, and in their memoirs they refer again and again to the importance of friendship, mutual help and the readiness to take a risk to save a friend, and the image of Fredy – all these helped them hold out, keep from despairing, survive, go back to their studies, acquire a profession, start a family and never to lose their faith in humanity.[39]

The children, the mothers, the elderly, the sick, and those unfit for work who remained in the family camp were killed in the gas chambers on 10 and 11 July 1944. Only the Indians, Eskimos, Snow White and the seven dwarfs on the walls of the children's barracks remained.

♦

The management of the Polish Auschwitz-Birkenau state museum has allowed the wooden hut of the children's barracks with its brick chimney to crumble, and in camp B/2/b only its foundations remain today – a rectangular concrete frame. The electrified fence behind the hut is corroded with rust. In the German archives, no official records of its existence have ever been found. It is as if the children's barracks never existed. The children's singing was borne away on the wind.

39 Testimonies of the "Birkenau Boys" in: Freund, ed., *After Those Fifty Years.*

Roll Call

A thousand years of the history of Bohemia and Moravia Jewry are concealed in the names of Jews who perished in the Holocaust

Eighty thousand names are recorded in the two large, thick, black volumes of *The Terezin Memorial – The Jewish Victims of the German Occupation of Bohemia and Moravia 1941–1945*. The book was published in 1995 and is based primarily on the lists of the transports of deportees to the Łódź ghetto and the Terezin ghetto and from there to extermination.[1] Just reading the names – along with the dates of birth, dates of the transport to the ghetto and dates and places of death, if known – is like reading a thousand years of Jewish history in the heart of Europe, and for me, is also a return to a world that has not been forgotten, only covered with a thick layer of years. There I meet Grete Wambach, my classmate in the German elementary school in the Vinohrady quarter of Prague, a quiet motherless girl, dressed in dark clothing, shunned by the other girls. I visited her home once. I recall only a dark apartment,

The Czech language has diacritic marks that change the sound of the letter: č is pronounced as ch; š – sh; ž – zh. ř is a letter peculiar to Czech, in English it is replaced by the letter jr. ě is pronounced as ye (a drawn out e). The ´ accent above a vowel (á, é, í, ý) as well as ů means it is a long vowel.

1 *Terezinská Pamětni kniha: Židovské oběti nacistických deportací z Čech a Moravy 1941–1945* (Prague: Melantrich, 1995). This is the material that forms the basis of this chapter, and as I drew from it most of the data on the names, numbers and fate of the deportees, I think it unnecessary to cite it with each mention.

a father in a black suit and a stout taciturn aunt who kept house for them. To her death in Treblinka, in October 1942, 19-year-old Grete went alone. The same was true of Jankel Podpiska, a boy from Subcarpathian Ruthenia, alone in Prague, who came to us once a week for a home-cooked lunch and became attached to my mother. Like many refugees, Jankel was sent to the Terezin ghetto on the first transports in January 1942, and two months later, on 11 March, was sent to Izbica in the Lublin district where all trace of him vanished. He is the only Podpiska in the book.

Behind every name there is a living person, and even if I knew each and every one of them, there would not be enough time in the dwindling years of my life to write about them all. So I will only try to link the names with the history of the Jews of Bohemia (known in Hebrew writings as Biham) and Moravia (known as Maharin), the two Bohemian crown lands that, with the occupation on 15 March 1939, became a German protectorate. In particular, I will try to link the names with the history of the Jews of Prague, called in Hebrew "city and mother." To Israeli tourists, present-day Prague is a charming city whose residents are genial, but that city was capable of showing much cruelty to her Jews in the past. Riots, expulsions, murder, the confiscation of property, prohibitions against engaging in various trades, restriction to a closed ghetto, a special hat, a yellow patch on the left sleeve – for all the abuses of the Nazi rule there were recurring precedents in the history of Czech Jewry, with the exception of the modern technical innovation: death on an assembly line.

♦

Abel, the first victim of murder since the expulsion from the Garden of Eden, casts a long shadow on all those who bear his name. The first two letters of the name are the first two letters of the Latin and Hebrew alphabets, the beginning of all beginnings. That name was also the first in most of the lists of transports to the Terezin ghetto, in the form common to Czech Jews – Abeles, with the patronymic suffix 'es', i.e., the son of Abel. Over time, the word 'son' was foregone, but the relationship remained. Arthur Abeles opens the list of the first transport that left on 16 October 1941 from Prague to the Łódź ghetto. There were two with that name, one born in 1897, the other in 1884, and neither survived. Altogether, 160 Abeleses and another 13 Abels, male and female, were among those leaving for the unknown. Simon Abeles – a name that even the most assimilated among Prague's Jews remember with horror – was not among them. Little Simon's grave in the Tyne church bordering on the Old Town square, and a memorial plaque, commemorate him to this day: a martyr for his Christian faith.

Simon's grandfather, Moses Bumsla Abeles, was the head of the Prague community. His grandson was raised in the home of his father Lazar, a glove merchant, and his fourth wife. Church legend has it that little Simon was attracted to Christianity and secretly baptized, and therefore was murdered by his father. The truth apparently is less uplifting. On 21 February 1694, 12-year-old Shimele was sent to buy a herring, brought it home without the milt, and also refused to eat it because in general he was a poor eater. Löbl Kurzhandel, a relative who lived with the Abeleses and helped educate their children, punished him by a hard hit and in doing so broke his neck. Alarmed, Lazar Abeles and Löbl Kurzhandel claimed Simon had died of a sudden attack of spasms and buried him hastily. That, however, did not save them. It turned out that in July 1693, Simon had secretly visited the home of a converted Jew, Johann Fanta, who had smuggled him, disguised, into the nearby Jesuit monastery where Simon had expressed his desire to learn everything about the Christian religion and to convert to Christianity. His motive is not clear. Perhaps it was because of the harsh atmosphere in the home of his father and stepmother, perhaps because of his refusal to wear the stiff pleated collar that Bohemian Jews were forced to wear at the time to distinguish them from the Christians. Simon Abeles was entrusted to a convert named Franz Kawka, but late in the fall, Lazar Abeles discovered his son's hiding place, took him home, and by means of persuasion and threats attempted to return him to the religion of his forefathers. In the eyes of the Church and the authorities there was only one explanation for Simon's death: he was martyred in the name of Jesus. Lazar Abeles hung himself in prison on 16 March 1694 to escape torture.

Kurzhandel pleaded his innocence, but finally, under torture, he confessed to the killing, although he refused to admit that religion had motivated him, and was sentenced to death in an Inquisition trial. In his last moments, pressured by the priests, Kurzhandel expressed his willingness to convert to Christianity and he was granted special dispensation. Instead of dying slowly, on the rack, he was granted a quick death. He was buried under the Christian name Jeronymus in the St. Peter church in Prague. He was nineteen at the time of his death.[2] The name Kurzhandel does not appear in the book of the dead. Of the 160 who bore the name Abeles who arrived in Terezin from the Protectorate, 11 survived in the ghetto – four of them because they were married to non-Jews and were deported to the ghetto only in the last months of the war – and three came back from the extermination camp: 14 in all, less than a tenth. One of them, Karel, changed his name after the war to Brožík, just to be safe.

At that time, in the seventeenth century, Jews could still save themselves by converting to Christianity. Conversion not only saved their lives, it also opened many doors to them. A Jew who agreed to convert was free to live wherever he wished, to engage in the occupation of his choice, to travel wherever he wished, and marry whenever he wished. In the Middle Ages, conversion sometimes saved lives. In the nineteenth and early twentieth century, conversion was first and foremost a way to acquire a career, since Jews had a hard time obtaining the title of professor or a senior government position.

Not everyone converted for practical reasons. There were also those who were captivated by the loving, redeeming religion, attracted by the Church and all its beauty. Dr. Ernst Kalmus, chief physician of the Prague police force, bore the ancient Jewish name that derived from Kalonymus, the name of a family that moved from Italy to Germany in the sixteenth century. The name appears

2 Alexander Putik, "The Prague Jewish Community in the Late 17th and Early 18th Centuries," *Bohemiae Judaica* XXXV (2000), pp. 55–56; Egon Erwin Kisch, *Pražský Pitaval* (Prague: Státní nakladalelstvi Politické Literatury, 1958), pp. 110–119.

among those of Bohemian Jews in the sixteenth century and is also engraved on tombstones in the ancient cemetery of Prague, like the tombstone of Rachel, daughter of Kalonymus from Venice.[3] Dr. Kalmus converted to Christianity in the early twentieth century, and chose the Protestant church of the Moravian brothers. His children were born as Christians and his oldest was called Ernst, like him, an indication of how totally cut off he was from Jewish customs. But it did not help: 73-year-old Dr. Kalmus and his wife Elsa were sent as Jews to the Terezin ghetto on 24 October 1942, and only two days later were sent onwards to the gas chambers of Auschwitz. The Christian God also let them down.

In the Reich, Jews who did not have distinctly Jewish names were forced to take a middle name – Israel for men, Sarah for women – another way of distinguishing them from the pure race. Although this rule was not fully implemented in the Protectorate, from the Nazi point of view it was justified. In fact, the names of the persecuted attest to how intertwined the lives of all inhabitants of Central Europe were, Christians and Jews alike. The list of deportees includes Jews with the same names as members of the Nazi leadership: Himmler, Hess, Rosenberg, Müller, Pohl, Todt, Frank, Funk, Koch[4] – as well as Wagner, the high priest of Germanic music. There is even a Sheindel Hittler among those going to their death, although she spelled it with a double t. Jakob Edelstein, the director of the Palestine Office in Prague and deputy head of the Prague community during the occupation, was called in to the Gestapo headquarters one day (in 1939 or 1940) and asked to translate a letter in Yiddish written by a Jewish shoemaker, Alois Hittler, to his sister. Edelstein believed that the Gestapo was interested in Alois only because he had the same surname as the Fuhrer.[5] The

3 Otto Muneles, *Inscriptions from the Ancient Jewish Cemetery in Prague* (Hebrew) (Jerusalem: The Israeli Academy of Sciences, 1987), tombstone No. 27.

4 H. Himmler, Head of SS; R. Hess, Hitler's deputy; A. Rosenberg, Minister for Occupied Areas in the East; H. Müller, Head of Gestapo; O. Pohl, Chief of the Main Office for Economy and Administration; P. Todt, Head of the Todt organization; H. Frank, Governor General of the General-gouvernement; R. Funk, President of the Reich Bank.

5 Testimony of A. Tarsi, Hachotrim 1976, author's archives.

names of the SS officers Seidl, Burger, Rahm, commandants of the Terezin ghetto; Bergel, the violent, drunken deputy commandment of the ghetto; and Brunner and Fidler, SS men on the staff of the Center for Jewish Emigration,[6] were also the names of their prisoners, members of the inferior race. They were called Eichenbaum and Eichler and Eichner, but Eichmann, the name of the head of the Center, the "oak man" as the Jews sometimes called him, was not one of their names.

♦

The Jews of the Hapsburg monarchy, a loosely enforced tyranny as its subjects often depicted it, tended to grant their children the same names as members of the imperial family – Rudolph, Franz, Leopold, Friedrich, Karl, Ludwig, Otto, Maximilian (Max) and in particular Josef, a very useful name, both Jewish and imperial. The girls were called Elizabeth, like the wife of the Emperor Franz Josef. She was a delicate woman, an admirer of Heine, who in 1898 was stabbed to death by an anarchist. The name Ferdinand, also one of the names of the Hapsburg dynasty, was, however, given to very few Jews, perhaps one out of every hundred who were called Karl or Rudolf. The shadow of Ferdinand of Aragon who expelled the Jews from Spain cast a shadow over that name, as did that of his grandson, Ferdinand I of the Hapsburg dynasty, who was educated at the court of his grandfather in Spain and, like him, wanted a kingdom free of heretics. The attitude of the Emperor Ferdinand I (1503–1564) towards the Jews of Bohemia was schizophrenic: he wanted and needed the large sums of money they paid in the form of heavy taxes, but he did not want the Jews themselves. In addition to his Christian revulsion, the Emperor was aware of the accusation that the Jews were spying for his enemies the Turks, whom he fought for many years (and to finance his war, he levied many special taxes on the Jews). In 1541, Ferdinand issued an order expelling the Jews from Prague and the entire area of the Bo-

6 Siegfried Seidl, Anton Burger, Karl Rahm, Karl Bergel, Alois Brunner, Hans Fidler.

hemian kingdom. Nonetheless, in exchange for a large ransom he granted wealthy Jewish families letters of protection that enabled them to continue living in his kingdom for various purposes.[7] At first he granted the letters to twelve families and later raised their number, extending the validity of the protection repeatedly. He also issued an order that the Jews should be allowed to leave in an orderly fashion, taking their belongings and property with them. This, however, did not prevent suffering, robbery and murder on the roads. Some of those who were expelled went eastward, to neighboring Poland; some hoped to hold out until the worst was over. This havoc went on for twenty-five years, until the Emperor died. Ironically enough, in July 1565, his son, Prince Ferdinand, ordered his head groom to pay the Jewish horse merchant, Jakob of Prague, 300 schock[8] for the purchase of eight–ten horses for a wagon to carry the body of Ferdinand I to Bohemia.[9] The Jews had learned from history to hold on until the danger had passed, until the evil rule was replaced, until, with God's help, the tyrant died (compared to his father, Ferdinand II showed mercy towards the Jews).

With regard to the Empress Maria Theresa, who, following in the footsteps of her forefathers, also expelled the Jews, the Jews' memory was shorter. Hundreds of women on the list of transports, particularly those born during the monarchy, were called Theresa; some, like her, were even named Maria Theresa. The young Empress rose to power in 1740 and a year later the Jews of Prague held a festive procession on the occasion of the birth of her firstborn son, the crown prince. That did them no good: Maria Theresa was embroiled in a war with Prussia over control of the Silesia region, in which the Prussians conquered Bohemia and entered Prague.

7 In 1559 Ferdinand instructed his son, the Duke of Bohemia, to collect the 5,000 thaler the Jews holding a letter of protection had undertaken to pay, and to transfer that sum to Vienna. See: Gottlieb Bondy–Franz Dworsky, *Zur Geschichte der Juden in Böhmen, Mähren und Schlesien* (Prague, 1906), no. 1289 (this is a collection of documents, and the number appearing after its name is the number of the document contained in it).

8 An ancient measure (kopa in Czech) worth 60 units (coins, eggs, etc.).

9 Bondy-Dworsky, *Zur Geschichte der Juden*, no. 461.

After the Prussian army withdrew, the fact that the Prussian king had extended his protection not only over the priesthood, the university and the students, but also over the Jewish Town, as the Jewish quarter in Prague was then called, was interpreted as proof that the Jews had taken his side and spied for him. The Empress, a devout Catholic, needed no evidence. In 1748, despite the opposition of the nobility, all too aware of the Jews' financial value, she ordered the expulsion not only of the Prague Jews but of all the Jews of Bohemia. The writers of chronicles at the time described the heartrending spectacles they witnessed when the Jews left. The expulsion order was rescinded years later, following pressure from within and without.[10] In 1780, her eldest son, the Emperor Joseph II, built a fortress in northern Bohemia to ward off the Prussian army, which had expansionist aspirations, and gave it the name Theresienstadt. As it turned out 160 years later, he had indeed suitably commemorated his mother's name.

Most of the first names chosen by the Jews of Bohemia and Moravia for their sons and daughters during the Enlightenment, at the end of the monarchy and in the time of the Czechoslovakian republic, expressed the spirit of Jewry in the crown lands. These were neutral names that aroused no malice – "rishes" in Jewish parlance [from the Hebrew word *rishut*, meaning evil], the epithet they used then for antisemitism – on the part of either the Czechs or the Germans, and they did not make their bearers conspicuous. Joseph, Karl, Rudolf, Otto, Emil, Franz, Georg (Jiří in Czech) were common names for men; Anna, Julia, Olga, Irma, Trude, Berta, Martha – for women, as well as, strangely enough, Maria, the holy mother, perhaps because that was such a common name in their surroundings, perhaps because only one letter differentiated it from the name Miriam in Hebrew. Generally, out of a natural sense of restraint (and also because of repeated prohibitions by the Church in previous generations), most of the Jews, even the assimilated ones, did not choose distinctly national Czech names of saints, rulers and heroes from the legendary past, such as Bořivoj, Spytihněv, Přemysl, Vladislav, Svatopluk, Václav, Libuše, Ludmila,

10 Bondy-Dworsky, *Zur Geschichte der Juden,* no. 681.

and others.[11] As for the ancient Germanic names, they were very fond of the name Siegfried, the hero of the legend of the Nibelungs.

In the seventeenth century, the Jews had only one first name, and they still stuck to biblical names or those taken from the symbols of the tribes of Israel. According to tax books from 1665 to 1667 that include 1,950 people, the most popular names among Prague's Jews then were: Moses (154); Leib, i.e., Arieh (144); Hirsch (115); various forms of Jacob, such as Jokel and Jekel (104); David (71); Abraham (65); and Samuel (50).[12] As for the women's names, here the barrier was broken much sooner, and already in the fifteenth century they often took Czech names that were translations of their Hebrew names: Růža (Varda), Dobrá (Tovah), Sláva (Tehila), Veselá (Aliza), Květná (Pirchia).

Very few of the Jews of Bohemia and Moravia born after 1918, in the time of the Czechoslovakian Republic, had only a Hebrew first name. The Hebrew name given them at their circumcision was generally used only at the time of their barmitzvah ceremony, their wedding (if it wasn't a civil marriage), and their death. However, there were still those who had distinctly Hebrew names: Moses or Mojžís, Israel, Simon, Salomon or Šalomoun, Izak or Isaak, Nathan, Abraham, Nachman, Benjamin, Chaim, Esther, Chaya, Leah. To judge by their surnames, I would say most of them were refugees from Eastern Europe and their offspring who had settled in Czechoslovakia. I believe that among those leaving for the Łódź ghetto in the first five transports, between 16 October and 3 November 1941, Hebrew names were more common because these transports included refugees and many welfare cases, most of whom came from east of the state.

Ruth and David were in fashion during the 1920s and 1930s, short names popular everywhere in the world.

♦

11 The absurd combination Bořivoj Abeles could appear only in a satire like that by Karel Švensk, the actor and director of cabarets in the Terezin ghetto.

12 Otto Muneles, "Zur Namengebung der Juden in Böhmen," *Judaica Bohemiae* II/1 (Prague: Státní Zidovské Muzeum, 1966), p. 11.

Despite assimilation, despite the desire not to be different, the majority of Czech Jews continued to carry the names of their forefathers, a distinct mark of identity. On the list of deportees there are about 625 Jews whose names are various forms of Levy (Löwy, Lewitus, Levitus, Lewin, Levin, Lewy, Levit, Lewitt, Levy, Lövy, Lovi, Lowidt, Lowy, Levitner, Levinsky) and about 500 with the name Cohen (Coen, Cohn, Kann, Kohn, Kohner, Kahn, Kan), plus 350 whose name is Katz, not all of whom knew their name had nothing to do with a cat, but were the first letters of the Hebrew *kohen-tzedek*, righteous priest. Even a Christian priest could have the name Cohen: Theodor Kohn (1845–1905), Archbishop of the city of Olomouc in Moravia, who was born into a poor Jewish family, kept his ancient Jewish name even when he reached his high position in the Church.

The list of deportees includes several Hebrew surnames, such as Shabbat (Sabath, Sabat, Sabbath); Jomtov (Jontof) – festive day; Reach – an acronym for rabbi and cantor; Aharon (Aron); Solomon; Nathan; Ashkenaz; Margolis (Margaliot) – pearls; and Koref (*karov* – relative – in the Ashkenazi pronunciation). In addition, there were uniquely Jewish names: Bondy (jomtov in Spanish); Altschul, Altschuler and Asch (from the old synagogue in Prague, where the Sephardi synagogue stands today); Kantor, in its diminutive form, Kantůrek (cantor); Justitz (judge). There were also names with a patronymic or matronymic suffix (s or sh) – Pereles, Teweles, Jeiteles, Pascheles, Muneles, Fleckeles, Karpeles and Abeles, which has already been mentioned. This suffix is equivalent to the suffix "son" (Mendelson, Jacobson), "kin" (Dvorkin, Halkin) or "witz" (Davidowitz, Salomoniwitz) in other diasporas. All these names are linked to the history of the Jews of Bohemia and Moravia – Pascheles was the name of a family of book dealers and publishers; Jeiteles a family of rabbis, doctors and scientists – and most of them are also included in the list of transports.

The name Roubíček or Robitschek with a Czech ring belongs only to Jews, and it apparently originated from the name Reuven. This name appears more than 400 times on the list of those sent to be exterminated. In the midst of the transports, a clerk of the Prague Jewish community said to Joseph Roubíček, hero of the novel *Life with a Star* by Jiří Weil,[13] "Three weeks ago the Cohens went, now it'll be the turn of the Roubíčeks." That is how they were called up to the transports: groups of Jews with the same name, straight out of the card file. Fifteen Josef Roubíčeks went to the transports, two married to Christian women who were brought to the ghetto only in 1945; one of them who was sent to Auschwitz survived. The hero of *Life with a Star* also survived. He did not report for the transport, but instead went underground with the help of his Czech friends, as did the author of the book.[14]

Over the generations, all the pure Hebrew surnames from the sixteenth and seventeenth centuries disappeared – names like Shir haShirim, Sagi Nahor, Shalit, Talit, Kadosh, Teumim, Malakh, Rofé, Anokhi, Arokh, Peretz, Tzoref, Karov, Katzav, and Shochet, that are engraved on tombstones in the ancient Prague cemetery.[15] Some of them became extinct, some appear, in German translation, on the list of deportees: Blinder instead of Sagi Nahor, Zwillinger instead of Teumim, Engel instead of Malakh, Heilig instead of Kadosh, Lang instead of Arokh, Goldschmied instead of Tzoref.

In the time of the monarchy, a Jew from Bohemia or Moravia who wanted to succeed, to improve his lot in life, to have a career, moved to the capital Vienna. The families of many of the famous Jewish scholars and artists in Vienna hailed from Bohemia, and nearby Moravia: Freud, Mahler, Karl Kraus; the writers Herman Baruch, Franz Werfel, Leo Perutz; the philosophers Josef Popper-Lynkeus and Edmund Husserl; the leader of the Austrian Social Democrats, Victor Adler, and Bruno Kreisky, the Chancellor of Austria from 1970 to 1973. Some of their family members continued to live in the crown lands; in 1918 these became Czechoslovakia, which was reduced to a Protectorate and finally, for them, reduced further into the Terezin ghetto and into the lists

13 Jiří Weil, *Life with a Star*, Northwestern University, Evanston, Ill, November 1998.

14 Jan Podlesák, "Stříbrnou polnicí zpívejte píseň svobody: Život a dílo Jiřího Weila, *Židovská ročenka* (1989–1999), p. 108.

15 Simon Hock–David Kaufmann, *Die Familien Prags nach den Epitaphen des Alten Jüdischen Friedhofs in Prag* (Pressburg, 1892).

of transports, which included eight Werfels, fifty-five Freuds, and 106 Mahlers (one named Gustav). If they had not escaped in time, Sigmund Freud, Franz Werfel and other famous men would have followed the same path, because Jews from Vienna were also sent to the Terezin ghetto and from there to extermination.

When they became associated with the Czech national liberation movement at the end of the nineteenth and beginning of the twentieth century, the Jews of Bohemia and Moravia began to translate their names – often into the Czech source from the Middle Ages. Albert Österreicher (1862–1935), the beloved Czech Jewish writer and creator of the charming characters Modche and Rezi, chose the pseudonym Vojtěch Rakous, a verbatim translation of his German name. Schwarz became Černý; Kurtz, Krátký; Sonnenschein, Slunsky; and Wasserman, Vodička. This tendency intensified in the time of the Republic and became a sweeping wave at the end of World War II. A change of name was not always helpful: Rudolph Slánský, originally Salzman, general secretary of the Communist party after the war, was arrested and tried first and foremost as a Jew. His roots, which no ideology could uproot, are attested to by a story from his interrogation. Eugen Löbl, the former Minister for Foreign Trade, was among the accused in the 1951 show trial. He was one of the few not sentenced to death and hence able to write his memoirs. After days and nights of interrogation, when his strength had run out, Löbl confessed to the crimes attributed to him and was required to repeat his confession before the main accused, the prisoner Slánský, who was also then only a shadow of his former self. After each sentence in his confession, such as: "As a member of the group of conspirators under Slánský's leadership, I did..." he added the Hebrew word *oser* (forbid) as Czech Jews did when they wanted to deny what they had just said (sometimes, they said *az oser*). Slánský understood and for a moment his face lit up. They both knew: the verdict had been decided before the trial.[16] Indeed, when the outer layers were removed, all

16 Wilma Iggers, ed., *Die Juden in Böhmen und Mähren* (Munich: C.H. Beck, 1986), pp. 367–370.

that was left were two Jews accused of poisoning wells, just like in the Middle Ages.

♦

If I mentioned in connection to one name or another that it appeared in the fourteenth or fifteenth century, that does not mean it did not exist even earlier. However, sources from the time of the early settlement of Jews in Bohemia are scarce, and they rarely contain first names of individuals. Our earliest knowledge about Jewish merchants in Prague from around the year 965 comes from a Jewish traveler of Spanish or North African descent, Ibrahim ben Yakub. It is known that the Jews in Bohemia fought alongside the Christians against the pagans[17] and, until they found more respectable occupations, engaged, among others, in the slave trade. It is also known that they were regarded as *servi camerae Regis* (servants of the royal chamber), the property of the ruler, and thus enjoyed his protection (for which they paid). The first Jew mentioned by name is Podiva, which means strange, and the castle he built in the eleventh century is called Podivín to this day. Podiva converted to Christianity, but it is not clear whether he built his castle before or after his conversion.[18] Hedwig Podivin, born in 1920, was sent to Terezin only in January 1945 and listed as "married to an Aryan." Kosmas, the first Bohemian historiographer (who died in 1125), who does not conceal his dislike of Jews, tells about the massacre and forced conversion of the Jews during the First Crusade (in 1096), but does not relate that they had weapons and bravely resisted their attackers with the help of the Duke Boleslav, nor does it mention that they returned to Judaism after the storm died down.

Lists of names from the first centuries of Jewish settlement in Bohemia and Moravia were lost in repeated fires and pogroms. From the sixteenth century, population censuses of Jews were occasionally carried out (in particular for tax purposes and for restricting their right of residence), and all the real estate transactions of

17 Bondy-Dworsky, *Zur Geschichte der Juden*, no. 3.
18 Bondy-Dworsky, *Zur Geschichte der Juden*, no. 4.

inhabitants of the Jewish Town in Prague (as well as in other cities) were recorded in the municipal ledgers of the neighboring Old Town, as was customary for the Christians. Most of these records were preserved. They contain not only records of purchases and sales of a whole house or an apartment inside a house, but also of one room, which was often inhabited by an entire family. The overcrowded conditions inside the walls of the Jewish quarter of Prague were horrendous: according to a 1702 census, 11,517 Jews lived there, 20 and even 30 families in one house. This overcrowding was surpassed only in the Terezin ghetto, 240 years later, when up to 57,000 people were confined in an area of less than 800 square meters.

Only from 1783, during the reign of the Emperor Joseph II, were the births, marriages and deaths of the Jews registered in an orderly manner, like those of the Christian populations, under the supervision of the priesthood.[19] The order that duplicate copies of the registry books be kept did not change throughout the generations and proved its effectiveness during World War II. Although during Nazi rule some of the Jewish registry books were destroyed, at least the copies were preserved, sometimes in hiding places.

Anyone taking pride in a centuries-old family tree based on the registry ledger of inhabitants cannot know for sure who his forefathers were (not only in Czechoslovakia, and not only among the Jews). Soldiers of the invading, occupying and retreating armies, as well as forbidden love, often resulted in extramarital pregnancies that were concealed by a hasty match and by adoption. In previous centuries such family secrets were kept deep inside the drawers of the cupboard or of the heart. And the truth – if it were ever disclosed – was learned only generations later. One example is the story of the März family. Early in March 1811, at the height of the Napoleonic campaigns eastward, after the battle at Austerlitz

19 Vladimir Hrubý, "Entstehung und Entwicklung der Jüdischen Matriken in Böhmen," *Bohemiae Judaica* XVII/2 (1981), pp. 91–95. I possess a poverty certificate issued in 1857 to Františka Windspruch. The certificate for the Jewish woman was written in Czech and in Gothic letters by the priest of the village of Nalešice (from Irma Polak's estate).

(Slávkov) in Moravia and before the Russian campaign, an infant was found on the border between the Christian part and the autonomous Jewish quarter of the city of Ungarisch Brod (Uherský Brod in Czech) in southern Moravia. The community adopted the infant, and he grew up as a Jew and bore the name David März.[20] Seventeen of his descendants were on the transport that left Uherský Brod on 31 January 1943. None of them survived.

Deserters from the French army who came to the region during the Napoleonic War early in the nineteenth century settled in Bohemia, married Czech women (or met these women before deserting), and taught the Czech villagers how to expand their use of domestic knitting machines and to manufacture not only colorful stockings that were part of the Czech folk costume, but also fezzes, the traditional craft of the Huguenots, the French Protestants. Several Jews from the city of Strakonice in southern Bohemia, where they lived from the fifteenth century and perhaps earlier, financed this home industry, found ways to improve the manufacture of felt, and laid the foundations for the fez industry of Strakonice and Písek; later their products became well known worldwide. The Fürth and Zucker families were among the founders of this prosperous industry and were associated with it until the pogroms. One hundred Fürths and twenty-seven Zuckers left on the transports, from southern Bohemia too, where their forefathers had lived.

As if the repeated plagues, harsh religious oppression and aggressive missionary activity of the Jesuits were not bad enough, bitter internal struggles were fought among the Jews themselves. Sometimes these struggles were so unrestrained that Jews went so far as to inform on their co-religionists to the authorities. The well-known cross on the Charles bridge in Prague that bears the mocking Hebrew inscription in gold letters: "*Kadosh, kadosh, kadosh, Adonai tzva'ot*" ("Holy, holy, holy is the Lord of Hosts"), served for centuries as proof of the humiliation of the Jews. But some blame also falls on the Jews: Eliahu Backoffen, who in 1693 was forced to pay for this inscription as punishment for having blasphemed the

20 David Paul März, *The Geneaology of a Jewish Moravian Family (the März Family)*, (Hebrew) (Jerusalem: Private Publishing, 1983).

Christian faith, was the victim of a false libel. Abraham Aharon, a member of a faction competing for key positions in the community, informed on him, and Backoffen's trial in fact ruined his public standing.[21] Five Backoffens remained in the Protectorate; all five went to their deaths.

In the 1560s, the Jews of Prague were compelled by order of the Archbishop to visit St. Clement's church every week to hear the priest Heinrich Blyssemius from Bonn preach there in German and "Jewish." It turns out, however, that his effort was in vain, because the Jewish listeners closed off not only their minds but their ears as well.[22] Only three converted, one of whom was Moses Černý (black), a wealthy Jew. He was baptized in the church in the Castle complex and from then on was called Jeronymus. His wife and son Jakob, however, "remained faithful to their Jewish heresy." Dinah, Černý's wife, known in the Czech sources as Zdena, died in 1580 and was buried in the old cemetery: "Here lies dear Dinah, with God's help she rose early, to pray with fervor." Her son Jakob, known as Koníř (namely a horse dealer), remained a Jew, had children, bought a house in the Jewish Town of Prague for himself and his eldest son Aaron, and that same year also purchased the house of his father, the Christian Jeronymus, that stood between the homes of Samuel Portugali and Yakov Uher (Ungar).[23] Almost three centuries later (280 years to be exact), twenty-six Jews, all from Prague, carried the name Konirsch (Konjirsch, Koníř). None of them survived.

♦

The names of the Jews bear witness to their wanderings. The country of their origin is often added to their Hebrew name to distinguish between all the Moses, Abrahams, Jacobs, Isaacs – Hungarian, German, Austrian, Italian, English, Turkish, sometimes

21 Putik, "The Prague Jewish Community," p. 80.

22 Bondy-Dworsky, *Zur Geschichte der Juden*, no. 627.

23 Muneles, *Inscriptions from the Ancient Jewish Cemetery*, Tombstone No. 124; Bondy-Dworsky, *Zur Geschichte der Juden*, no. 462.

in German: Türk, Engländer, Welsch, Österreicher, Deutscher, Ungar; sometimes in Czech: Wallach, Rus, Rakous, Uher, Němec, Turek (in 1510 it was still common to write: "Zalman known as Turk"). They continued to bear the designations of their country of origin as surnames – and they are all included on the list of transports. Poland was the closest, so Jews expelled from Bohemia and Moravia fled there; and from Poland came Jews persecuted in pogroms, like Bogdan Chmielnitzi's Cossack revolt in the mid-seventeenth century that devastated hundreds of Jewish communities in Eastern Europe. Polák, and its diminutive form Poláček, little Pole, was therefore a very common name: over a thousand expelled Jews of Bohemia and Moravia bore that name, thirty-five of them called Josef Polák. Their last journey took them back to the land their forefathers had left.

Sometimes, instead of the name of their country of origin, their city of origin in another country was added to the first name: The city of Vienna (Wien, Wiener) was the most popular of these (137 such names appear on the transport lists). Frank, to denote an origin in Franconia, namely France, was not unique to the Jews of Bohemia, but more than 250 of the deportees had that name in one of its derivative forms (Frank, Frenkel, Franke, Fränkl). One of them was Jakob Frank, with the same name as the founder of the messianic sect of Frankists who, in the eighteenth century, agitated Bohemia and Moravia's Jews and found disciples and supporters among them.[24] In March 1942, 79-year-old Jakob Frank was taken from the city of Brno, where his predecessor had found refuge in 1786, to the Terezin ghetto, where he died four months later.

The names Böhm or Czech, Čech, also attested to the wandering of the Jews. Only a Jew who left Bohemia for another country was called Böhm there, and when times changed and the rulers were replaced by others, he or his offspring returned to the land that seemed the lesser of two evils. About 200 Jews with the name Böhm, Čech or Czech, again left their homeland on their way to the unknown. One of them was 72-year-old Dr. Ludwig Czech,

24 From 1773 to 1777, Frank found refuge in Brno with the help of his cousin Shendel Dobruschka. See also note 55 below.

leader of the German Social Democrats in Czechoslovakia and Minister of Social Welfare on behalf of that party. It was the tangle of identities personified: a Jew whose name is Czech, who headed the largest German party in Czechoslovakia (until the victory of Henlein's Nazi party in 1935) and died in July 1942 as a prisoner in the ghetto.

In previous centuries, the distances between one place and another seemed greater, and even a Jew who came to Prague from one of the regions of the Bohemian kingdom bore a stamp of foreignness: Morawetz, Moravec – for someone from Moravia; Hanák – for someone from the fertile region of Haná in Moravia; and Sachs, Sachsl, Saxl, Sax – for someone from neighboring Saxonia with which the Jews of Bohemia had strong commercial ties, particularly through Leipzig, the city of fairs. Even though Slovakia was also a neighboring country, none of the Jews in the Protectorate were called Slovak. Several of them did bear the name of its capital, Pressburg, in German. The newness of recent arrivals was denoted in their names – Novák, Nováček, Novotný, Neumann – and they carried these names for generations; 570 remained new until their deportation.

The source of hundreds of surnames of Czech Jews was the city, town or village where their forefathers lived – Pacovský, Rychnovský, Turnovský, Utitz, Kolín, Pribram, Nachod – and so on. Sometimes, the name of the place of origin was preserved in Hebrew initials: ל"ש (Lasch) – for Jews from Lichtenstatdt, נ"ש (Nasch) – for those from Neustadt. Several Jews whose name came from their place of origin became world renowned. The name Pulitzer, founder of the prestigious American prize for journalism, refers to Police, Politz in German, the village in Moravia from which his family came (eighteen Jews with the name Pulitzer left on transports). The surname of the Petscheks, the wealthiest Jews of Czechoslovakia, the local version of the Rothschilds, originated in the town of Petschau (Bečov in Czech) in northern Bohemia. Their money also helped them during the German occupation: no one with the esteemed name of Petschek remained in the Protectorate until the transports began. Their capital ransomed them.

Some Jews bearing surnames that originated in Czech towns

achieved greatness. The name Brandes or Brandeis comes from the city of Brandýs on the banks of the Elba River, northeast of Prague. The most famous man with that name is Louis Dembitz Brandeis, the son of parents who emigrated from Prague to the United States (in the wave of emigration of Bohemian Jews following the failure of the 1848 revolution), who became the first Jewish justice in the United States Supreme Court. For generations, the Brandeises were among the most respected Jews of Prague. The names of about 200 of them are engraved on tombstones in the old cemetery; sixty with that name remained trapped in the Protectorate.

For centuries, only a few Jewish families were permitted to live in Taus (Domažlice in Czech), a city in southern Bohemia. Their descendants, however, must have been very fecund and dispersed throughout the whole land because the name Taus, Tausk, Tausik, Domažlický, Taussig was one of the most common among Czech Jews. One of them was Jakob Tausk, a poor teacher from Prague, Shabbetai Zevi's trusted disciple, who in 1666 wrote in Yiddish "A New Fine Poem on the Messiah: to gladden the hearts of the Jews awaiting redemption."[25] More than 550 Jews bearing the name of the city of Taus in its various forms are on the list of transports, including 17 Anna Taussigs and 15 Karl Taussigs. The conductor of the new Czech national theater in Prague, inaugurated in 1881 to bolster the spirit of the Czechs in their struggle against the Austrian monarchy, was Adolf Taussig, a native of Taus (1841–1903), but he preferred to be called Adolf Čech.

The name Kapper symbolized the aspiration of Bohemia's Jews to be an inseparable part of the Czech nation. Siegfried Kapper, a physician and writer (1821–1879), the son of a glazier, thought of himself as a Jewish member of the Czech nation even though he wrote most of his literary work in German: "Only do not say I am not a Czech/Like you I am a son of the Czech soil!" he wrote in the periodical, *České listy* ("Czech Leaves") in 1846. However, Karel Havlíček Borovský, the proponent of Czech nationalism, rejected Kapper's ideas of interaction. Judaism, he stated, is not only a ques-

25 Gershom Scholem, *Shabbetai Zevi* (New Haven: Princeton University Press, 1976), p. 538.

tion of religion, but also of race and nationality, and anyone who wants to be a Czech must desist from being a Jew; and if he wants to be an assimilated Jew, he had best stick to German. Kapper was not dissuaded; he did not give up his Judaism, and became one of the fathers of the Movement of Czech Jews. The Association of Czech Jewish Academics bore his name.[26] Nor was anyone saved by Czechness: sixteen Kappers were deported from their homeland because they were members of the Jewish people.

The name of the city of Hořovice, 50 kilometers southwest of Prague, where Jews had settled as far back as the fifteenth century, flourished more than all the others. The entire tribe of Horovský, Gurwicz, Gurewitsch, Hurwitch, Horvitz, Hurwitz, Horwitz, Horowitz, and Ish-Horowitz sprang from there, established a dynasty of rabbis and judges in Poland, Lithuania, Austria, Hungary, Bohemia and Moravia, and spread throughout the world, even to Palestine. Isaiah ben Abraham Halevi Horowitz, "Ha-Shela ha-Kadosh," immigrated there after the death of his wife in 1621 and settled in Jerusalem. In the sixteenth century, the Horowitz family was one of the wealthiest families in Prague and, thanks to its affluence, enjoyed many privileges, including the right given in 1535 to Aaron Meshulam Horowitz, known as Zalman Munka, to establish a private house of prayer, today's Pinkas synagogue in which the names of all the victims of the Holocaust in Bohemia and Moravia are inscribed, including thirty Jews with the venerable name Horowitz.

Today Libeň is a suburb in Prague, but in the past it was a village in the shadow of a noble castle and served as the first station for Jews when they were repeatedly expelled from the capital, particularly during the expulsion ordered by Maria Theresa. In the nineteenth century, the inhabitants of Libeň whose place of residence became their surname spread throughout the monarchy. Unlike the majority of the Jewish population, the Liebens of Prague (their original family name was Menaker, remover of veins, because the cattle dealers of Libeň supplied kosher meat to the Jewish quarter

26 Josef Vyskočil, "Die tschechisch-jüdische Bewegung," *Bohemiae Judaica* III/1(Prague: Státní Židovské Muzeum, 1967), pp. 36–39.

of Prague) were still strictly religiously observant in the twentieth century. Among them were Dr. Salomon Hugo Lieben, a historian and the founder of the Jewish museum in Prague (in 1906), and Dr. Salomon Lieben, a humanitarian physician whose clinic was open to everyone in need. After the German occupation when all the general hospitals were closed to Jews, Dr. Lieben converted the Jewish orphanage in Prague into a hospital and rented an apartment in the Old Town to house the old people who had been thrown out of the general institutions. He was arrested by the Gestapo (his family believed the reason was a research book he had written to prove that kosher slaughtering was less cruel than any other method) and in 1942 died in the Dachau concentration camp.[27] In 1942–1943, the other Liebens, forty-eight in number and still imbued with religious faith, were sent to the Terezin ghetto and from there eastward. Two returned from the extermination camps.

♦

This was an educated Jewry. Of every one thousand deportees there was an average of fifty to one hundred with degrees as doctors or engineers, and the degree stayed with them even after they had been divested of everything else. Next to their names on the list of transports, they are faithfully recorded: Dr.Ing., JUDr., MUDr. On the transport designated B, which left for the Łódź ghetto on 21 October 1941 with one thousand men, women and children, there were 293 doctors and engineers, some of them with two degrees, and quite a few women with an academic degree. In fact, in Czechoslovakia, people used to joke that every Jewish mother wants to be able to say "my son, the doctor," but it took hundreds of years until Jews were allowed to attend the University of Prague, which was founded in 1348 and run by the Catholic Jesuit establishment. The Emperor Charles IV graciously granted the university that bore his name several Jewish homes close by to be used as student dormitories – and those were the first to supply rioters

27 Bondy, *Elder of the Jews*, p. 148; Mordechai Livni (Lieben), interview with the author, Tivon, October 2000.

in repeated pogroms against the Jewish Town. Universities in Italy and Germany had a less rigid attitude toward Jewish students, and it was there that Jewish doctors from Bohemia earned their first academic degrees: Salomon Gomperz (1662–1728) and Abraham Kisch, son of Jakob the pharmacist (1725–1803).[28]

Since time immemorial, there have been Jewish physicians who were not certified medical doctors but had learned the profession from their fathers. These Jewish physicians were highly respected, and even though they were forbidden to treat Christian patients, they were often called into the home of a nobleman or even to the royal court. The Jewish doctor Angelik, probably originally Malakh or Malakhi, treated King Vladislav and in 1489 also gained the right to purchase a house in the Small Quarter at the foot of the Hradčany castle so he would be close to the royal court.[29] The names of sixteen doctors in Prague between 1482 and 1561 are known, all of them registered under their Hebrew name: Abraham, David, Moses, Ben Meir, Meir ben Daniel. One of the first tombstones (in the year 1492) in the ancient Jewish cemetery of Prague belongs to Gedalia: "A very capable physician, righteous too, always prepared a good deed to do." A later, more opulent tombstone (1665) is that of Joseph Solomon Rofé (Del Medigo) – a mathematician, astronomer and master of many languages: "The glorified rabbi, scholar, divine, and mighty one among physicians, great teacher and rabbi Joseph Rofé of Candia [Crete], head of the rabbinical court in Hamburg and the district of Amsterdam, son of the revered Reb Elijah Delmegido, of blessed memory."[30]

There were families in Prague – Jeiteles, Leon, Gumperz, Kisch – that produced physicians for generations. On the Ck transport that left Prague on 22 December 1942, was one of them: Dr. Joseph Kisch, and his wife Maria. His surname came from the name of the Bohemian village Chiesch or Chýše, but for centuries

28 Bondy-Dworsky, *Zur Geschichte der Juden*, no. 166.

29 Guideo Kisch, "Die Prager Universität und die Juden," *Jahrbuch der Gesellschaft für die Geschichte der Juden in der Čechoslovakischen Republik (JGGJ)* (Prague: Samuel Steinherz, 1929–1937), pp. 1–67.

30 Muneles, *Inscriptions from the Ancient Jewish Cemetery*, Tombstone No. 9, 220.

Kisch or Kysch families lived in Prague and from there went out into the world, among other countries to England. There, Herman Michael Kisch enlisted in His Majesty's service in India, and his son, Frederick Herman, is the famous Lt. Colonel F. H. Kisch, a member of the Zionist executive and Weizmann's right-hand man, who fell in World War II. A moshav, forest and streets in Israel are named after him. The Kisch family produced rabbis, scholars and historians, but the best known in modern times is probably Egon Erwin Kisch (1885–1948), the "Raging Reporter," the father of investigative journalism who exposed scandals (such as the case of Colonel Redl). Kisch, a loyal Communist, managed to escape the Nazis' clutches in 1939, first to the United States and later to Mexico. However, twenty-two other members of the Kisch family went in the opposite direction. None of them returned.

Even after the Jews gained permission to study at the German University of Prague in the eighteenth century, it took many more years until they were also allowed to defend their doctoral theses publicly as did the other candidates for a degree, and close to one hundred more years until Jews were also accepted to the academic staff. Wolfgang Wessely was the first to be appointed full professor (of rabbinical Hebrew and literature) in 1861. According to a venerable custom, the most senior member of the academic staff was elected as Rector when the position was vacated by the death of his predecessor, and when a Jewish professor was next in turn for that honor he was expected to politely refuse to accept such a distinguished position. In 1922, however, the senior member of the staff was Professor Samuel Steinherz, a medieval historian, and he was not prepared to play by those rules. He declared that he felt himself to be a German who acted like a German, so there was no way out but to elect him Rector. His appointment, however, provoked student demonstrations and unrest on the academic staff of the Charles University. A year later, Prof. Steinherz saw fit to resign.[31] From then on, he devoted his major studies to the history of Bohemian and Moravian Jewry. In July 1942, 85-year-old Prof. Steinherz was sent to the Terezin ghetto and died there in Decem-

31 Kisch, "Die Prager Universität," p. 29.

ber of that year. On 22 September, he still managed to deliver a lecture in the ghetto entitled, "Small Pictures from the Life of the Jews in Bohemia."[32] Ghettos, persecutions, expulsions: everything happened, everything passed, everything recurred.

Leopold Hilsner (1869–1928), a somewhat odd shoemaker from the town of Polná, was the victim of the last traditional blood libel in Bohemia. In 1899, he was accused of murdering the Czech girl Anežka Hrůzová for ritual purposes and was sentenced to death. His sentence was commuted to life imprisonment, and Hilsner stayed in prison for eighteen years until he was granted amnesty in 1916. He never married nor did he have any children. During the years of the false libel, his mother Maria used the surname Himmelreich, but his name and the name of the affair, known as Hilsneriáda, stirred emotions in Bohemia and Moravia, arousing a wave of virulent antisemitism and mass psychosis. It was never erased from the historical memory of either Jews or Czechs. The only Hilsner left in the Protectorate was Růžena, born in 1860. On 6 July 1942, she left Prague for the Terezin ghetto and died there two months later. In September 2000, a museum of Jewish history in Polná, first mentioned in written sources in 1532, was opened in the ancient synagogue there. There are no longer any Jews in Polná.

In the days of the mass hysteria and window breaking following Hilsner's trial, Vojtěch Rakous wrote:

> In fact, if a man should decide to convert to Christianity… only to think that a few drops of holy water will suffice so that no only he, but also his children and their offspring, will escape all the evil, all the humiliations and the suffering… a few drops will suffice so that the slave will become a man! If only we wanted that! But we do not want that! Do not want that! We have it no worse than our forefathers did! Antisemitism is as old as Judaism.[33]

32 Elena Makarova, Sergei Makarov, Victor Kuperman, *University over the Abyss* (Jerusalem: Verba Publishers, 2000), p. 450.

33 Vojtěch Rakous, *Rozbitá okna, Židovská Ročenka*, (Prague, 1990–1991), p. 54.

The Jews began admiring Tomáš Garrigue Masaryk, the founder of the Czechoslovakian Republic and its first president, during Hilsner's trial when he fearlessly came to Hilsner's defense, to defend Christian faith against prejudice, as he defined his action. His opponents claimed he had received bribes from the Jews; Czech students demonstrated against him, and the Czech press went wild. As Masaryk told the writer Karel Čapek in the 1930s: "During the war, I understood why that was beneficial: the world press is controlled by Jews or partially financed by them. They knew me from the Hilsner trial, and now they returned the favor, and wrote about our cause with sympathy or at least fairness. From a political standpoint, that helped us very much."[34] Behold, even this eminent humanist and protector of the Jews was not free of prejudice when it came to the Jews' control of the world (if only he'd been right!).

The name Masaryk comes from the word *masař*, meaning butcher, an occupation Jews were permitted to engage in to serve the community even in the days when they were banned from most other trades. There are also Masaryks among the deportees, but the name was written somewhat differently (Masarik, Massarek) and a great many more, about four hundred, bore the name in its German forms: Fleischhacker, Fleischmann, Fleischner, Fleischl, Fleischer. It was clear to the Christians: the Jewish slaughtering laws necessitated the existence of Jewish butchers. Hence the Jewish butchers of Prague were among the first to be given the right to organize into a guild with its own emblem and pennant, which was proudly carried in festive processions.[35] In 1541, there were only two tailors, one seamstress, one wood carver, three bookbinders, one builder of mousetraps and four barbers, but there were sixteen butchers, one of whom was called Isak Krava, namely cow, and

34 Karel Čapek, *Hovory s T.G. Masarykem* (Prague: Borový, 1946), p. 74.

35 In 1593, during the reign of the Emperor Rudolph II, the Jewish butchers of Prague were obliged to supply 22 pounds of first-quality beef and veal for the lions kept by the Emperor on the palace grounds. According to the imperial orders, they were promised reimbursement for the meat. See: Bondy-Dworsky, *Zur Geschichte der Juden*, no. 890.

another was registered only on the name of Tele – a calf.[36] Four hundred years later there were still 24 Jews named Kuh (cow in German) and ten Kalb (calf in German) among the deportees, and another 140 named Rind (beef), Lamm (lamb), Beran and Widder (a ram in Czech and German).

The name Benesch, Beneš, Benisch, like that of Edward Beneš, Masaryk's right-hand man and the second president of the Czechoslovakian Republic, scion to a venerable Christian family, was shared by 186 of the deportees. The name derives from a pet name for Benjamin, and it has existed among Czech Jewry since the fifteenth century. In a list from 1546 that included the name Beneš, the name Jakub Kadeřavý, which means curly-headed Jacob in Czech, also appears. Curls remained the hallmark of the Jews, because Czechs usually had straight fair hair. Their nickname was translated into German – Kraus, one of the most common names among the Jews of Bohemia and Moravia. More than seven hundred Krauses reported for the transports, fourteen of whom were Karl Kraus, like the name of the caustic Viennese satirist, a native of Bohemia, who had nothing good to say about Jews either. He was fortunate enough to die in 1936.

In order to distinguish between Moses and Moses, Isaac and Isaac, the most common Jewish names often had nicknames attached to them that related to their owners' physical and other traits. A list of Jewish moneylenders from 1497 to 1501 included Lame (Chromý) David, Small (Malý) Samuel, Limping (Kulhavý) Moshe, Hot-tempered (Vzteklý) Peitel, and Bulge-eyed (Vokatý) Jon. There was also someone called Deaf (Hluchý) Judel, Dry (Suchý) Moshe, Toothless (Bezzubý) Isak, Crooked-mouth (Křivoústý) Enoch, and Crazy (Blázen) Simon.[37] For obvious reasons, their offspring did not continue to bear those nicknames, except for the deaf and the small: Tauber or Taub and Klein, a typical Jewish name, that of 650 of the deportees. There were fewer Jews

36 Jan Heřman, "Die Wirtschaftliche Betätigung und die Berufe der Prager Juden vor ihrer Ausweisung im Jahre 1591," *Bohemiae Judaica* IV/1 (Prague: Státni Židovské Muzeum, 1968), p. 57.

37 Bondy-Dworsky, *Zur Geschichte der Juden*, no. 294, 296.

named Gross (large) and Lang (long). Another hallmark was black and white: more than 560 Schwarzes and Černýs are included in the memorial book, in addition to dozens with black hair or black beards (Schwarzkopf, Schwarzbarth), and close to 670 Weisses, in addition to dozens with white hair or white beards (Weisskopf, Weissbarth).

♦

The Hapsburg monarchy is the cradle of the complex bureaucracy of ancient tradition (which is nowadays called Kafkaesque). It naturally wanted to introduce some order and put an end to the confusion that typified the names of the Jews, who often changed their names, so that the same man was known as both Shalom Teplitz and Shulem Shulklopper (synagogue beadle); another was registered both under the name Samuel Peperish and the name Zangwil Patsche, and even when they had a permanent surname, it was written in various forms (Moischeles, Mohscheles, Moscheles) in different languages. On 23 July 1787, the Emperor Joseph II issued an order (a Patent, as it was then called): "To prevent all the disorder that is certain to arise among a group of people in legal and political proceedings, as well as in their private lives, if the families do not adhere to a permanent surname and individuals do not bear a known first name, we decree that:" — and here came seven clauses that stated in detail the duty of the head of every Jewish family in the crown lands to report to the local authority by 30 November 1787 the permanent surname he had chosen. The report was required to be in writing, in German, and it had to note the surname and first name used until then in its German form. From that time on, they were forbidden to change their names, and penalties were set — heavy fines and even expulsion — for anyone who failed to fulfill the instructions of the Patent.[38] The imperial order also required that records be kept of the births, marriages and deaths of the Jews in German and forbade the use of Hebrew or Yiddish in public or legal documents. This was the age of the Germanization

38 Muneles, "Zur Namengebung der Juden," p. 9.

of the Jews – imposed on them but also often desired by them, because German was the language of culture, and for many, Vienna was the city of their dreams. There was, after all, a class division: the Czechs were the peasants and tradesmen, the Germans were the bourgeois, and the nobility were cosmopolitan. The Jews had only aspirations.

The Jews of Bohemia and Moravia were given the opportunity to choose a name, and the officials chose one only for those who failed to do so. Consequently, complex, often meaningless or derisive names, such as Reibeisen (grater), Krummholz (crooked wood) or Gartentzaun (fence), were relatively rare in comparison to Galicia, which was also part of the Austro-Hungarian monarchy. I assume that most names of this type came to Czechoslovakia from there. Generally, the Jews of Bohemia and Moravia preferred brief names that were not hard to pronounce, such as Freund (556 in the transport lists), Heller (575), Spitz and Spitzer (522), Stein and Steiner (more than one thousand).

Currency trade and money lending were the main occupations in which Jews were allowed to have contacts with Christians, and many Jews did engage in them, particularly lending money against interest – an occupation forbidden to Christians for religious reasons. The Christians needed loans, but they hated the lenders and the interest payments, which were high (as much as 86 percent per annum) because of the great risk that the money might not be repaid. On repeated occasions, one ruler or another would cancel all the promissory notes held by the Jews in order to relieve himself of the burden of debt; sometimes the notes were burned together with the homes of the Jews; and many times orders were issued setting the permitted rate of interest, but they were not observed because the needs of the market determined the rate. It is doubtful that in the twentieth century those with the name Kauders or Kauder knew that in ancient German it meant usury. The transport lists included 135 Kauders plus several dozen Borgers (lenders) and Wechslers (money changers). The only Kauders family to survive Terezin in entirety, thanks to the father's professional knowledge in electronics, changed their name to Klíma after the war. The eldest son, born in 1931, is the Czech writer Ivan Klíma, a member of the circle of dissidents during the Communist regime. Only years later, through one of his protagonists, did he reveal to his readers that he had spent his childhood in the Terezin ghetto.

With the rising competition by Christians in the money market (and there were Christians who preferred to borrow money from Jews than from members of the nobility or the monasteries, because in their view they exploited them less), the Jews had to find other means of livelihood. Although they were permitted to engage in trades only within the Jewish community, and Christian artisans, fearing competition, did not take Jews as apprentices to learn their trade with them, the Jews did acquire occupational skills, sometimes with the help of tradesmen from Poland, where the Jews were freer. When the barriers were broken, Jews proudly took the names of the trades they engaged in: Glaser (glazier), Färber (painter), Knöpflmacher (button maker), Schleifer (grinder), Stecklmacher (heel maker), Kürschner (furrier), Gerber (tanner), Perlhefter (baster of pearls), Goldsticker (gold embroiderer), Töpfer (potter), Schnurmacher (string maker), Schneider (tailor), Drechsler (turner), Mautner (collector of toll fees on roads and bridges), and Lederer (leather worker). Recorded in the memorial book are two hundred Mautners, six hundred Lederers, and along with them, bartenders, or those who served beer and brandy (Bierschenk, Brandweinschenk) – a common Jewish occupation – who were called by the Hebrew initials ב״ש, pronounced Basch, to shorten their names or to conceal their line of work (98 with this name appeared on the transport lists).

There were also Jewish occupations needed specifically by the community: Schuldiener (beadle), Taucher (ritual bathhouse attendant), Koch (cook), and various kinds of musicians (who, despite the prohibition, were also invited to celebrations of Christians and even of the nobility[39]): Fiedler, Geiger, Horner, Zimbalist, Musikant, Spielmann. In 1941, an entire orchestra was still left: 300 men, women and children had the names of musicians, and

39 At the wedding of the noble Peter Vok von Rosenberg in 1580, "the dance orchestra of the Jews from Prague played very beautifully," see: Bondy-Dworsky, *Zur Geschichte der Juden*, no. 1331.

another 350 were called Singer, which means both a singer and a cantor. People engaged in the world of books were the aristocracy of the artisans: Schreiber (writer), Buchbinder (bookbinder), and especially Drucker (printer). The printing of Hebrew books had a long tradition in Prague, where the first Hebrew book, *Sefer zemirot uvirkat hamazon* (The Book of Sabbath Songs and Blessing of the Food) was printed in 1514. The printer was Gershom ha-Kohen, the founder of a dynasty of printers called Gershons. Gershom ben Solomon ha-Kohen is recorded in contemporary Czech sources under the name Herman Impresor (namely, Gershom the printer), to whom in 1527 Ferdinand I granted the monopoly to print Hebrew books[40] – most likely in exchange for a hefty payment to the king's treasury. Thus the Hermans (Herrmann, Hermann), my mother's family name, entered into the history of Czech Jewry. Eight hundred people bearing this name were on the lists of transports – but not a single Gershon or Gershom.

Some of those engaged in the various occupations ought to have been recorded in the feminine gender because women also worked in commerce and certain trades. In 1729, the population census of residents of the Jewish Town of Prague recorded 2,229 wage earners, including a large number of women who engaged in the same occupations as men: there were thirty-seven male butchers and seven female butchers in the city; sixty-four men and ten women dealt in money changing. Along with the tailors – the most popular occupation in the Jewish Town at the time – there were scores of seamstresses, one of them an expert in sewing trousers. There were female shoemakers, cooks, merchants, furriers, agents, one water carrier, one printer, two midwifes and one doctor – Zelda, the daughter of Loebel the barber.[41]

When the competition between the Christian artisans and tradesmen and their Jewish counterparts, some of whom also sold

40 Salomon Hugo Lieben, "Der hebräische Buchdruck in Prag im 16 Jahrhundert," *Die Juden in Prag*, Prag, 1927, pp. 93–99. See: Bondy-Dworsky, *Zur Geschichte der Juden*, no. 522.

41 Jaroslav Prokesch, "Die Prager Judenkonskription vom Jahre 1729," *JGGJ* IV (1932), pp. 297–332.

their products, grew more intense, the former repeatedly applied to the authority, asking not only that it prohibit the Jews from engaging in trades and commerce, but that it also expel them from the city (and not only from Prague), or at least reduce their number and impose a *numerus clauses* in commerce. In a request submitted in 1791, representatives of the Old and New Towns of Prague claimed that competition with the "avaricious" Jews had led to the economic ruin of Bohemia. To be on the safe side, they also added an accusation that they poisoned medicines and wells.[42]

For centuries, "in the good old days," the only commerce Jews were allowed to engage in, in addition to dealing with money, was trading in used objects. The heart of this commerce was the flea market in the Old Town of Prague, the Tandelmarkt, where the Jews leased a place for stalls and storerooms from the Christians, the citizens of the Old Town. All traces of this livelihood of the past, engaged in by thousands of Jews, seem to have been erased. In the Protectorate, during the deportations only twenty-four still bore the name Tandler, from the word *Tand*, meaning things of no value. The name Kaufmann, a merchant, designated a different status that could be preserved (187 on the transport list).

The name of the foodstuff they dealt in – salt, sugar, rye, pepper, spices, wine (Salz, Zucker, Korn, Pfeffer, Gewürz, Wein) – stuck to the Jew, at first as a nickname and later as an enduring surname. In 1348, the Emperor Charles IV founded a new city (Nové Město, Neustadt) that bordered on the Old Town of Prague, fixed its boundaries, and exempted those settling there from paying taxes for twelve years. Jews, along with their sons and daughters, were permitted to live there and they too were exempt from taxes, on condition that they lived there permanently and built their houses from stone.[43] On the slopes above the new city, the king's vineyards were planted (to this day the quarter is called Vinohrady in Czech, Weinberge in German), and the Jews also grew grapes and manufactured wine. After some time, they were expelled from the new city, but the name Weinberger remained. It was the name

42 Bondy-Dworsky, *Zur Geschichte der Juden*, no. 249.
43 Bondy-Dworsky, *Zur Geschichte der Juden*, no. 57.

of the well-known Jewish Czech composer, Jaromír Weinberger (1896–1967) and of the former U.S. Secretary of Defense, Caspar Weinberger, as well as of more than 200 Jews who left on the transports.

The Jews of Prague are mentioned in this study more frequently than the Jews of the villages, towns and other cities, not only because Prague was the largest Jewish center but because more material on it is available. There is just as much to write about the Jews in most of the cities of Bohemia and Moravia, on the expulsions, the pogroms, and the repeated attempts to integrate. In the sixteenth century, the Jews were forbidden to live or stay in the silver mine cities, such as Kutná Hora, because they were accused of smuggling silver and damaging coins. There were cities – Jihlava, Litoměřice, Brno, Olomouc, Žatec and others – from which the Jews were exiled "in perpetuity" that sometimes lasted until the nineteenth century. In Eger in northern Bohemia, the community was destroyed and rebuilt five times from the thirteenth century until it was finally annihilated during the Nazi period; twenty-five Jews bore the name of that city until their death. In one place they were burned at the stake, in another their homes were set on fire. In many places, the Christian citizens asked the King for the right to live in a city that was free of Jews – and always the Jews started all over again, made do with very little, used connections with their families and other Jews dispersed throughout Europe for their commerce, and became established until the next blow, and still kept multiplying – as much as they were allowed. For from the eighteenth century, the Familiants' Law was in force, which limited the number of Jewish families in Bohemia to 8,541 and in Moravia to 5,106, and only the eldest son was permitted to marry and establish a family. The other sons had to remain bachelors or emigrate, or they could live as a married couple in secret, in constant danger of punishment and expulsion – a danger that also hung over the head of the rabbi who married them.

The great rabbis whose names were linked with Prague were not born there, nor did they remain there to serve until their death, either because of squabbles inside the community, or because of informers or arrest, they were called to serve elsewhere, or old age. David Oppenheim was born in 1664 in Worms in Germany and was called to the rabbinate of Prague in 1702. Later he also served as the chief rabbi of half of the state of Bohemia, but his name was always linked with Prague and he was buried there in 1736. His tombstone is inscribed with words of praise: "Had a fine command of the Babylonian and the Jerusalem Talmud as well as the Tosafot: David revealed the Talmud to others… David was a shepherd and leader for fifty years, edified many pupils, and wrote innumerable books."[44] David Oppenheim is in fact regarded as the father of Jewish bibliography. Because of the strict censorship imposed on books belonging to Jews, he prudently removed his collection of books and rare manuscripts from the boundaries of the monarchy, and it is now in the Bodleian Library in Oxford. The censors examined not only books before they were printed and sold, but also books already kept in the houses of study and in private homes. Censors with a knowledge of Hebrew examined every book; any reference to the Talmud or the Kabbalah was unacceptable, because those books were considered damaging to the Christian religion. Thousands of rejected books were set on fire.[45] Until the transports began, seventy-five Oppenheims remained in their forefathers' chosen land, and most of them came to the same end as the books.

His name indicates that R. Jonathan Eibenschütz's family descended from the ancient community of Ivančice in Moravia. In 1715 as a young rabbi he came to Prague, where he became head of the yeshivah and a popular sermonizer. Later he became the city's chief rabbi, a genius in Talmud and Kabbalah, and an adjudicator who did not barricade himself inside the past. In 1742 or 1743, when the city was under siege by the French army, he permitted the Jews of Prague to work building fortifications on the Day of Atonement, because in his view, no religion should stand in the way of the state's final objective or place any obstacles in its path.[46]

44 Muneles, *Inscriptions from the Ancient Jewish Cemetery*, Tombstone No. 232.

45 Bondy-Dworsky, *Zur Geschichte der Juden*, No. 1340.

46 Ludwig Singer, "Zur Geschichte der Juden in Böhmen in den letzten Jahren Josefs II," *JGGJ* VI (1934), pp. 230, 249–270.

The last to bear his name, Martin and Helena Eibenschütz and their 17-year-old daughter Mariana, left the city of Ostrava on 26 September 1942 for the Terezin ghetto. Two weeks later, they were killed in Treblinka.

In the distant past, the Jews, all religiously observant, knew they had to work in order to earn a living, and the yeshivah students who flocked to Prague from the neighboring countries also worked as teachers in the homes of Jewish families. Their yeshiva in Prague was often proudly called the "Jewish university." In 1806, that aroused the ire of the authorities; a university is worthy of the name only if it contains four faculties; at most a yeshiva could be defined as a "High School of Talmud."[47] In 1839 the subject was raised again, when the head of the community, Moses Landau, applied to the Prague authorities for permission to establish a theological faculty of Judaism. The rabbis and community leaders, named Landau or Landa, came to Prague from other countries: Ezekiel Landau, known as "Noda bi-Yehudah" after one of his works, was born in Poland, but the name originates in the city of Landau in western Germany from which the family spread throughout the world. He and his learned descendants are buried in what was considered the new Jewish cemetery at the edges of the Žižkov quarter. The enlightened Communist regime later destroyed that cemetery with the exception of a few famous graves, and constructed a television station whose tower pierces the heavens like a threatening fist. Five Landaus were on the transports, including 14-year-old Dan and his parents, who on 26 April 1942 left for Terezin on the transport designated Am and two days later were sent from there to extermination in Zamość. Of the one thousand deportees in the Am transport, sixty-one survived.

And the greatest of them all — the rabbi, educator, mathematician and philosopher, scion of a distinguished family that originated in Worms, Germany: the Maharal of Prague (1525–1609). But if a stranger had asked a Jew in Prague during the Republic where the Maharal's grave is, he would have shrugged his shoul-

47 František Roubik, "Zur Geschichte der Juden in Böhmen in den ersten Hälfte des neunzehnten Jahrhunderts," *JGGJ* VI (1934), pp. 295–314.

ders; he wouldn't have known that name. In Prague they called Judah ben Bezalel Rabbi Löw; the few Talmudic scholars then in Prague wrote the name Liwa, and the greatest injustice done to this man, an intellectual before his time, is the close connection made between him and the legendary figure of the Golem, who may or may not have existed. The statue of the Maharal, by the Czech sculptor Ladislav Šaloun, that stood in the Old Town was removed during the time of the Nazis, hidden and returned to its place after the war. But the bearers of the Maharal's name met with a different fate: 136 Loews or Löws were on the transports and only 13 returned at the end of the war. Each day, hundreds of non-Jews place notes on the Maharal's grave in the old cemetery asking for his benevolence, which was of no avail to his people in their time of greatest need.

The zoology in the names of the Jews is not always easy to explain: Arye, Zeev, Dov (Löw, Wolf, Beer, Bär), meaning lion, wolf and bear were linked to the Bible and to the Tribes of Israel and they symbolize strength and power, but among the Jews of Bohemia and Moravia the most popular names of animals were actually the fox (Fuchs), a symbol of cunning (477 on the list), and somewhat less so the hare (Haas, Zajíček), light-footed and quick to flee (200). One was Hugo Haas (1901–1961), a popular actor in theater and film in the Republic, who in 1939 managed to flee to the United States through France. His brother, Pavel Haas, a musician and composer who never stopped creating, even in the Terezin ghetto, was sent to Auschwitz in October 1944 at the age of forty-five.

The tradition of using animals' name as surnames is not unique to the Jews of Bohemia and Moravia, but is prevalent throughout Central and Eastern Europe. However, some zoological errors have occurred in this practice: Hirsch is the noble deer with the impressive antlers (Ayal in Hebrew), and not Zvi (gazelle) as it is often translated back into Hebrew. And even worse, one of the most common zoological names in Central and Eastern Europe was Adler (the name of 409 deportees), based on the assumption that it is the correct translation of the biblical *nesher*, the proud eagle that symbolizes great size, confidence and speed (also admired by the Germans), but in the Bible the reference is usually to the vulture (*a'yit*, in Hebrew, *Geier* in German), and that bird evokes a totally different association, that of a carrion eater.

In addition to Adler and Vogel (bird), other birds accepted by the Czech Jews were the goose (Gans), the main supply of kosher fat and meat for the holidays; and the rooster (Hahn), symbol of masculinity (247 on the lists). Also used were storks, doves, jackdaws, jays, quails (Storch, Holub, Kafka, Wachtel or Sojka) and a few others. The best known goose of all was David Ben Solomon Gans (1541–1613), an astronomer and mathematician, the first historian of Judaism in Bohemia, author of *Nechmad ve-naim* and *Zemach David*. Gans was born in Lippstadt in Westphalia, but he became well known in Prague (he was even invited three times by the court astronomer Tycho Brahe to the observatory of the Emperor Rudolph II, who took an interest in the sciences and alchemy), and he was buried in the old cemetery in 1613. A goose is inscribed on his tombstone.[48] Most of those with the name Gans or Ganz in the memorial book, 190 in number, have no tombstone.

Kafka, *kavka* in Czech, means a jackdaw, and in fact, a drawing of the bird, the smallest of the ravens, was the trademark that adorned the envelopes of the business owned by Hermann Kafka, located on the main square of the Old Town of Prague, and in his youth, his son Franz often used these to send letters.[49] In my interpretation, that is the nickname that the Czech peasants, whose folk costume is colorful and bright, gave to the Jewish peddlers who regularly came to the villages (and each peddler had his own territory) because of the Jews' black clothing, which was visible from a great distance. The name was common among the Jews of Bohemia. On the back of a tombstone in the ancient cemetery in Prague there is an inscription (from 1623): "Buried here is the exalted old man, the honored Reb Mordechai, the dear son of the honored teacher and rabbi, Moses Kafkis of blessed memory ('s' is a patronymic suffix)." An inscription in memory of his wife Hinde, who lies next to

48 Muneles, *Inscriptions from the Ancient Jewish Cemetery*, Tombstone No. 185.

49 Max Brod, *Franz Kafka – A Biography* (New York: Da Capo Press, 1964), p. 3.

him, states that Kafkis was "the caretaker of the lower synagogue."[50] He is also mentioned under the name Moses Kafka in the will of the well-known court Jew Mordechai Meisel. The convert Franz Kawka is linked to the 1694 scandal surrounding Simon Abeles. On the long list of residents of the ghetto whose homes and property went up in flames in the great fire of 1754, Nathan Kafka appears with the notation that the damage caused him amounted to 400 florins (a small sum compared to the property of wealthy Jews like Israel Simon Fränkel whose damage amounted to 20,000 florins).[51] Joseph Kafka is on a list of residents of Prague's Jewish Town for the year 1808, who provided lodgings for young men who came from other countries to study at the yeshiva and serve as tutors.[52] The fact that Hermann Kafka, Franz's father, came from the village of Ossek near Strakonice means nothing: because of the expulsions and restrictive decrees, Jews often moved from Prague to the estates of nobles who gave them refuge, and then returned. Close to 200 with the name Kafka were on the transports, including four whose first name was Franz. One of them, with a doctoral degree, survived. Kafka's three sisters are registered under their husbands' names: Ottla David (sent to Auschwitz on 5 October 1943), Gabriela Hermann (sent to the Łódź ghetto on 21 October 1941), and Eli Polak (sent to Łódź on 31 October 1941). All three perished.

Brod (a water crossing in Czech), like the name of several cities in Czechoslovakia and Moravia, was also a typical Jewish name. In 1631, one of the Czech Jews mentioned was Moses Brod Polizeimacher, namely policeman. Ninety-five people bearing the name Brod left on the transports, including Otto Brod, the brother of Max Brod, Kafka's friend. Otto Brod, born in 1888, also an author, delivered a series of lectures in Terezin: on Voltaire's attitude towards Jews, the messianic movement, Heine, and his brother Max.[53] He was sent to Auschwitz on the last transport, which left on 28 October 1944.

50 Muneles, *Inscriptions from the Ancient Jewish Cemetery*, Tombstone No. 191.

51 Wenzel Žaček, "Nach dem Brande des Prager Gehttos im Jahre 1754," *JGGJ* (1934), p. 190.

52 Roubik, "Zur Geschichte der Juden in Böhmen."

53 Makarova et al., *University over the Abyss*, p. 379.

In addition to the general name for fish (Fischl, Fisch), which was also a substitute for Ephraim, and pike (Hecht), the Jews were mainly attracted to the carp (Karpeles, Karpfen, Karpe), a freshwater fish commonly found in the lakes of Bohemia and Moravia. In its Czech form, Kapřík, it appears on a list of Jewish tradesmen in Prague as far back as 1505. Rabbi Joel Kapřik or Karpeles was a member of the community committee from 1638 to 1639; Leibl Karpeles immigrated to Palestine in 1700 with the disciples of Judah HaNasi and was buried in Tiberias. Altogether, 137 bearers of the various forms of that name left on transports and were never buried.

The name Meisel derives from a nickname, and in fact, in writings from the time of Mordechai ben Samuel (1528–1601) there is sometimes a notation "known as Meisel." This term of endearment was not specific to Mordechai; even in relation to a Meir or a Moses, it was sometimes written "known as Meisel or Moisel." But the sound brings to mind the word Mäusel, a small mouse, and in fact Mordechai Meisel was occasionally called by that nickname in Hebrew (*akhbaron*). The inscription on his tombstone in the ancient Prague cemetery reads, among other things: "A doer of good deeds to all human beings: he built a synagogue, a very magnificent building, and almshouses and bathhouses. He paved streets with stones in the Jewish Town, made a bet midrash for scholars and was charitable to thousands."[54] In marked contrast to the age-old Jewish custom of lavishing exaggerated praise on the deceased when writing the inscription on a tombstone, in the case of Mordechai Meisel, the wealthiest Jew of his time, it is all true, as visitors to the synagogue that bears his name and the community assembly hall he built can see for themselves to this very day. His immense wealth, about half a million florins (the histo-

54 Muneles, *Inscriptions from the Ancient Jewish Cemetery*, Tombstone No. 176. One of many testimonies to Meisel's connections with the imperial court. In 1581, Marcus Meisel, a Jew from Prague, applied to the court bureau to be paid, with interest, the amount of 2,000 thaler he had lent three years earlier to the Empress Maria, through the head of the kitchen, to cover the needs of the imperial kitchen. Silver utensils from the imperial household served as collateral. See: Bondy-Dworsky, *Zur Geschichte der Juden*, No.803.

rian Heinrich Graetz described him as "the first Jewish capitalist") was confiscated by Rudolph II, the Emperor in whose service and under whose protection he acted. His heirs, according to his will, first among them his two nephews, were left with nothing. However, the family name, written in various ways – Meiseles, Maisels, Maisl, Meisl – remained, and it is found among rabbis and savants in Poland and Lithuania as well as among Czech Jews in the modern age; 115 bearing that name left for the Terezin ghetto and the extermination camps.

♦

Karel Poláček, the most popular Jewish author of the 1930s, gave his protagonists, most of them Jews – if not specifically declared as such, then based on their worldview and their petit bourgeois way of life – strange names such as Michelup or Načeradec. To us, his faithful young readers, these names seemed to be distinctly his own inventions, but that was not the case. They too appear in the lists, and with them Karel Poláček himself, who, although he passed the selection, died somewhere in Germany at the beginning of 1945 at the age of fifty-three. Among the deportees there was one named Brettschneider, like the bullying plainclothes policeman in the first chapter of *The Good Soldier Schweik* by Hašek, not to mention the dissolute military chaplain Otto Katz, whose orderly was Schweik. Ten Otto Katzes suffered the fate of the Jews.

A main character in two of Karel Čapek's books (among the deportees there was also a Karel Čapek from Kolín) in whose home the Friday men's circle (Pátečníci), of which Poláček was also a member, convened was called Bondy. There was no need to say he was a Jew; Bondy was the name of Jews, sometimes rabbis, sometimes Czechs of the Mosaic religion, sometimes Zionists. The Bondys held key positions in the Jewish community in Prague in the seventeenth century, and headed a faction that struggled to gain these positions; later they produced historians, industrialists, entrepreneurs, and physicians. There were 360 with the name Bondy or Bondi among those leaving on the transports. Nine of them were called Josef Bondy, like my father.

Very few names of Jews expelled from Spain and Portugal who come to Bohemia and Moravia, usually through northern Italy, were preserved over the generations: Rappaport (21 on the list), Luria (43), Bak (a family of printers in Prague). No one remained with the name of Avigdor Karo, who lamented the massacre of Prague's Jews in 1389 and whose tombstone (from 1439) is the oldest legible tombstone left above ground in the old cemetery. The descendants of Del Medigo, Anselmo, and Portugali have all vanished. Of the highly influential Todras family, only Irma remained in Bohemia, and she died in the Trawniki camp at the age of sixty-two. The origin of the Ramhal's family name, Luzzatto, is in the region known in Czech as Lužice, Lausitz in German. In the fifteenth century, the family moved from there to the area of Venice and added a more Italian ring to their name. Two bearing this name who wandered back were among those leaving on the transports: 18-year-old Ernest was sent to Auschwitz in the fall of 1944, and Hedwig came from Prague to Terezin on 12 September 1942 and ten days later met her death in the Maly Trostinets camp in the Lublin district.

In his book, *By Night Under the Stone Bridge*, Leo Perutz, a native of Prague, and son of a family of industrialists (sixteen Perutzes were on the transports), tells the story of Berl, a dealer in used goods from Prague, who bought curtains made of expensive fabric four days before the commander of the imperial forces, Albert von Wallenstein, published an order forbidding the purchase of items from soldiers without the permission of their commander. It turns out that the curtains were stolen by a soldier from the palace of the aristocratic family of Liechtenstein. After the order was published, Berl returned the curtains through the beadle of the old synagogue. Nevertheless, he was sentenced to death by hanging alongside two dogs, as a mark of humiliation.[55] As a matter of fact, this incident actually happened late in 1621, at the height of the Thirty Years War. At the last minute, the Prague community managed to ransom the man sentenced to death by paying an enormous sum of money that was brought to the Town Hall of the Old Town in dozens of sacks.

55 Leo Perutz, *By Night Under the Stone Bridge* (New York: Arcade, 1990).

General von Wallenstein used the money to establish a home for Jews who wanted to convert to Christianity.[56] The name of the ransomed man was Josef Thein, the same as the name of the church that borders on the square of the Old Town (*týn* in Czech means a stronghold) adjacent to the Jewish quarter. Fifty-seven Jews still bore that name at the time of the deportations.

♦

Since the Jews were obliged to inform the authorities which permanent surname they had chosen, one can assume that it generally reflected their own wishes. Certainly no government official would have forced them to take noble or distinguished names. Apparently, many Jews wanted to be called Kaiser (emperor), König, Král (king in German and Czech), Prinz (prince), Baron, Graf, Herzog, Kníže, and Fürst, all the ranks of nobility of Central Europe. Secret aspirations, defiance, the desire to be like everyone else – today we have no way of knowing what determined their choice. And that is how they went to their death: more than 400 kings and barons, at least according to their names. To the credit of the nobles in Bohemia and Moravia, they were often more tolerant toward the Jews than the emperors were, if not out of sympathy, then for practical considerations: Jews who were allowed to live on their estates increased their incomes, particularly as leasers of land, as holders of a concession to manufacture alcoholic beverages, or as dealers in horses and grain.

The lists of transports include a number of Jews who bore the names of the noble families of the empire: Lichtenstein, Kinský, Dubský, Mansfeld, Rosenberg – but without the title. There were, however, true aristocrats among the Jews of the crown lands. The first among them – and among all the Jews of the Austrian monarchy – was the merchant and court Jew, Jacob Bassevi (1570–1634), originally from Italy. One of the wealthiest men in the Jewish Town of Prague, Bassevi bought many houses there and built himself a

56 Vladimir Sadek, "Die jiddische Version der Familienmegilla 'Vorhangpurim' aus dem Jahre 1623," *Judaica Bohemiae* IV/1 (1968), pp. 73–78.

palace, which was destroyed during the "restoration" of the Jewish Town, namely the destruction of the greater part of that quarter at the end of the nineteenth and the beginning of the twentieth century. In 1622, Bassevi was elevated to the nobility and given the title von Treuenberg. The inscription on the elaborate tombstone of his second wife (who died in 1628) in the old cemetery in Prague reads: "Hendel, wife of the generous community leader, benefactor of the generation, our honored teacher and rabbi, Jacob Bassevi." And this was a true statement: Bassevi did a great deal for the Jews of Prague. During the Thirty Years War, however, he got into some trouble involving the minting of a low-value coin, found refuge with his partner General von Wallenstein and after his death, was buried in Jungbunzlau (Mladá Boleslav in Czech, called Bumsla by the Jews).[57] Chaim Popper (1721–1795), a banker and entrepreneur who came from the Bohemian village of Březnice, was raised to the nobility and given the name Joachim von Popper.[58] Moses Porges (1781–1870) was the owner of the largest factories for the manufacture of cotton cloth in the monarchy, and was called Edler von Portheim. In the eyes of the royal court, the major entitlement of the three (and of other holders of noble titles in Bohemia and Moravia, such as Israel Hönig, who had a monopoly on tobacco in the whole of Austrian empire, known from 1789 as Edler von Hönigsberg) was their great wealth, from which the royal treasury also benefited. Perhaps because of their keen intelligence to which they owed their success in life, perhaps because of their great wealth and their deeds of charity the three also filled key roles in the life of the Jews in the crown lands. The house of Bassevi-Treuenberg died out; the Popper and Porges families produced many illustrious men — rabbis, physicians, artists, scientists, musicians, and in-

57 Käthe Spiegel, "Die Prager Juden zur Zeit des dreissigjährigen Krieges," in *Die Juden in Prag* (Prague: Die Loge Praga des Ordens B'nai Brith, 1927), pp. 138–139.

58 His sister's two sons, of the Dobruschka family, who converted to Christianity and took the name Schönfeld, emigrated to Paris where they called themselves Frey. Later they were executed for monetary fraud during the stormy days of 1794. They are buried in a mass grave with Danton, one of the heads of the French Revolution. See: Kisch, *Pražský Pitaval*, pp. 44–60.

dustrialists. A long procession of Poppers (361 appearing on the lists) and Porgeses (187) left – a pack on their back, a suitcase in their hands – on the transports to the unknown. Among the deportees from Prague there was one true member of the nobility: Paula von Kurz zum Thurn. At the age of sixty-seven, she was sent to the Terezin ghetto, where she died a year later.

The Guttmann family was among the wealthiest of the Jews of the crown lands. In 1840, David Guttmann, a 17-year-old boy from Lipnik in Moravia, took a lump of coal from the deposits near the city of Ostrava and traveled to Vienna to meet with the Rothschilds who owned the steel plants in adjacent Vítkovice. His initiative paid off and the result was the metal and mining plants of Vítkovice, jointly owned by the Rothschilds (51 percent) and the brothers David and Wilhelm Guttmann (49 percent). Although the name Guttmann commanded the respect that the Jews of Bohemia generally reserved for the names of the very wealthy, it also provoked derision: the painter Robert Guttmann, a well-known figure in Prague, walked through the streets of the city looking much like the Parisian version of a bohemian – long hair, a kerchief tied around his neck, a cape on his shoulders and a portfolio of paintings under his arm. The bourgeois Jews of Prague did not think his paintings respectable enough to hang on the walls of their homes. But today he is assessed differently: Guttmann, who painted with the naiveté of a child, was an authentic artist who carried with him the memory of the Jewish Town before it was destroyed in the early twentieth century. Those of his paintings that remained are kept in the Jewish museum of Prague. He himself, der Maler Guttmann, a dedicated but impecunious Zionist, who walked on foot to the Zionist Congresses, was sent to the Łódź ghetto on 26 October 1941, at the age of sixty-two, and there he died in March 1942. The first exhibition of his paintings was held in 1967, twenty-five years after his death. Three hundred good people – the literal meaning of the name Guttman – left on the transports, and with them others named Guth, Gutwilling, Gutfreund and Gütig, written in various ways, all attesting to their and their forefathers' longing for goodness. Among those leaving there was not a single one with the name Böse or any other name meaning bad or badness. Only five had the name Zorn, meaning anger. There were those who were beautiful – Krása (106) and Schön (134) – but none who were ugly. Hundreds were rich, according to their names (Reichmann, Reicher, Reich), but those names were probably given them by others, because the truly wealthy would probably have preferred a name that would not tempt the evil eye.

A number of family names refer to character traits – sincere (Aufrichtig), honest (Ehrlich), decent (Redlich), faithful (Treulich), diligent (Fleissig), patient (Geduldig), disciplined (Gehorsam) – but one does not know whether the trait was noted because it was rare or because it was common. The names of all the good traits were also the names of the deportees: Egon Redlich was the head of the youth department in the Terezin ghetto, and on 28 October 1944 he was sent with his wife and infant son Dan on the last transport to leave the ghetto eastward, to the gas chambers of Auschwitz.

The names of the Jews evince their readiness to ignore reality, to hope for the best, to find some bright spots in their lives. They were called Felix, Seligmann, Šastný, Lustig, Freud, Frölhich, Glücklich and Veselý, names indicating happiness and those satisfied with their lot in life. Close to 800 Jews with names heralding happiness and joy left on the transports, but only five whose name was Trauer (sadness), one Smutná (sad) and thirty-eight with the name Kummermann, a man of sorrow. More than 700 bore the name of peace in various forms (Fried, Friedmann, Friedler, Friedl), and were caught up in an all-out war. The Jews searched for their good fortune: more than 360 of the persecuted bore the name Stern, meaning star or luck, and dozens more bore that name in various combinations (Sternschein, Sternlicht, Sternschuss). In days gone by, they assumed the name was a favorable sign – but no name can overcome absolute evil. Only eighteen of the deportees had the name Strach, which in Czech means fear.

♦

From the eighteenth century, many Jewish families earned their livelihood as jewelers and by dealing in gold, silver and precious stones. There are forty-six names on a list of members in the society of workers in gold, silver and jewels in Prague from 1805 to 1860, and it notes with whom the member learned his trade, what his apprenticeship was, and what his master craftsman work was (a long pair of "Jewish earrings" in the form of a drop, a ring with a large precious stone surrounded by three rows of small stones), when he earned membership in the society, and the number of apprentices working with him. Some of them bear the name Goldschmied, that is, a jeweler in gold, indicating that the profession was passed down in the family from father to son. Other names on the list are typical names of Bohemian Jews, such as Horowitz, Poděbard, Frankel, Kauders,[59] Gold, Silber (silver), Diamant (diamonds), Edelstein (precious stones), Rubin (rubies), Perl (pearls), and Bernstein (amber). All the materials of their craft were immortalized in the names of the Jews, including their various combinations: Silbermann, Perlhefter, Goldschmied, Goldscheider, and others. In 1940, by order of the German authorities, the Jews of the Protectorate were forced to hand over all jewels and objects made of gold, with the exception of wedding rings and dental crowns. Until the day of their death, they took with them only the names of the precious metals and stones.

There were names of Jews that became famous because of the products they manufactured. The most outstanding was Waldes-Kohinoor, the commercial name of the snap fastener that took the world by storm, whose logo was a girl who had a snap in one eye like a monocle. In the 1930s, the factory owned by Jindřich Waldes, born in 1878, exported half of the world's consumption of snap fasteners. Waldes refused to emigrate during the occupation and was imprisoned in the Buchenwald concentration camp. In 1941 he was ransomed by his wealthy family abroad, but he died on his way from Lisbon to Cuba.[60]

A status symbol among the rich ladies of Prague were dresses made by the owner of the Lavecká salon; men throughout the Re-

59 *Mitgliedsverzeichnis der jüdischen Gold, Silber und Galanteriearbeiter — Zunft in den Jahren 1805–1860*, the author's archives.

60 Arno Pařik , "Mecenáš Jindřich Waldes," *Roš Chodeš* 12 (1999), pp. 12–13, 17.

public were dressed by Sborowitz, the largest manufacturer and exporter of ready-made clothing in Czechoslovakia, whose main factory was in Prostějov in Moravia. The Kolben-Daněk factories were among the leading plants in the metal and aircraft industry in Czechoslovakia. In June 1943, their founder, Dr. Emil Kolben, was sent at the age of eighty-one to the Terezin ghetto, where he died three weeks later. Delicious cucumbers pickled in vinegar were made by the Wertheimer factory in Znojmo in Moravia; the well-known "Griotte" cherry liqueur was produced by Leo Vantoch. And so on in a paean to the enterprise and diligence of the Jews of Bohemia and Moravia, whose last chapter, with all the well-known trade names, is contained in the memorial book.

One of the industrialists who managed to flee Czechoslovakia in time and immigrated to Palestine was Egon Propper. There he founded a small plant, called Osem, which manufactured noodles. The Moller family established the Ata textile plants. However, the best-known name of a Czech Jew in Israel is not that of an industrialist or of a wealthy family. It is the name of Dr. Albert Ticho (which means silence in Czech), a Jerusalem eye doctor, a pioneer in ophthalmology in the Holy Land, who immigrated to Palestine in 1912. Others were too late: thirty-nine Tichos left on transports, some of whom had lived until their deportation in Boskovice, Dr. Ticho's place of birth.

The Jews are not the only ones to change their names, but in their case they did so frequently and often repeatedly throughout their wanderings, out of a desire to be accepted and absorbed in each new place. The seesaw between German and Czech names did not end with the Holocaust. In the overall atmosphere of Czech hatred for everything German, the survivors who returned to Czechoslovakia hastened to get rid of their family names if they had a German ring: Kurzbacher was changed to Krátký, Freudenfeld to Franěk, Lengsfeld to Lenek. And the same was true of the survivors who immigrated to Palestine. Out of Zionist zeal and the longing for a new chapter in life, Lieben became Livne, Tressler became Tarsi, Brammer, Barnea, and Fischer, Ophir. When changing their names, the majority kept the first letter of their previous surname or the letters it was composed of. The past was not completely erased.

♦

From their point of view, the Germans were doing the right thing when they divested the prisoners in the camps of their names and turned them into numbers. A name is an identity, a belonging, continuity, the promise of a future. There are those who believe that the Jews of Central Europe committed a fatal error and showed weakness in going to the transports in an orderly manner. If the deportations had been carried out in a disorganized way, perhaps more Jews would have fled. No one can maintain that today with any certainty. After all, the final outcome in the towns of Poland, where the Jews were taken out of their homes and hiding places indiscriminately, was the same. But it is hard to associate the Jews of Bohemia and Moravia with chaos. There was something in order and regularity that you could rely on, even during times of trouble. The Jews of Bohemia and Moravia were accustomed to leading orderly lives according to laws, rules and habits. They accepted the transports, which were efficiently arranged by lists, families and cities, as the lesser of two evils. In retrospect, after many decades, looking now at the memorial book, I think there was a glimmer of some good in the orderly way they left. At least, the names of the dead, their date of birth and some trace of their fate remained. In Eastern Europe, thousands disappeared without anyone knowing their names anymore. At least that: for all the 80,000 Jews of Bohemia and Moravia who perished in the Holocaust, with a few exceptions, their names – some proof of their existence – remained: on the walls of the Pinkas synagogue, in the memorial book and in the two computerized card files.

The idea of commemorating the names of all the Jewish Holocaust victims of Bohemia and Moravia on the walls of the Pinkas synagogue in Prague was apparently conceived by Hana Volavková, director of the Jewish museum after World War II. A Ph.D. in art history, she was on the staff of Jewish specialists who, in 1942–43 at the height of the war, were ordered by the SS apparatus under Eichmann to prepare an exhibit of Jewish history in the ancient synagogues of Prague, probably intended to be the Central Jewish Museum of the exterminated Jewish people. Volavková was the only member of the staff to survive. Because of her non-Jewish spouse, she was deported to Terezin only three months before the end of the war.[61]

The names project required immense preparation: first, an alphabetical index of all the deportees according to the lists of transports, a record of the deceased and the survivors in the Terezin ghetto and the remaining documentary material that was preserved.[62] In a pre-computer age, this was an enormous task, and it took years. The hostility towards the Germans and the German language in those years, as well as the assumption that during the German occupation people were forced to Germanize their names, dictated the way they were recorded. The names of all the women were written with the suffix ová or á, as is customary in Czech (Rubinsteinová, Rychnovská), even if they came from German-speaking families. But the main flaw is that all the first names were written in their Czech version, so that even those called Ernst, Franz, Georg, Ignaz, Rosalie, Elizabeth or Johanna throughout their lives, had their names written in the index – and afterwards on the walls of the Pinkas synagogue – as Arnošt, František, Jiří, Hynek, Růžena, Eliška and Jana. What is written on the walls cannot be changed. To turn the clock back, at least on the computerized index, would mean many years of painstaking work, a task that is still politically and emotionally charged. And it is not possible to ask the dead what they would like.

The two volumes of the memorial book were prepared with the aid of computers and a large staff of experts. Nonetheless, while it was being printed, it turned out that some errors had been made, particularly in the breakdown between the deceased from every transport and those who survived. In 1958, a small bibliophilic book, *Žalozpěvy 77.297 obětím* ("A Lament to 77,297 Victims") by Jiří Weil, was published in Prague. It is dedicated to the Jews of Bohemia and Moravia whose names are inscribed on the walls of

61 Arno Pařik, "Židovské uměni a památky v dile Hany Volavkové," *Židovská ročenka* (1989–1999), pp. 132–138.

62 Letters to the author from Anita Franková, researcher at the Jewish Museum in Prague, September 2000.

the Pinkas synagogue. The book contains excerpts of unrhymed poetry, biblical verses, quotations, documents and illustrations. This supposedly accurate number of Holocaust victims probably reflects what was known at the time the book was written. Today, despite all the computerization, no one is able or prepared to fix the exact number of victims. Some of the camp inmates, liberated when they were nearly dead and transferred to hospitals in different countries, remained in foreign lands, psychologically incapable of returning to the countries of their birth. They did not bother to inform the information center in Prague of their existence, so they were counted with the dead. A computerized index was also prepared at Beit Terezin in Givat Chaim-Ichud, with far more modest means than those in Prague, and was mainly the work of volunteers. Years after its completion, it still requires some corrections since new information is constantly becoming available. It will probably never be possible to obtain the names of all the Jewish victims of the Protectorate of Bohemia and Moravia, down to the last one, because not all of them found their death through the transports; some died in Gestapo prisons and some were killed in local acts of abuse, some were arrested as political prisoners or apprehended in the underground, and some were victims of informers – and some of these names sank into the abyss of oblivion.

Five synagogues remained standing in Prague. The Pinkas synagogue, the second oldest, was selected as the commemoration site. Even now, years later, it seems to have been the right choice. The older Altneuschul, which is small and replete with tradition, could not be touched. The others are ornate, with architectonic elements that are too prominent. The Pinkas synagogue has no ornamentation and its curved walls were blank, but most important, it borders on the ancient cemetery, sunk between the level of the street, which over the generations rose following destruction and rebuilding, a place suitable for crying out: "Out of the depths I cried to you, oh Lord" – and you didn't reply.

The restoration of the synagogue and the work of inscribing the names on the walls, according to the last place of residence before the transport, in alphabetical order by family name, with the names of members of the same family usually written one after the other, was completed in 1959. But not too long after, problems began. Because of the low level, groundwater seeped into the foundation and walls of the synagogue and the names began to peel and fall off. The Pinkas synagogue was shut down in 1968 for repairs – and reopened only after the fall of the Communist regime, in whose view it was not Jews who were murdered during the German occupation, but rather "victims of the fascist regime." Since closing down the Jewish commemoration site for ideological reasons would have led to negative reactions in the Western world, the need for ongoing repairs of long duration served as a convenient pretext.[63]

Technical means of insulating the walls were found only after the 1989 revolution. The names were rewritten on the walls, and the commemoration site was reopened on Holocaust Day in 1996. So there is a site, there is a memorial book; only the Jews no longer exist. The Holocaust survivors who remained in Czechoslovakia after the war are slowly dying out, some married non-Jews and concealed their Jewishness to cut themselves off from the past or to avoid causing their children any harm during the Communist regime. In the revived democratic era, they were joined by some converts to Judaism, and some Jews came from the United States, from Israel and other countries to earn a living and business purposes. The communities in the small cities ceased to exist a long time ago. Today there are approximately 4,000 Jews in the Czech Republic, many of whom came from other areas and bear other names. What is left of the Jewry of Bohemia and Moravia are the treasures of the Jewish museum in Prague, synagogues that serve mainly to exhibit them, cemeteries, books and names – and a vacuum that will never be filled.

♦

Sometimes I ask myself why I am so preoccupied with the past, when the present is so fateful and turbulent, so full of experiences,

63 "Information on the Course of the General Restoring of the Memorial Placed in the Pinkas Synagogue," *Bohemiae Judaica* XIV/2 (19778), pp. 118–119

both good and bad, when I ought to think first of all about the future. And I always answer myself: I'll just finish this one bit of research, and then I'll be done with the past, this will be the last article I'll write on the Holocaust. Maybe I'm addicted to the past, maybe I am searching in it for a refuge against the demands of the present that call for action, for an ideological stance, civic involvement. Perhaps I am evading the burden of personal responsibility for the future. But who knows, perhaps a knowledge of the past can also fortify us for what is yet to come?

Major Dates in the History of the Jews of Bohemia and Moravia During Nazi Rule

28 October 1918 — Establishment of the Czechoslovak Republic, comprising three separate parts, Bohemia and Moravia, Slovakia and Subcarpathian Ruthenia, and containing a large German minority.

1 October 1938 — Following the Munich agreement between Nazi Germany and England and France, the German army captures the border areas known as Sudetenland. Most of the Jews of Sudetenland flee into the interior of the country.

1939

15 March — In violation of his commitments under the Munich agreement, Hitler occupies the western part of Czechoslovakia, which becomes the Protectorate of Bohemia and Moravia. Slovakia becomes a fascist satellite state.

According to official statistics, 118,310 Jews, 14,350 of whom belong to other religions but are considered Jews under the racial laws, live in the Protectorate.

July — A Central Office for Jewish Emigration (*Zentralstelle für jüdische Auswanderung*), like those in Vienna and Berlin, opens in Prague, under the command of Adolf Eichmann. Its declared

	purpose is to cleanse the Protectorate of Jews through their emigration.
1 September	World War II breaks out, German forces invade Poland.
October	Following the occupation of western Poland, 5,000 men are sent in two transports from the city of Moravská Ostrava to a marsh area near the town of Nisko in the Lublin district, in an abortive attempt to set up a "Jewish colony" based on the method of "annihilation by means of deportation." In April 1940, 516 men are sent back.
End December	19,016 Jews have emigrated from the area of the Protectorate.
1940	
8 August	Jewish pupils are forbidden to attend schools in the new school year. During the year, an endless list of laws and orders are published, with the intent of ousting the Jews from economic life, restricting their movements and humiliating them. In the course of the year, 6,176 Jews emigrate from the Protectorate.
1941	
1 September	The Jews of the Protectorate are ordered to wear a special insignia: a yellow Star of David with the word *Jude* in the center.
October	Based on a special census, there are 88,105 Jews in the Protectorate.
16 October	The first transport of 1,000 Jews from the Pro-

tectorate leaves for the Łódź ghetto. After that, another four transports of 1,000 persons each leave between 21 October and 3 November.

3 November — 1,000 Jews from Brno, the capital of Moravia, are sent to the Minsk ghetto.

24 November — The advance unit (AK1) of 345 Jewish men leaves to prepare the fortress city of Terezin (Theresienstadt in German), 60 kilometers north of Prague, as a Jewish ghetto. There are seven barracks in the city, and it has 3,800 inhabitants.

4 December — A second advance unit (AK2) of 1,000 men arrives in Terezin.

Jakob Edelstein, formerly director of the Palestine Office in Prague, who was appointed the Elder of the Jews (*Judenältester*), arrives in the ghetto with 22 staff members (Stab). Contrary to what was agreed, transports begin arriving at the ghetto that same day, without anything having been prepared to receive them.

6 December — Living quarters for women and children are set up in separate barracks from the men's quarters, and they are forbidden to meet.

31 December — 7,350 inmates are in the Terezin ghetto.

1942

9 January — The ghetto is stunned: contrary to expectations, the Terezin ghetto is only a transit station. The first transport leaves Terezin to the East. The destination: the Riga ghetto.

A stream of transports begins to leave, mainly to the extermination camps in the Lublin region: Majdanek, Sobibór, Maly Trostinets in the Minsk region, and others. Only a few survive.

10 January — Nine young inmates of the ghetto are hanged for violating prohibitions issued by the German command. The second execution takes place on 26 February 1942.

20 January — At Wannsee near Berlin a conference is held on the "Final Solution for the Jewish Problem." There, Reinhard Heydrich raises for the first time the plan to bring the elderly and the World War I disabled from the Reich and Austria to the Terezin ghetto.

27 May — An attempt to assassinate Reichsprotektor Reinhard Heydrich takes place in Prague. He dies on 4 June.

2 June — The first transport of old people arrives from Berlin and is followed by hundreds of additional transports.

10 June — Thirty ghetto inmates are sent to the village of Lidice to bury the men executed there as punishment for Heydrich's assassination.

A penal transport as reprisal for Heydrich's assassination passes through Bohušovice, the train station closest to Terezin. There are 1,000 persons on the transport.

27 June — The last local residents of Terezin leave. The area of the ghetto is expanded, buildings of living quarters are added. The inmates are allowed to go out into the street, with the exception of the area reserved for the SS command and the Czech police. Families can meet after work.

August	The overcrowded conditions in the ghetto are at their worse: 1.6 square meters per person. The mortality rate is constantly rising.
7 September	The crematorium of the Terezin ghetto, whose construction began in May, is in operation. It has the capacity to burn up to 160 bodies a day.
26 October	The first transport leaves Terezin for Auschwitz-Birkenau. From now on, that is the destination of all the transports.
December	Of the 3,500 children and teenagers aged 3–16, about 2,000 live in children's homes.
31 December	There are 50,006 inmates in the ghetto. In the course of the year, 101,761 inmates have been brought to the ghetto, 54,228 of them from the Protectorate. During the same time period, 43,871 have been sent eastward. Following the transports of the elderly from the Reich and Austria, a third of the population is over 65.
1943	
31 January	By order from Berlin, Dr. Paul Eppstein from Berlin replaces Jakob Edelstein as Elder of the Jews. His deputies are Jakob Edelstein and Benjamin Murmelstein from Vienna.
February	The typhus epidemic spreads.
9 April	After six young men escape (three of them are caught), a collective punishment is meted out to the entire ghetto, in the form of a curfew after work and a prohibition against engaging in cultural activities and switching on a light.

21 April	A bank of "the self leadership of the ghetto" is established and special currency is printed. This is the first stage in the campaign to "beautify" the ghetto in preparation for a possible visit by a delegation of the International Red Cross.
1 May	The name Terezin ghetto is cancelled. From now on the ghetto is called "the area of the Jewish settlement."
10 May	The punitive curfew is cancelled.
28 June	Representatives of the German Red Cross and the Nazi administration visit Terezin under the guidance of Adolf Eichmann.
24 July	6,422 inmates are hastily evacuated from two barracks to make room for storage of the archives of the Reich Security Head Office, on the assumption that the Allies would not bomb the ghetto.
24 August	1,300 children from the Bialystok ghetto arrive in Terezin, most of them in a deplorable condition. The inmates of the ghetto are forbidden to have any contact with them, with the exception of counselors, doctors and nurses who volunteered to care for them. It is rumored that they are intended for an exchange with the West.
6 September	A transport of 5,007 men, women and children leaves for a new work camp, which is in fact Auschwitz-Birkenau. The people from Terezin do not undergo a selection, and the men and women are interned in the same camp, known as the "family camp."

5 October — The first Danish Jews arrive in Terezin (a total of 460, and they are protected against transports to the East).

1,260 children from Bialystok leave the ghetto with 53 escorts. In the ghetto everyone assumes they are leaving for the West. In fact, they are taken directly to the gas chambers of Auschwitz.

9 November — Edelstein is arrested and held in the commandant jail under suspicion that he helped inmates escape.

11 November — A roll call of all the inmates of the ghetto is held outdoors on a cold wintry day outside the walls of the fortress.

15 December — A transport of 2,504 persons is sent to the family camp, and three days later is followed by another transport of 2,503 persons.

31 December — There are 34,655 inmates in the ghetto. During the year, 16,388 have been brought to the ghetto, 18,328 sent to Auschwitz, and 12,696 died in the ghetto.

1944

8 March — 3,792 men, women and children, survivors out of the 5,000 inmates of the September transport, are led from the family camp in Birkenau to their death in the gas chambers.

15–18 May — Three transports of 7,500 persons are taken to the family camp.

20 June — Jakob Edelstein and the members of his fam-

	ily are shot to death in the main camp of Auschwitz.
23 June	A delegation of the International Red Cross and the Danish Red Cross visits the ghetto for half a day and is favorably impressed by the show prepared especially in their honor, without discerning the true reality that exists in the ghetto.
2–12 July	The family camp in Birkenau is liquidated. About 3,000 men and women are sent to work; the rest, about 7,000 in number, are killed in the gas chambers.
16 August	Shooting of the propaganda film on the Terezin ghetto begins.
27 September	Paul Eppstein is arrested and shot to death in the Gestapo prison in the Small Fortress. Benjamin Murmelstein is appointed the third Elder of the Jews.
28 September	The liquidation deportations from the Terezin ghetto to Auschwitz begin. They continue until 28 October 1944 and include 18,000 men, women and children. In the last transport, nearly the entire leadership of the ghetto is taken for extermination.
November	11,068 persons remain in Terezin. These are mainly women, "prominents," Danish Jews and those who have professions or trades considered by the Germans to be essential.
23 December	The first transport from Sered arrives at the ghetto with 416 Jews from Slovakia. Another

three transports follow. In the course of the year, 7439 inmates have been brought to the ghetto; 25,995 have been sent to Auschwitz and Bergen-Belsen (a small group).

1945

26 January
Jews who until now were protected against transports because of their Aryan spouses begin to arrive in the ghetto.

5 February
1,200 inmates are freed from the ghetto and reach Switzerland.

15 April
The Danish Jews are freed and taken to Sweden by the Swedish Red Cross.

20 April
The first survivors of the death marches start to arrive in the ghetto. Most of them are on the verge of death. Many are ill with typhus and the epidemic spreads through the ghetto.

8 May
The Red Army liberates the Terezin ghetto. There are more than 30,000 inmates in Terezin, half of them survivors of death marches.

November
The last liberated inmates leave Terezin.

Summary

At the start of the German occupation, there were 118,310 Jews in the Protectorate on the basis of the racial laws. At the end of the war, only 3,030 Jews remained, most of them because they were married to Aryans.

A total of 7,002 Jews were deported on transports to the Łódź ghetto, to Minsk and to Ujazdow; only 291 of them survived. Altogether, 73,468 Jews from the Protectorate were brought to the

Terezin ghetto; 6,152 of them died there, and 6,875 were liberated there, in particular those with non-Jewish spouses who were brought to the ghetto only after the deportations to extermination.

From Terezin, 60,382 inmates were taken to extermination.

Only 3,097 survived until the liberation.

Index